Foundations for Learning

CLAIMING YOUR EDUCATION

Third Edition

Laurie L. Hazard

BRYANT UNIVERSITY

Jean-Paul Nadeau

BRISTOL COMMUNITY COLLEGE

Boston   Columbus   Indianapolis   New York   San Francisco   Upper Saddle River
Amsterdam   Cape Town   Dubai   London   Madrid   Milan   Munich   Paris   Montreal   Toronto
Delhi   Mexico City   São Paulo   Sydney   Hong Kong   Seoul   Singapore   Taipei   Tokyo

Editor in Chief: Jodi McPherson
Editorial Assistant: Clara Ciminelli
Vice President, Director of Marketing:
  Margaret Waples
Executive Marketing Manager: Amy Judd
Production Manager: Meghan DeMaio
Creative Director: Jayne Conte

Cover Designer: Suzanne Duda
Cover Image: Fuse/Getty Images
Full-Service Project Management/Composition:
  Revathi Viswanathan/PreMediaGlobal
Printer/Binder/Cover Printer:
  R. R. Donnelley & Sons
Text Font: Berkeley-Medium 10.5/12

Credits and acknowledgments borrowed from other sources and reproduced, with permission, in this textbook appear on appropriate page within text.

Microsoft® and Windows® are registered trademarks of the Microsoft Corporation in the U.S.A. and other countries. Screen shots and icons reprinted with permission from the Microsoft Corporation. This book is not sponsored or endorsed by or affiliated with the Microsoft Corporation.

Many of the designations by manufacturers and seller to distinguish their products are claimed as trademarks. Where those designations appear in this book, and the publisher was aware of a trademark claim, the designations have been printed in initial caps or all caps.

Library of Congress Cataloging-in-Publication Data

Hazard, Laurie L.
Foundations for learning : claiming your education / Laurie L. Hazard, Jean-Paul Nadeau.—3rd ed.
    p. cm.
  Includes bibliographical references and index.
  ISBN-13: 978-0-13-231806-8 (alk. paper)
  ISBN-10: 0-13-231806-7 (alk. paper)
  1. Study skills. 2. Learning, Psychology of. 3. Academic achievement. 4. College student orientation. I. Nadeau, Jean-Paul, 1968– II. Title.
  LB2395.H394 2012
  378.1'70281—dc22

2011002002

10 9 8 7 6 5 4 3 2

www.pearsonhighered.com

ISBN-10: 0-13-231806-7
ISBN-13: 978-0-13-231806-8

Dedication

*To our children, Grace, John, Andrew, and Alison,
whose giggles and smiles at the end of the day
help sustain this project.*

LAURIE L. HAZARD holds an Ed.M. in Counseling and an Ed.D. in Curriculum and Teaching from Boston University. She is the Director of the Academic Center for Excellence at Bryant University, the Curriculum Coordinator for their First-Year Experience (FYE) course, and teaches in the Applied Psychology Department. Laurie, an award winning educator, was selected by the National Resource Center for The First-Year Experience and Students in Transition as a top ten *Outstanding First-Year Student Advocate.* She also received the *Learning Assistance Association of New England's Outstanding Research and Publication Award.*

Laurie has been designing curricula for FYE and study skills courses for more than twenty years reflecting her area of expertise: the personality traits and habits of students that influence academic achievement. She has done extensive work assessing the effectiveness of learning assistance programs and FYE courses. She has been a Guest Editorial Board member for the *Learning Assistance Review.* Publications by Laurie and her co-author include: *Exploring the Evidence, Volume III: Reporting Outcomes of First-Year Seminars*, a monograph published by the National Resource Center for The First-Year Experience and Students in Transition and "What Does It Mean to be 'College-Ready'?", an article which appears in *Connection: The Journal of the New England Board of Higher Education.*

Laurie's expertise has received national media attention. Her interviews include: "Prepare college-bound kids for hard work ahead," which appeared in the *Chicago Tribune* in 2007 and "Study Tips for College Students" in *Seventeen Magazine* in 2008. Most recently, in March 2010, Laurie was interviewed by Associated Press columnist Beth Harpaz for her article "Colleges Don't Like Senior Slump in High School."

JEAN-PAUL (JP) NADEAU earned his Ph.D. in Rhetoric and Composition from the University of Rhode Island and has been teaching first-year composition, basic writing, and literature courses since 1992. Currently he is an Associate Professor of English at Bristol Community College, located in Southeastern Massachusetts, where he is also Chair of the English Department's Portfolio Assessment Program. He recently co-authored a longitudinal study of first-year writers, *Community College Writers: Exceeding Expectations (Southern Illinois University Press, 2010).* JP has given dozens of presentations at local and national conferences during the last fifteen years, including the Conference on College Composition and Communication, the Learning Assistance Association of New England Conference, and the Northeast Writing Centers Association Conference. He was recipient of the 2006 Learning Assistance Association of New England Outstanding Research and Publication Award along with his co-author. In that same year he was awarded a research grant from the Calderwood Writing Initiative at the Boston Athenaeum.

BRIEF CONTENTS

PART III   Implementing Strategies and Habits for Peak Academic Performance

CONTENTS

PART III   Implementing Strategies and Habits for Peak Academic Performance

CHAPTER SIX

Developing Communication Skills   125

As a first-year student, I found college to be an environment that was so overwhelming, it was almost impossible to stay focused on the reason why I was there in the first place: to earn a degree. How was I expected to handle the substantial workload assigned outside the classroom when I was given the freedom to do whatever I wanted whenever I wanted? As a traditional 18-year-old student, my parents were no longer around to look over my shoulder to make sure I was doing my homework; it was solely up to me to actively take part in my education.

The pursuit of a college education was a conscious choice I made to improve myself in areas that stretched far beyond the classroom. By the end of the first week of classes, it became quite clear that I could not be successful by just being there. I had to claim my education as my own. A great deal of responsibility comes with the privilege of having the opportunity to earn a college degree. Maintaining a healthy social environment, practicing time management and effective study skills, and preparing for the tasks assigned were must do's for me and anyone else who expected to claim their education and achieve their goals. To build a solid college experience and eventual professional career, I needed a base to build on.

The one thing that helped prepare me was a class all first-year students were enrolled in that year called "Foundations for Learning." The class was geared specifically toward the issues that all students face and designed in a way that readied me for challenges I would encounter throughout my first year. For example, just as I was trying to figure out what my school was all about, Chapter One described the inner workings of a collegiate institution and what was expected of me from my professors.

I thought I knew it all in high school, but college was very different with much higher expectations. The text *Foundations for Learning* not only explained to me what it meant to be a college student, but it also taught me the necessary skills I needed to be a successful individual. I learned in Chapter Two that surrounding myself with the right friends who shared the same interests and supported me as an individual was one of the most important decisions I would ever make. With guidance in creating the right social environment, I was now ready to focus on achieving my goals.

The remaining chapters in the textbook coached me through effective methods of understanding how I personally learn best, specific study tactics for different types of tests, writing papers, note taking, and, most importantly, time management. By learning how to manage my time effectively, through a structured schedule, I found I had ample time to get all my work done, spend time with my friends, and participate in on-campus activities. This has made my college experience both enjoyable and increasingly productive. As a junior, I still hit bumps in the road, whether it is preparing for a complex presentation in my investments class or finding an effective way to read through a difficult novel in philosophy. At first I thought the book used in *Foundations for Learning* was just a textbook, but I realize now that I can use it throughout college as a reference for working through problems I will face in the future.

As I read this book, I realized it actually works. The principles and skills I learned and implemented as a result have guided me toward earning an exceptional grade-point average thus far. By accepting the fact that I did not know everything about school, I was able to acquire effective tools to improve my life as a whole. More than a textbook, *Foundations for Learning* provides guidance on what is necessary to be successful beyond college. *Foundations for Learning* gave me the tools to take my college experience to the highest level. I believe the good habits I have developed will undoubtedly extend into my career in the future. It is now up to you to claim *your* education.

—*Daniel J. Fiandaca*
Student Reviewer

WHAT'S NEW IN THIS EDITION

he third edition of *Foundations for Learning: Claiming Your Education* aims to help a broader range of students by sharing a more diverse range of student experiences and asking a broader range of questions about students' learning processes and attitudes.

- "Adjust Your Mindset" and "Adjust Your Strategies" sections. These sections begin each chapter by asking questions to help students consider their current and emerging attitudes and behaviors relative to forthcoming chapter content. As opposed to earlier editions (which included only a few of these questions under the title "Make it Personal"), the separation serves to emphasize the distinction between attitudes and behaviors, a key theme in the text.

- "First year diaries: Adjustment reflections" sections. Each chapter now ends with between one and three journal entry chunks from actual students enrolled in a first-year experience course. Entries are explicitly linked to key chapter concepts.

- Broadened audience. While previous editions were aimed squarely at students attending residential, four year institutions, this new edition broadens the audience base to include students attending two-year colleges, commuters, and adult learners. Changes include, but are not limited to, examples and student narratives originating from these subject-positions.

- Additional visual aids. New visual aids will help students understand difficult concepts. These include a sample syllabus, a breakdown of variations of the 8-8-8 formula, and a graphic representation of Freud's theory of personality, among others.

- Attention to emerging technologies. Educators are increasingly aware of the influences technology such as Blackboard (and other course delivery software), Facebook, Twitter, and texting is having on student learning. This edition speaks to these influences, helping to prepare students to manage their cyber-presence in college.

- New emphases in key sections. The "Planning, Prioritizing, and Procrastination" and "Developing Malleable Mindsets and Metacognitive Skills" chapters have undergone extensive revision. The former now more firmly emphasizes the need for behavior management, offering advice on how to manage behavior to achieve goals in a new section titled, "Overcoming Procrastination." The latter has a reworked "Theories of Intelligence" section that includes a new category: emotional intelligence. Brain function is also discussed here for the first time.

This book is written with the central idea that *all* students have the ability to succeed in higher education. We presume from the outset that every individual can cultivate the habits of mind necessary for academic achievement regardless of their intelligence quotients, past educational records, high school grades, and college boards. For many years, such indicators have been used to predict college success and achievement. We contend that, once you are admitted to an institution of higher education, they don't really matter all that much. You may be thinking, "Well then, what does matter?" This textbook argues that what matters most are your attitudes and the behaviors you enact as a result of those attitudes.

At its core, this text is based on the psychology of adjustment. Psychology is the study of behaviors and mental processes. Behaviors are what you do, what's observable by others. Mental processes are thoughts, attitudes and feelings. If you think of yourself as lazy, you may have a negative attitude and not feel like doing much of anything let alone studying; however, if you conceive of yourself as a hardworking student, you will more likely enact behaviors that are congruent with the definition of hardworking such as reading, going to the library, and utilizing services on your campus. Your mindset, then, influences how you behave. Reflecting on your mindset in an honest way will enable you to make necessary adjustments for your new role as a college student.

We therefore encourage you to take an in-depth look at your attitudes toward education and learning and how they might affect your college experience. Our best advice is to keep an open mind, accepting you will likely experience many changes over the course of this academic year. Reading this book with the mindset, "I already know what I'm doing, this is just a waste of time," a somewhat negative attitude, will result in little, if any, introspection and change. But if you enthusiastically accept the challenge to evaluate your current attitudes and study habits, for instance, you will find more efficient and effective methods of accomplishing your academic goals.

You will notice that this textbook is written in a style common to academic texts. Research is referenced to support the concepts presented in each chapter. This approach is purposeful, modeling one type of writing you will be asked to do in college; it also allows you to make a more informed decision regarding whether to embrace or reject individual ideas and strategies presented. Indeed, without this research, we would be imploring you to just do it, which doesn't reconcile well with the self-reflective, evaluative stance we are suggesting students should take toward their education. Instead of imploring you to just do it, rather, we implore you to be ready for new ideas and willing to try new strategies. Allow time for the ideas to resonate and the strategies to become part of your repertoire of skills before you make the informed decision to accept or reject what you have learned.

We deliberately selected the topics in the text based on years of professional academic support experience and student feedback. Recognizing that the student standpoint is critical, you will notice many student voices and narratives presented in the text. These are the words and stories of real students from several different two- and four-year institutions of higher education. Although their situations may differ from those you may have faced in the past or will face in the future, observing their responses to various situations can help you negotiate events and circumstances in your own college career. You have the opportunity to benefit from understanding the ways in which other students who have come before you have achieved their successes and persevered through failures.

Observing many such students has given us incredible insight to what exactly it is that students need to know to be successful in higher education particularly during the first year. To that end, the chapter topics were thoughtfully chosen as a result of years of working with students and pinpointing the salient features of what attitudes and habits are necessary to make the grade during the first year.

Acknowledging that the student standpoint is critical, so too is it essential for you to clearly understand the new context in which you will be learning. Chapter One explains this context, offering you entree into the social institution of higher education, a scholarly community. Understanding this context is crucial because it will provide you with insight into your professors' vantage point, an appreciation for your role and responsibility within the scholarly community, and a keen awareness of the vital conventions of this community.

Once you become familiar with the inner workings of your institution of higher education and those working, teaching, and learning there, you will need to consider your position as an individual within it. Who are you as a person, and how will that affect the way you function at college? Getting a solid handle on your thoughts and feelings surrounding this question is what Chapter Two is all about: reflecting on your developing academic self-concept. Chapter One, then, is about the institution of higher education, and Chapter Two is all about you as the individual and how you fit into it. As you begin to solidify this understanding of yourself and how you will approach your new environment, Chapter Three asks you to turn outward toward others, considering their diversity and reflecting on what you can learn by being open to those who are different from you. Once you understand the institution, your position within it, and gain a reconceived appreciation for those around you, you have the initial cornerstone of your "foundation for learning."

In the remaining chapters, the text exposes you to a variety of skills and strategies you will most definitely want to master to do well in your college-level coursework. A wide variety of topics, such as time management, how to combat procrastination, identify your learning style, write a research paper, and prepare for exams, are discussed. These topics beg the question of whether you have already mastered these skills and strategies. Certainly, some of you will say you have done so. A wise professor adopted a clever mantra when using this text for his course. He granted to his students that some of them may already know "how to" manage their time, but the larger question was whether they were actually doing it, and could they do it in the same way in this new context. His mantra was, "You may know how to do it, but are you actually doing it?" He would raise this simple question each time his class met.

Indeed, at the heart of *Foundations for Learning* is this mantra. The question of whether you are actually applying the skills and strategies that have been recently taught to you (or the ones you "already know") is embedded in each chapter. Each chapter implores you to revisit your attitudes and the behaviors you choose to enact as a by-product of those attitudes. Each chapter reminds you to engage in a serious self-reflection. Which attitudes do you possess that will either propel you toward or inhibit you from getting the most out of your college experience?

What is at stake here is learning. Learning is a relatively permanent change in behavior due to experience. This definition of learning presumes from the outset that during your first-year, you will undergo permanent changes in behavior, but you will find that this is entirely up to you. Social-cognitive theorists identify three ways in which learning takes place: through direct experience, self-produced experience, and vicarious experience. Direct experience means that you have to earn a "C" on a paper before you decide to change the behavior of composing papers the night before they are due. Self-produced experience means that you inherently recognize the task of writing a college level paper will require different strategies, and perhaps you use a trial and error approach to adjust to this awareness, thus producing your own consequences. Finally, vicarious experience is the idea that learning takes place through observation, modeling, and taking the advice of those who have experienced college success before you.

It may come as no surprise that most people learn by direct experience. Our hope is that you may consider shifting your mindset to learning primarily through vicarious experience. That is, consider the research in this book that discusses the study habits that the most successful college students utilize, for example. Reflect on the experiences of those students who came before you. Learn what strategies work best and what pitfalls to avoid by vicariously experiencing the triumphs and challenges others have encountered during their first-year. Finally, once this advice is heeded, self-produce your own consequences.

ACKNOWLEDGMENTS

I, Laurie Hazard would like to thank Nancy Nyhan, one of the founding members of the Learning Assistance Association of New England. As a graduate student, you were my mentor, friend, and colleague. Thanks for your support and encouragement. Thanks also to Maureen Foley-Reese and Eileen Maguire, special friends and colleagues who have always recognized my passion for working with students and who have encouraged me to persist in my professional career despite all of the obstacles. To Linda Wells, Dean of the College of General Studies (CGS) at Boston University, your annual speech to incoming students about joining a community of scholars and taking personal responsibility for their education was a major influence on Chapter One of this text. Thanks to Robert Emery, Assistant Dean of the College of General Studies and Director of the CGS Writing Center at Boston University. Your early design of the Learning Assistance Program at CGS has been a model to emulate. You will be missed, Dr. Emery. Finally, thanks to all of my family and friends for your positive words and enthusiasm.

I, Jean-Paul, would personally like to thank those people who got me excited about teaching at the college level, including William Kelly of Bristol Community College, who helped give me the confidence I lacked; Howard Tinberg, also of BCC, who taught me so much about writing center work; and Nedra Reynolds of the University of Rhode Island, who showed me how much there was to learn about writing and teaching.

We would both like to acknowledge the assistance of our countless students who possessed the ability and humility to reach out and ask for help. You have provided us with incredible insight to what enables students to be successful during their first year and beyond. Our student reviewer, Daniel Fiandaca, showed us through his energy and enthusiasm that if you choose to "claim your education," the first-year experience can be completely transformative. We must also thank Kim Brugger from Pearson Custom and Carolyn Gogolin from Prentice Hall for cheering us along.

We offer a very special thanks to Richard Light, Walter H. Gale Professor of Education, at Harvard University. Hearing you speak at Bryant's Convocation let us know we were on the right track. Thank you for your thoughtful review of this text and for the positive feedback. Thanks to Dr. Ashton Trice for his permission to use the Trice Academic Locus of Control Scale. Giving students insight into this attitudinal variable and its influence on academic achievement has given many first-years the opportunity to reflect on their role in taking responsibility for their education. Thanks to Dr. Craig Jones and Dr. John Slate for their permission to use the Study Habits Inventory. Offering students the ability to self-assess their utilization of study skills has provided the reality check that many first-years need.

Thanks also go to Sharon Alex for her tireless efforts designing a wide variety of materials to teach students note-taking skills. To Heidi Brown and Will White, former learning specialists at the College of General Studies, thanks for your instructional materials. Special thanks to Clara Ciminelli, editorial assistant, former editor Sande Johnson who faithfully continues to support this project, and Jodi McPherson, Editor in Chief, who will see it through.

Thanks to our project managers, Annette Joseph, Olivia Johnson, and Revathi Viswanathan who kept us on task with our deadlines. Truly, a heartfelt thanks to Amy Judd, Executive Marketing Manager, who gave terrific feedback on the cover, and who insures the book gets into the hands of students.

We would both like to acknowledge the many contributions of Bryant faculty and staff, whose questions and suggestions encouraged us to reflect on the intersection between theory and practice. Finally, thanks to all of the students who shared their stories with us. Without your original stories and composites of your experiences, the portraitures, reflections, and narratives would not be as powerful as they are. Thank you.

INSTRUCTOR SUPPORT – Resources to simplify your life
and support your students.

Book Specific

Online Instructor's Manual This manual is intended to give professors a framework or blueprint of ideas and suggestions that may assist them in providing their students with activities, journal writing, thought-provoking situations, and group activities. The test bank organized by chapter includes: multiple choice, true/false and short-answer questions that support the key features in the book. This supplement is available for download from the Instructor's Resource Center at www.pearsonhighered.com/irc

Online PowerPoint Presentation A comprehensive set of PowerPoint slides that can be used by instructors for class presentations or by students for lecture preview or review. The presentation includes all the graphs and tables in the textbook. The presentation contains bullet point PowerPoint slides for each chapter. These slides highlight the important points of each chapter to help students understand the concepts within each chapter. Instructors may download these PowerPoint presentations from the Instructor's Resource Center at www.pearsonhighered.com/irc

MyStudentSuccessLab Are you teaching online, in a hybrid setting, or looking to infuse exciting technology into your classroom for the first time? Then be sure to refer to the MyStudentSuccessLab section included in the coming pages of this Preface to learn more. This online solution is designed to help students build the skills they need to succeed at www.mystudentsuccesslab.com

Other Resources

"Easy access to online, book-specific teaching support is now just a click away!"
Instructor Resource Center - Register. Redeem. Login. Three easy steps that open the door to a variety of print and media resources in downloadable, digital format, available to instructors exclusively through the Pearson/Prentice Hall 'IRC'.
www.pearsonhighered.com/irc

"Choose from a wide range of video resources for the classroom!"
Prentice Hall Reference Library: Life Skills Pack (ISBN: 0-13-127079-6).
Contains all 4 videos, or they may be requested individually as follows:
- *Learning Styles and Self-Awareness*, 0-13-028502-1
- *Critical and Creative Thinking*, 0-13-028504-8
- *Relating to Others*, 0-13-028511-0
- *Personal Wellness*, 0-13-028514-5

Prentice Hall Reference Library: Study Skills Pack (ISBN: 0-13-127080-X).
Contains all 6 videos, or they may be requested individually as follows:
- *Reading Effectively*, 0-13-028505-6
- *Listening and Memory*, 0-13-028506-4
- *Note Taking and Research*, 0-13-028508-0
- *Writing Effectively*, 0-13-028509-9
- *Effective Test Taking*, 0-13-028500-5
- *Goal Setting and Time Management*, 0-13-028503-X

<u>Prentice Hall Reference Library: Career Skills Pack</u> (ISBN: 0-13-118529-2).
Contains all 3 videos, or they may be requested individually as follows:
- *Skills for the 21st Century – Technology*, 0-13-028512-9
- *Skills for the 21st Century – Math and Science*, 0-13-028513-7
- *Managing Career and Money*, 0-13-028516-1
  Complete Reference Library - Life/Study Skills/Career Video Pack on DVD (ISBN: 0-13-501095-0).
- Our Reference Library of thirteen popular video resources has now been digitized onto one DVD so students and instructors alike can benefit from the array of video clips. Featuring Life Skills, Study Skills, and Career Skills, they help to reinforce the course content in a more interactive way.

<u>Faculty Video Resources</u>
- Teacher Training Video 1: *Critical Thinking*, ISBN: 0-13-099432-4
- Teacher Training Video 2: *Stress Management & Communication*, ISBN: 0-13-099578-9
- Teacher Training Video 3: *Classroom Tips*, ISBN: 0-13-917205-X
- Student Advice Video, ISBN: 0-13-233206-X
- Study Skills Video, ISBN: 0-13-096095-0

<u>Current Issues Videos</u>
- ABC News Video Series: *Student Success Second Edition*, ISBN: 0-13-031901-5
- ABC News Video Series: *Student Success Third Edition*, ISBN: 0-13-152865-3

<u>MyStudentSuccessLab PH Videos on DVD</u> (ISBN: 0-13-514249-0).
- Our six most popular video resources have been digitized onto one DVD so students and instructors alike can benefit from the array of video clips. Featuring Technology, Math and Science, Managing Money and Career, Learning Styles and Self-Awareness, Study Skills, and Peer Advice, they help to reinforce the course content in a more interactive way. They are also accessible through our MSSL and course management offerings and available on VHS.

"Through partnership opportunities, we offer a variety of assessment options!"
<u>LASSI</u> - The LASSI is a 10-scale, 80-item assessment of students' awareness about and use of learning and study strategies. Addressing skill, will and self-regulation, the focus is on both covert and overt thoughts, behaviors, attitudes and beliefs that relate to successful learning and that can be altered through educational interventions. Available in two formats: Paper ISBN: 0-13-172315-4 or Online ISBN: 0-13-172316-2 (access card).

<u>Noel Levitz/RMS</u> – This retention tool measures Academic Motivation, General Coping Ability, Receptivity to Support Services, PLUS Social Motivation. It helps identify at-risk students, the areas with which they struggle, and their receptiveness to support. Available in paper or online formats, as well as short and long versions. Paper Long Form A: ISBN: 0-13-512066-7; Paper Short Form B: ISBN: 0-13-512065-9; Online Forms A,B & C: ISBN: 0-13-098158-3.

<u>Robbins Self Assessment Library</u> – This compilation teaches students to create a portfolio of skills. S.A.L. is a self-contained, interactive, library of 49 behavioral questionnaires that help students discover new ideas about themselves, their attitudes, and their personal strengths and weaknesses. Available in Paper, CD-Rom, and Online (Access Card) formats.

<u>Readiness for Education at a Distance Indicator(READI)</u> - READI is a web-based tool that assesses the overall likelihood for online learning success. READI generates an immediate score and a diagnostic interpretation of results, including recommendations for successful participation in online courses and potential remediation sources.
Please visit www.readi.info for additional information. ISBN: 0-13-188967-2.

<u>Pathway to Student Success CD-ROM</u>
The CD is divided into several categories, each of which focuses on a specific topic that relates to students and provides them with the context, tools and strategies to enhance their educational experience. ISBN: 0-13-239314-X.

<u>The Golden Personality Type Profiler</u>
The Golden Personality Type Profiler™ helps students understand how they make decisions and relate to others. By completing the Golden Personality Type Profiler™ students develop a deeper understanding of their strengths, a clearer picture of how their behavior impacts others, and a better appreciation for the interpersonal style of others and how to interact with them more effectively. Using these results as a guide, students will gain the self awareness that is key to professional development and success. ISBN: 0-13-706654-6.

"For a truly tailored solution that fosters campus connections and increases retention, talk with us about custom publishing."
<u>Pearson Custom Publishing</u> – We are the largest custom provider for print and media shaped to your course's needs. Please visit us at <u>www.pearsoncustom.com</u> to learn more.

STUDENT SUPPORT –
Tools to help make the grade now, and excel in school later.

"Now there's a Smart way for students to save money."
CourseSmart is an exciting new choice for students looking to save money. As an alternative to purchasing the printed textbook, students can purchase an electronic version of the same content. With a CourseSmart eTextbook, students can search the text, make notes online, print out reading assignments that incorporate lecture notes, and bookmark important passages for later review. For more information, or to purchase access to the CourseSmart eTextbook, visit www.coursesmart.com

"Today's students are more inclined than ever to use technology to enhance their learning."
Refer to the MyStudentSuccessLab section of this Preface to learn about our revolutionary resource (www.mystudentsuccesslab.com) This online solution is designed to help students build the skills they need to succeed.

"Time management is the #1 challenge students face." We can help.
<u>Prentice Hall Planner</u> – A basic planner that includes a monthly & daily calendar plus other materials to facilitate organization. 8.5x11.
<u>Premier Annual Planner</u> - This specially designed, annual 4-color collegiate planner includes an academic planning/resources section, monthly planning section (2 pages/month), weekly planning section (48 weeks; July start date), which facilitate short-term as well as long-term planning. Spiral bound, 6x9. Customization is available.

"Journaling activities promote self-discovery and self-awareness."
<u>Student Reflection Journal</u> - Through this vehicle, students are encouraged to track their progress and share their insights, thoughts, and concerns. 8 1/2 x 11. 90 pages.

"The Student Orientation Series includes short booklets on specialized topics that facilitate greater student understanding."
S.O.S. Guides help students understand what these opportunities are, how to take advantage of them, and how to learn from their peers while doing so. They include:
- Connolly: *Learning Communities* ISBN: 0-13-232243-9
- Hoffman: *Stop Procrastination Now! 10 Simple and SUCCESSFUL Steps for Student Success*, ISBN: 0-13 513056-5
- Jabr: *English Language Learners* ISBN: 0-13-232242-0
- Watts: *Service Learning* ISBN: 0-13-232201-0

For Students!

Why is this course important?

This course will help you transition to college, introduce you to campus resources, and prepare you for success in all aspects of college, career, and life. You will:
- Develop Skills to Excel in Other Classes
- Apply Concepts from College to Your Career and Life
- Learn to Use Media Resources

How can you get the most out of the book and online resources required in this class?

Purchase your book and online resources before the First Day of Class. Register and log in to the online resources using your access code.

Develop Skills to Excel in Other Classes
- Helps you with your homework
- Prepares you for exams

Apply Concepts from College to Your Career and Life
- Provides learning techniques
- Helps you achieve your goals

Learn to Use Media Resources
- www.mystudentsuccesslab.com helps you build skills you need to succeed through peer-led videos, interactive exercises and projects, journaling and goal setting activities.
- Connect with real students, practice skill development, and personalize what is learned.

Want to get involved with Pearson like other students have?

Get involved with Pearson

Join www.PearsonStudents.com
It is a place where our student customers can incorporate their views and ideas into their learning experience. They come to find out about our programs such as the **Pearson Student Advisory Board, Pearson Campus Ambassador**, and the **Pearson Prize** (student scholarship!).

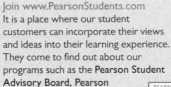

Here's how you can get involved:
- Tell your instructors, friends, and family members about **PearsonStudents**.
- To get daily updates on how students can boost their resumes, study tips, get involved with Pearson, and earn rewards:

  f Become a fan of **Pearson Students** on Facebook

  t Follow **@Pearson_Student** on Twitter

- Explore **Pearson Free Agent**. It allows you get involved in the publishing process, by giving student feedback.

See you on **PearsonStudents** where our student customers live. When students succeed, we succeed!

MyStudentSuccessLab is an online solution designed to help students acquire the skills they need to succeed. They will have access to peer-led video presentations and develop core skills through interactive exercises and projects that provide academic, life, and career skills that will transfer to ANY course.

It can accompany any Student Success text, or be sold as a stand-alone course offering. To become successful learners, students must consistently apply techniques to daily activities.

How will MyStudentSuccessLab make a difference?

Is motivation a challenge, and if so, how do you deal with it?
Video Presentation – Experience peer led video 'by students, for students' of all ages and stages.

How would better class preparation improve the learning experience?
Practice activities – Practice skills for each topic - beginning, intermediate, and advanced - leveled by Bloom's taxonomy.

"I liked that it gives students the opportunity to discover the content and I think that's the key, not only in face-to-face teaching, but also online as well."

Meg Hunter, Gateway Technical College (Wisconsin)

What could you gain by building critical thinking and problem-solving skills in this class?
Apply (final project)
– Complete a final project using these skills to create 'personally relevant' resources.

As an instructor, how much easier would it be to assign and use MyStudentSuccessLab
if you had an Implementation guide?
Instructor Guide – Describes each activity, the skills addressed, an estimate of student time
on task, and a grading rubric for the final Apply activity.

MyStudentSuccessLab Feature set:

Topic Overview: Module objectives.

Video Presentation - Connect: Real student video interviews on key issues.

Practice: Three skill-building exercises per topic provide interactive experience and practice.

Apply - Personalize: Apply what is learned by creating a personally relevant project and journal.

Resources: Plagiarism Guide, Dictionary, Calculators, and Assessments (Career, Learning Styles, and Personality Styles).

Additional Assignments: Extra suggested activities to use with each topic.

Text-Specific Study Plan (available with select books): Chapter Objectives, Practice Tests, Enrichment activities, and Flashcards.

MyStudentSuccessLab Topic List -

1. Time Management/Planning
2. Values/Goal Setting
3. Learning How You Learn
4. Listening and Taking Class Notes
5. Reading and Annotating
6. Memory and Studying
7. Critical Thinking

8. Problem-Solving
9. Information Literacy
10. Communication
11. Test Prep and Test Taking
12. Stress Management
13. Financial Literacy
14. Majors and Careers

MyStudentSuccessLab Support:

• Demos, Registration, Log-in - www.mystudentsuccesslab.com under "Tours and Training" and "Support."

• Email support - Send an inquiry to MyStudentSuccessLab@pearson.com

• Online Training - Join one of our weekly WebEx training sessions.

• Peer Training - Faculty Advocate connection for qualified adoptions.

• Technical support - 24 hours a day, seven days a week, at http://247pearsoned.custhelp.com

A 'one-stop shop' for student success.

This website offers a compilation of Pearson's training, resources, and support options all in one convenient place.

We provide variety of Training options to meet your needs. Events and Workshops around the country as well as Online Webinars. MyStudentSuccessLab Technology training is available too.

A wealth of Resources are available to address a range of interests, including assessments, online catalog, customized solutions, Instructor Resources, and Student Resources. Technology is addressed, whether you're teaching online, hybrid, or just need an engagement tool.

For Support, always contact your local sales professional, however, the SSCD Team is here to help anytime including Customer Service, Technical Support, Editorial, Events, Marketing, Specialists, and Faculty Advocates.

Welcome to the Pearson SSCD Online Community where we connect, empower, and renew with one another. Regardless of your institute origin, teaching background, or experience level, we strive to ensure there are resources available to support our mission—infusing success for EVERY student and instructor!

www.pearsonhighered.com/sscd4success

Many parents and students all over the globe believe in the value, the usefulness, of earning a college degree. Students believe that earning a college degree will help prepare them for a future career, and parents hope a college diploma will secure better lives for their children (Boyer, 1987). But a college education means more than salary, status, or security; it means learning about yourself and the communities around you.

Most students believe college will help them become educated and trained for a career, and they think the chief benefit of a college education is its effect on earning power (Levine, 1989). This *Foundations for Learning* textbook will challenge you to examine other ways your education will benefit you beyond considering your potential gross income.

A key concept explored in the chapters that follow is making personal choices. One important choice that students often forget they have made is the decision to attend college. The bases for these decisions differ from student to student. As one first-year student explains:

> I am in college so I can further my education, and get a better job so I can better myself in the long run. I don't always like being here, but I know I have to go to school somewhere. I mean, it's just, what do you have if you don't have an education? You don't really have much.

Another student says, "My mom went to the University of North Carolina, Chapel Hill. She had the same college experience I'm going to have. I see my mom is successful, and I think, I'll do the same thing. I'll be successful." As you read this textbook, think about your decision-making process: why did you decide to attend college, and what do you hope to get out of the experience?

The central philosophy of *Foundations for Learning* is that of "claiming an education," the idea that learning in college demands that students engage with the material presented (Rich, 1977). Your perception of college may be that you'll sit quietly, taking notes lecture after lecture, but you will likely find college to be quite different from your initial expectations. Instead of thinking about college as a place where professors dump information into you that you then "know," *Foundations for Learning* will help you see that learning is more than mere collection and absorption—and more than doing the minimum amount of work required. Learning involves making connections, taking calculated risks, and being open to change; and these concepts are discussed in the context of your new environment. This textbook will help you better prepare for learning in a new environment, as well as for the challenges presented by college or university professors.

You'll be encouraged to claim your education in many ways, including working to gain membership in a scholarly community, reflecting on your academic self-concept, developing your planning abilities, becoming more aware of the ways in which you think and learn, communicating more effectively in writing and in class discussion, and approaching classes and exams in a manner that enables deep processing as opposed to rote memorization. These topics are presented in the context of current research as well as the voices of first-year students, highlighted by the experiences of actual college students in student narratives, reflections and student portraiture boxes in each chapter.

Two other concepts stressed repeatedly across chapters are the ideas of being open to change and being able to self-reflect. As you'll read in Chapter One, the transition from a high school to college environment means rethinking your attitudes and behaviors related to learning. As you make this transition, you will be most successful if you are able to reflect periodically on these attitudes and behaviors—*and* if you have the motivation, and, ideally, the humility, you will be able to work toward making any necessary changes. If, for example, you understand the theory surrounding breaking down large assignments into manageable pieces, but don't ever put the theory into practice, you won't benefit.

Institutions of higher education recognize the need to support students as they face the increasing academic demands of college, resulting in first-year experience courses, academic success centers, academic advising, tutoring services, writing centers, and other student-centered initiatives. Discussing effective ways to maximize first-year students' capabilities for academic success—indeed, how to get the most out of the opportunities just noted—is the primary goal of the *Foundations for Learning* textbook. This text focuses on the process of learning how to learn, developing academic performance techniques, and cultivating the habits of mind for lifelong achievement and success.

Chapter One will help you clarify your responsibilities as a college student and what professors and college/university staff expect of you, both in and out of the classroom. You will find at the college level that you will be asked to take a significantly more active role in your own learning than you did in high school. In the college environment, if you choose not to do the reading in chemistry, for example, your teacher won't make you stay after school; instead, you will be unable to contribute to the class discussion, have to squeeze in this reading at a later date, and feel like you have fallen behind. And, if you choose to read an unassigned text about a subject mentioned briefly in your Western civilization class, you won't necessarily be given special recognition or credit. Discovering and exploring your interests is what college is all about.

Chapter One asks you to clarify your responsibilities as a college student and think about how you will handle meeting the heightened academic expectations of higher education. Chapter Two will help you conduct a more in-depth exploration of what Chapter One asks you to do. Chapter Two asks you to reflect on your thoughts and feelings about your continuing role as a student and how those thoughts and feelings may influence your ability to meet the many demands you will be facing. Further, Chapter Two challenges you to explore your relationships with your family, your peers, and your new relationship with your college or university, and how these relationships will contribute to your role as a student. Chapter Three asks you to consider how the diversity of your campus will influence your developing self-concept.

Chapter Four centers on prioritizing your time as a college student. Eleanor Roosevelt once said, "If you want something done, ask a busy person," implying that people who have a lot to do, and get it all done, must be highly organized. Procrastination, the enemy of those of us who need to manage our time systematically, is also addressed.

In Chapter Five, the focus shifts to metacognitive strategies. Metacognition means "thinking about how you think." Here, you will read about strategies that help you learn about how you think: by using writing, namely writing to learn and journal writing, as well as reading, including a technique called "text annotation." Chapter Six covers developing communication skills with a focus on college-level writing. Writing the research paper is another activity introduced in this chapter, including suggestions regarding how to select a topic, how to gather useful information, and how to cite sources properly. Other important communication skills are discussed here as well, including becoming a participant in class discussions and making effective in-class presentations.

In an effort to help you get more out of studying than the ability to recall information for a 24-hour period, Chapter Seven explores numerous active reading, note-taking, and study methods that will help you benefit from what you have learned long into the future. These methods include how you read a textbook before you go to class, listen and take notes during lectures, and review your notes and readings after you've attended a lecture. You'll also see the importance of synthesizing the notes you've taken in class with the material from your readings. Of course, students often prefer to study in groups, and Chapter 7 also explains how to conduct productive study group sessions. Finally, Chapter 7 outlines a step-by-step process for responding to various types of exam questions.

Once you've mastered the habits and skills in Chapters One through Seven, Chapter Eight illustrates how you can continue to apply them in your life after college.

The *Foundations for Learning textbook,* then, offers insight into how to be a successful college student so you don't have to learn everything the hard way. If you read this textbook with an open mind and are willing to implement the many strategies, suggestions, and advice offered, you are likely to discover new ways to engage with peers and course material. In other words, you will adapt more easily to your new environment. You will also be reminded of what is expected of college students—and the importance of your attitude toward your own education. As you turn these pages, read actively, be willing to change, and thereby begin your journey toward membership in a community of learners.

REFERENCES

Boyer, E. (1987). *College: The undergraduate experience in America*. New York, NY: Harper & Row.

Levine, A. (1989). *Shaping higher education's future: Demographic realities and opportunities 1990–2000*. San Francisco, CA: Jossey-Bass.

Rich, A. (1977). *Claiming an education*. Speech delivered to the students of Douglass College, Rutgers University, New Brunswick, NJ.

CHAPTER ONE

Becoming Part of a Scholarly Community

In This Chapter

Adjust Your Mindset

- Do you possess intellectual curiosity?
- What do your professors expect of you?
- What are your responsibilities as a member of the campus community?
- What do you do when you come across something you don't understand?
- How does working with others result in scholarship?
- What is academic honesty, plagiarism, and intellectual property?

Adjust Your Strategies

- What can you do to develop intellectual curiosity?
- How do you find out what your professors expect of you?
- What document on your campus outlines your responsibilities as a member of the campus community? Where would you find it?
- What role do you play in the learning process? What campus resource can help you clarify that role? Where are they located?
- What personnel on your campus are in the best position to help you understand the concepts of academic honesty, plagiarism, and intellectual property?

lot has been going on at your college or university before your arrival on campus. Students have been working on case studies, conducting chemistry experiments, composing book-length master's theses, and having discussions about Foucault over coffee. Residence hall directors and student affairs personnel have developed a growing understanding of the needs of students, and food services management has worked on providing a diverse and healthy menu for students. The director of the library has been continually updating the library's print and online offerings, and the information technology department has worked to ensure that classroom labs are equipped with the latest technology. Students from the local community as well as those from across the country and all over the globe have traveled the same sidewalks and traversed the same corridors you now do.

So how will you react to this bustling campus and its ongoing conversations? Indeed, experts who study student success would encourage you to get involved with your campus community and be an active participant in this dialogue. Picture yourself walking into an enormous room full of people talking; listen for a while if you would like, but don't forget to offer your own contributions. Rhetorician Kenneth Burke's (1973) explanation of this concept has been referred to as the Burkean parlor:

> Imagine that you enter a parlor. You come late. When you arrive, others have long preceded you, and they are engaged in a heated discussion, a discussion too heated for them to pause and tell you exactly what it is about. In fact, the discussion had already begun long before any of them got there, so that no one present is qualified to retrace for you all the steps that had gone before. You listen for a while, until you decide that you have caught the tenor of the argument; then you put in your oar. Someone answers; you answer him; another comes to your defense; another aligns himself against you, to either the embarrassment or gratification of your opponent, depending upon the quality of your ally's assistance. However, the discussion is interminable. The hour grows late; you must depart. And you do depart, with the discussion still vigorously in progress. (pp. 110–111)

In the pages that follow, you will enter into an ongoing conversation regarding the factors that lead to college success. Essentially, you will hear what experts in the field have to say regarding ways to "claim your education." For the philosophies and techniques addressed, you will be provided with research to support the advice offered. These research findings stretch back over 30 years in some cases, and it is important to consider the history regarding these concepts to apply them to current situations— your college education, in particular—in an educated way.

As a two- or four-year college or university student, then, you have the opportunity to join a **scholarly community**, a group of people working toward intellectual pursuits, but your membership is not guaranteed. You must work toward familiarizing yourself with the guiding principles of that community and aspire toward them if you are to be considered a peer in this environment.

You may be asking yourself, "Besides fellow classmates, who are my peers in this environment?" The answer may surprise you. Professors are experts in their respective fields—or scholarly communities—who are helping students gain access to, and membership in, these same communities. In the context of the classroom, for example, students are expected to engage in scholarly discussions with their professors, raise questions, and, at times, even challenge them.

For a moment, think about your professors' perspectives. From their vantage point, you have made a life-altering decision to attend college. As an adult, in control of your own destiny, you have chosen to enter into a scholarly community and work toward earning membership. This process is very different from attending high school, which is a compulsory endeavor. The assumption here is that college is a carefully arrived at, well-thought-out choice. You *want* to be in college. You are excited about, and interested in, many, if not most, of the topics presented to you; and you are highly motivated to master new bodies of knowledge.

You'll make many more choices now that you are attending college. You will also, for example, need to decide which courses you'd like to take, and the professor and student contract is one way you demonstrate your willingness to engage with the material in each of these courses.

> ### Student Portrait
>
> **Kay:** "I can't really talk to my professors. It's because they're kind of evaluating you and so like you go on a more personal basis with them. I don't feel very comfortable about it. My science teacher right now, I don't feel too comfortable around him 'cause I'm not doing too great in his class. It's like they're up there, and you're all the way down here. That's how it is to me."

THE PROFESSOR AND STUDENT CONTRACT

T eaching and learning are enhanced when teachers and learners have shared expectations regarding course outcomes. For this reason, college professors construct a **syllabus**, a document outlining the desired course outcomes and other relevant information for each course they teach. Syllabi are usually shared with students during the first week of class, if not the first day or earlier.

Each syllabus you are given will help you understand important information about the course and your professor: what goals you are expected to strive toward, what will be expected of you, how your work will be assessed, and perhaps even what a typical class meeting might involve.

It would be beneficial, then, to consider these syllabi carefully, understanding that your acceptance of their terms—even if this is conveyed through silent approval—is a prerequisite for being a student in that class. If you have questions about what you should expect after reading the syllabus, ask your professor. Conscious acceptance of, and continued adherence to, your course contract is part of being a responsible member of a scholarly community.

> ### Pull-outs:
>
> *Conscious acceptance of, and continued adherence to, your course contract is part of being a responsible member of a scholarly community.*
>
> *Active learning is about students becoming agents in their own educational process.*
>
> *Through collaboration, you'll learn when and how to make concessions to arrive at a final product that is truly the work of an entire group.*
>
> *Attribution is the key to avoiding plagiarism.*

Instructor: Dr. Laurie Hazard
Section: PY 260 B, MWF, 12:00 PM-12:50 PM, UNI 382
Office Hours: MWF 2:00–4:00 PM; TR 9:00–10:30 AM
Phone: (401)-232-6746
e-mail: lhazard@bryant.edu

Course Description

An introduction to the basic concepts and fundamental principles of human behavior using the historical background of psychology as a foundation, and present theory and research as a tool to explore principles of learning, human development, motivation, personality, interpersonal skills, and mental health.

WEEK	DATE	CHAPTER(S)	TOPIC	ARTICLE/ACTIVITY
Week 1	Sept 5	1	Introduction to Course Requirements	Information Sheets
Week 1	Sept 7	1	Introduction: Thinking Critically With Psychology	More Than One In Three College Students Diagnosed With Alcohol Disorders
Week 2	Sept 10	1, 2	Introduction: Thinking Critically With Psychology/Biology and Behavior	

Grading

Participation is worth **15%**. Talking through the new concepts in class will help you learn the complex material. Discussion as a mode of instruction is a critical piece. You are required to participate. Throughout the semester, I will make recommendations of outside support to help you fully participate and maximize your potential in class. Taking advantage of these opportunities will significantly bolster your participation grade.

Attendance is worth **5%**. Please refer to the Attendance Policy in the <u>Bryant Student Handbook</u> on page 8. All students are expected to attend every class, arrive on time, and remain for the entire class. Students will be responsible for all material and information given out during class time. This will be applicable whether a student attends a particular class. Similarly, there will be no make-up for any missed in-class activities or assignments due to the absence of the student. No late assignments will be accepted.

Homework is worth **20%** and will consist of a weekly written assignment synthesizing an article and chapter.

Exam (1) is worth **15%**. The first exam will consist of material from chapters 1–6. The *Final* is worth **25%** and will consist of material from chapters 7–10, and 12–15. Both exams will be a combination of objective items and short essays.

Research Paper is worth **20%**. Information will be furnished in class.

Keep your syllabi handy throughout the semester. These documents often include a listing of topics, assignments, and other information you'll need to be prepared for future class meetings. Your professor may very well include a list of all of your assignments on the course syllabus and not mention them again until they are collected for grading. This information can be quite useful when you are planning your schedule in an attempt to manage your time effectively and efficiently.

Look at your syllabi carefully. There is likely a section on each syllabus that explains exactly how you will be graded in the particular course. For example, where you see the list of your assignments, you may also see exactly what each assignment is worth toward your overall grade. That is, if a research paper is a graded component of the course, it may be worth 30%. You may have exams, quizzes, and group projects in your classes. What is each of those components worth toward your overall grade in the course?

Your syllabus may also provide you with some insight into the professor's personality and teaching style. To what extent are the course expectations outlined on the syllabus? Are the expectations described briefly or in great detail? Compare the styles of each of your syllabi. For professors who tend to provide less information on a syllabus, they may expect you to visit them during their office hours to discuss the course expectations in more depth. Professor's office hours are often recorded on a syllabus. On the other hand, for professors who give a wide variety of information on the syllabus, they may have anticipated common questions students might ask regarding course expectations. Their strategy is to provide the students with that information from the outset. The point is to analyze your syllabus carefully. Professors operate under the assumption that you have read it, and therefore, fully understand the course requirements.

The key is to remember that the syllabus is an essential component of being a responsible member of a scholarly community. **Responsibility** literally means your response-ability, that is, your ability to choose a response. Ultimately, how you choose to respond to the requirements of your syllabi, for instance, will dictate your academic experience. Will you embrace all of the suggested assignments and complete them to the best of your ability, or will you respond by skipping books on your supplemental reading list? As you will soon learn, your response to the syllabus has implications for how much you will learn each semester.

One last bit of advice regarding course syllabi: many times your syllabi will include guiding questions to focus your attention on certain topics or themes in a course. Pay close attention to such questions because it would not be unusual to see them again in some form on a test or exam. It will be up to you to determine, based on the delivery of course material, what questions will appear on a test or exam. To do so with reliability, you must be actively engaged with your professors in **intellectual discourse**, in other words, able to have a rational discussion about a particular subject with interested others. This type of conversation will necessitate asking questions and searching for answers, which will ultimately lead to more questions. As in the Burkean parlor, the idea is that the conversation does not end when you leave the (class)room. To experience such discourse, though, requires teachers and learners alike to possess the trait of intellectual curiosity.

INTELLECTUAL CURIOSITY

Y ou may need to reflect on previous experiences to determine if you possess intellectual curiosity. Peggy Maki (2002), an expert in higher education assessment, defines intellectual curiosity as "the characteristic ability to question, challenge, look at an issue from multiple perspectives, seek more information before rushing to judgment, raise questions, deliberate, and craft well-reasoned arguments" (p. 6). You may use what you have read so far in this chapter to help you determine if you do, in fact, possess a high degree of intellectual curiosity.

Start out by asking yourself, "If I come across something I don't know or don't understand, what do I normally do? Do I skip the concept and hope the professor will deliver the answer in the next class?" For instance, in the first paragraph of this chapter, when you encountered the last name of an individual, Foucault, did you attempt to investigate who this person was if you did not already know? If you did, you may have discovered that he was a French philosopher and social critic who himself possessed intellectual curiosity. As he reflects on why he was attracted to a scholarly environment, he muses,

> We did not know when I was ten or eleven years old, whether we would become German or remain French. We would not know whether we would die or not in the bombing, and so on. When I was sixteen or seventeen I knew only one thing: school life was an environment protected from exterior menaces, politics. And I have always been fascinated by living in a protected scholarly environment, in an intellectual milieu. Knowledge is for me that which must function as a protection of individual existence and as a comprehension of the exterior world. I think that's it. Knowledge as a means of surviving by understanding. (qtd. in Foss, Foss, & Trapp 1991, p. 210)

If you possess intellectual curiosity, you might read these statements and, if it's not immediately apparent, assume the reference in the first few sentences is to World War II. If you were not sure, you might investigate further. You might read this passage and wonder what it would be like for a 10- or 11-year-old to face his or her mortality; question Foucault's perspective that school life is protected from exterior menaces, and perhaps disagree with this assertion; consider what knowledge means to Foucault, and thereby reflect on your own definition of knowledge; or wonder what he means when he says that knowledge is a means of "surviving by understanding."

Indeed, an intellectually curious individual collects and processes information in an elaborate, sophisticated manner. This manner of thinking is a habit, a disposition; the intellectually curious individual is in a routine of thinking deeply. You may be concerned that when you read Foucault's passage, you did not "wonder" to the extent that was described. Perhaps you did not wonder at all. You may be feeling anxious that you do not possess a disposition toward intellectual curiosity, and, without this, cannot earn membership into a scholarly community.

Fortunately, like training your body to run a marathon, you can train your mind toward the disposition of intellectual curiosity. To do so requires a particular mindset; it requires you to be *active*. You need to begin by analyzing ways in which you learn, and start thinking about how you are going to approach the endeavor of joining a scholarly community.

ACTIVE VERSUS PASSIVE LEARNING

The distinction that will be made here between activity and passivity does not have to do with physical behaviors but with psychological mindsets. One of these mindsets is that of the **passive learner**. Individuals consciously or unconsciously subscribing to this philosophy expect faculty to teach them what they need to know (and *only* what they need to know). They want the library to have the journal article or book they need when they need it, and they wouldn't consider reading an essay or book that was not required reading in one of their classes. They glance through assigned material with minimal investment, expecting that the professor will offer a clear and concise summary and analysis of the reading. They may even expect the professor to tell them exactly what questions will appear on an upcoming test. After all, goes the thinking, what is all of that tuition money for, anyway?

A philosophy more beneficial to college students is that of the **active learner**. Active learners believe students are NOT at college to be acted on and led through a series of disjointed activities toward some fuzzy end indicated by the receipt of a diploma. Active learning is about students becoming agents in their own educational process. After all, who has a greater stake in this process than the student learner?

Active learning involves doing many of the activities suggested in this textbook. Take reading, for example, or, more precisely, *active* reading. Instead of passively highlighting most of a chapter with only a moderate level of comprehension, active readers engage more directly with the text. Some active readers perform text annotation, whereby the student's reaction to what is read is written in the margins of the text itself. In this manner, questions can be asked—questions to which the student sincerely seeks answers. These questions could be brought up in class or during faculty office hours.

The ardent active learner likely wouldn't wait until class to seek out answers, however. The active learner's intellectual curiosity would encourage her to search for an answer to that question: in the index of the text in question, in other works that author has written, in works by other authors on that same subject. The goal of an active learner is to come to a better understanding, the consequence of which is asking more questions and searching for more answers.

Similarly, active listening requires you to consider carefully what a speaker has to say. An active listener identifies a speaker's main idea as well as the rationale used to support that idea. Equally important is what may be lacking from the speaker's rationale. Rest assured, for example, that members of Congress, particularly those aligned with the opposing political party, listen actively to the president's State of the Union Address. They are interested in the president's focus: what topics have been emphasized, and which have been deemphasized or avoided entirely? They are interested in the reasoning and evidence employed by the president. Often times the State of the Union Address is followed by criticism made by members of the opposing party, criticism resulting from active listening. Active listening, then, as does active reading, leads to questions.

Even the most active of learners, at times, get stuck in their quest for answers. They may, at these moments, resist thinking about a problem in different ways, a concept that two psychologists, Friedman and Lipshitz (1992), termed "automatic thinking." Automatic thinking is efficient when dealing with routine activities and situations like getting dressed. Yet, as Friedman and Lipshitz note, the advantage of automatic thinking can become a disadvantage when in the face of change or uncertainty. They argue that automatic thinking leads people to rely on what they already know; it contributes to a tendency to ignore critical information and rely on standard behavior repertoires when change is required. That is, people will continue to do what they feel most comfortable doing even if it isn't working for them. They resist change.

Accepting the assertion that automatic thinking can be a disadvantage when in the face of change or uncertainty, how might automatic thinking affect you as a first-year student? One of the major changes you will confront as a first-year student is uncertainty in approaching studying for your college courses. You will likely find out that the study skills you utilized in high school will not produce the same results when you apply them to college-level courses. Practitioners who help first-year students develop college-level study habits report that, indeed, students tend to cling to their old, comfortable habits even if these habits don't produce the results for which the students had hoped.

Consider the first-year student, Colleen, who completed high school with a B+ average. For her first major college exam, Colleen does what she did in high school: she waits until the night before to study. She begins diligently to prepare index cards, recording an important definition on each card. She finds that with the large volume of information she needs to know, it is taking her a lot longer to make index cards than it ever did before. "That's okay," she says to herself, "I'm in college now; this *should* take a little longer." After four hours of making index cards, it is well past midnight. Poor Colleen has run out of time and is too exhausted to review the cards she has made. She's a little nervous, but reasons that she has spent twice as much time studying than she had ever done before, so she should be ready. She takes the exam. It's much more difficult than she expected, and she is confused by some of the questions. She earns a C on her first college-level exam.

This mediocre grade is a bit of a blow to her ego. After all, in her estimation, she is not a C student; she's at least a B student. In her view, this grade is a failure. She reflects on the experience in earnest and grants that she did run out of time making her index cards and did not have enough time to review. The next test comes along three weeks later and she sets about making her index cards well in advance, this time leaving ample time for review. At the end of her grueling eight-hour study session, she has each and every index card memorized backward and forward. She is ready for the test! In fact, she's energized and excited; she feels in total control of the material. Never has she been so dedicated to her studies. This amount of effort should surely yield an A. Once again, though, her exam is returned with a grade of 76 marked clearly at the top.

How could this happen? She worked so hard. She put in what she considered an inordinate amount of effort. For Colleen, studying for eight hours was unprecedented. This time, she feels angry, frustrated, and helpless. She did exactly what she was supposed to do! In her automatic thinking mode, she never considered that the grade might have resulted from *how* she was studying. Although she adjusted the length of time spent studying, her two approaches were nearly identical. With automatic thinking, people tend to see only what they know and ignore critical information. When it comes to change, they gravitate toward their comfort zones. Colleen never considered that making index cards or relying on memorization as a learning skill wasn't working. She automatically assumed that her personal failure resulted from the *time* she spent studying.

The negative consequences of automatic thinking can contribute to failure. Active thinking, argue Friedman and Lipshitz (1992), "enables people to see situations differently and to experiment with novel responses. It also enables them to become aware of how they select, interpret, and act on information about themselves and the contexts in which they act" (p. 119). Albert Einstein once said that the definition of insanity is doing the same thing over and over again and expecting different results. Becoming an active learner requires a student to experiment with new ways of learning, particularly if their old ways aren't yielding the desired results.

Changing requires a certain amount of risk taking. Changing from automatic thinking to active thinking is not easy; it requires students to take full responsibility for their own learning. That is not to say a student will have to attempt to **switch cognitive gears,** or go from one mode of thought to another, alone (Louis & Sutton, 1991, p. 119). On a college campus, there are many people who can help.

The faculty and staff of institutions of higher education want students to be successful. For this reason, they establish mechanisms by which students can bolster their understanding of course material outside of the classroom. Some of these mechanisms are faculty office hours, tutoring and writing centers, counseling centers, and language labs, all integral parts of the scholarly community. The prevailing thought on a college campus is that learning occurs both inside and outside of the classroom. To get the most out of your college experience, the expectation is that all students will engage in extensive out-of-classroom learning.

You may be required to utilize and/or familiarize yourself with some of these academic programs and services. More than likely, however, you will have quite a bit of choice as to when, how frequently, and for what purposes you do so. If, for example, your economics professor requires students to visit the tutoring center periodically during the course of the semester, it is up for students to decide what "periodically" will mean for them. Periodically could mean visiting the center to check your comprehension of material the day before each exam. For others, periodically might mean a weekly appointment. Some students will elect to work with a tutor after they've studied to make sure they are prepared for a test. Others will want to review class materials weekly to prevent the possibility of getting lost. Although the choice is up to you, it is strongly suggested that you consciously consider the way(s) you plan on using each service—in other words, to take response-ability, to be an active learner, and to claim these services as part of your education—and that you realize that the way you use a resource will affect what you get out of the experience.

Many times students' attitudes prevent them from seeking help. Some students who end up in academic difficulty at the end of the semester confess they were just too proud or embarrassed to ask for help. For some, the inability to ask for help may result in poor grades. In a scholarly community, the expectation is that you will be an active learner and that you will search for clarification using all available resources. If you use the study techniques suggested and talk with your professor during office hours, you are doing some of the right things. That is, you are taking the advice offered and claiming your education. Another way to claim your education is to utilize tutoring services offered at your institution. Tutoring isn't a quick fix; it involves an ongoing relationship with a fellow student or professional, a person with whom you can have productive dialogues regarding course materials. Tutors can help confirm what you *do* understand as well as help you gain a better understanding of what you *don't*.

COLLABORATION

What better way to join a scholarly community than by working with one or more individuals toward a common goal? You will be afforded many such opportunities, so resist any urge you may feel to play it safe, stay in your automatic mode of thinking, and make the collaborative effort an individual effort. In other words, don't try to complete a collaborative assignment or task by yourself. You will learn far more if you are forced to consider the opinions of others, assign tasks, track progress, and develop interpersonal communication skills in the process. If collaboration is successful, the work of a group surpasses what would have been possible through the work of a single individual. Andrea

Lunsford (2002) admonishes students to debate with group members: "Expect disagreement, and remember that the goal is not for everyone just to 'go along.' The challenge is to get a really spirited debate going and to argue through all possibilities" (p. 34).

What types of collaborative activities might you participate in, you ask? These might involve in-class group work, study groups, group presentations, debates, and group papers/projects, to name a few of the more common activities. These situations are unique in their own way; just think about how long you have to get the group dynamic sorted out for in-class group work as opposed to a semester-long group project. Although many students dread collaboration, what they tend to call "group work," you will likely learn much about yourself and others from these experiences. You'll be learning to synthesize ideas—those of your own and those of other individuals both in and outside your group. Through collaboration, you'll learn when and how to make concessions to arrive at a final product that is truly the work of an entire group. Eugene Raudsepp (1984) neatly sums up the benefits of collaboration:

> Effective teamwork encourages each member to contribute his knowledge to the overall effort. . . . This combination of experience and trading of ideas enables them to learn from each other. It stimulates them to learn more, and to consider a greater variety of variables when solving problems. It brings out most of their latent abilities and provides an atmosphere for continuous growth and development. . . . Cooperative action by each of them contributes to a total effect that is greater than the sum of their independent contributions. (qtd. in Beckman, 1990, p. 129)

DOING RESEARCH

A discussion about scholarly communities would not be complete without mentioning **research**. Scholars investigate what others have said and/or written about topics in which they are interested. They use libraries and the Internet to perform some of this investigation. They also use the references in the works they find to lead to other useful sources. In addition to these solitary activities, scholars also talk to peers, other scholars in their field—at meetings, conferences, on the phone, and in person. In these ways, scholars stay up to date regarding their particular interests, whether those include molecular biology or still photography.

The research that is accessed has to first be conducted. In other words, the study referenced in Joe's sociology paper initially had to be performed. This aspect of research is another important contribution of scholars, namely, adding to the body of knowledge in their particular field. Through new research, scholars hope to say something that hasn't (quite) been said, make connections across/through ideas, and/or offer an analysis of previous research that helps others view the research in new ways.

How do you fit in to all of this? Well, as a scholar-in-the-making, you will be engaging in both of the activities just mentioned. You'll be familiarizing yourself with the body of knowledge in a number of disciplines, and you'll also be making your own contributions to the ongoing conversation. If this seems like an impossible goal, consider that these contributions will likely be small at first, but that all contributions potentially move the discussion forward.

PLAGIARISM AND INTELLECTUAL PROPERTY

One topic that professors often bring up when talking to students about an upcoming research project is plagiarism. Have you ever had the experience of someone taking credit for your idea? This act is referred to as **plagiarism**, presenting someone else's ideas as if they were your own. Of course, presenting someone else's ideas is not, in and of itself, plagiarism. If it were, scholars would be working in isolation, not benefiting from each other's work. Researchers and scholars commonly refer to each other's ideas, giving attribution to the sources of those ideas—whether those ideas were discovered through an interview, newspaper article, book, Listserv discussion, or Web site. Attribution is the key to avoiding plagiarism.

Some institutions subscribe to a service such as Turnitin.com, a site that serves as a clearinghouse for student essays. Professors may request that you submit your essay electronically to this site. Turnitin.com then checks the paper to determine whether the work is original—or whether there is a case of plagiarism.

Whether your paper will undergo electronic scrutiny or that of your professors, you want to be sure you have credited others for their ideas. Your college or university likely has an academic honesty policy or even have an honor code outlined in your student handbook. Here you are apt to find some clear consequences for committing plagiarism. Your professors may have outlined this same information on their syllabi. Why is plagiarism considered such a serious offense? The primary reason is likely that producing scholarship—conducting research and publishing findings—is hard work that often takes years, and, many times, the efforts of multiple individuals. The result of this labor is called **intellectual property**. This property is unique in some way: It contains some new concept or data set, or perhaps argues against a previously established correlation. At any rate, it is important that those integrating this intellectual property into their own research acknowledge the efforts of the authors. We will talk more about plagiarism and the ethics of research.

CLAIMING AN EDUCATION

Think back to the concept of responsibility defined earlier in this chapter: the ability to choose a response. You possess the power of choice. You have the ability to choose how you will respond to the new environment of higher education and the opportunities offered at your institution. You are urged to take responsibility for your educational choices and be an active participant in the experience. The foundation for optimal learning experiences at the college level rests in your ability to recognize your role and responsibility as a student. The person who has perhaps encapsulated this idea best is Adrienne Rich, a famous poet.

In a convocation speech given in 1977, she implores students to actively claim their education. She explains,

> The first thing I want to say to you who are students, is that you cannot afford to think of being here to *receive* an education: you will do much better to think of being here to *claim* one. One of the dictionary definitions of the verb "to claim" is: *to take as the rightful owner; to assert in the face of possible contradiction*. "To receive" is *to come into possession of: to act as receptacle or container for; to accept as authoritative or true*. The difference is that between acting and being acted upon.

→ Claim!

Notice the distinction between "acting" and "being acted upon." What Rich is emphasizing here is that you have the choice to act on the new environment of your institution or you can allow your first year to unfold, merely go with the flow, and simply let your college education happen to you.

Psychologists like Albert Bandura and Walter Mischel make similar distinctions. Bandura coined the term **reciprocal determinism,** which identifies the notion that there is a relationship between the person and the environment. Students can certainly be influenced by the new situations they'll find in college, but they can also choose how to behave (Pervin & John, 1997). Mischel (1976) elaborates on the concept of reciprocal determinism in action:

> The image is one of the human being as an active, aware, problem solver, capable of profiting from an enormous range of experiences and cognitive capacities, possessing great potential for good or ill, actively constructing his or her psychological world, and influencing the environment, but also being influenced by it in lawful ways. (qtd. in Pervin & John, 1997, p. 404)

If you choose to take sole responsibility for your education and claim it, that is, take it as opposed to receive it, the way in which Rich suggests, you will have the capability of profiting from the great range of experiences that await you.

The argument here is that how you interact with this new environment is entirely up to you. It is ultimately your responsibility. You may be wondering what responsibility means relative to learning, and perhaps even living, at your institution. Rich's convocation speech clearly outlines for students what responsibility means in terms of higher education. What follows are just a few of the ways she describes the concept of responsibility. According to Rich, responsibility means:

- "Refusing to let others do your thinking, talking, and naming for you"
- "Learning to respect and use your own brains and instincts; hence, grappling with hard work"

- "Insisting that those to whom you give your friendship and love are able to respect your mind"
- Not "falling for shallow, easy solutions"
- "Insisting on a life of meaningful work"
- Having "the courage to be different"
- "Expecting your faculty to take you seriously"
- "Refusing to sell your talents and aspirations short"

Rich's definition of responsibility acts as great advice for how you might think about conducting yourself during your first year. Which pieces of advice can you see yourself putting into action? Consider the first bit of advice, "refusing to let others do your thinking, talking, and naming for you." You might think, "Well, that depends on who the *others* are." The answer is whomever you have well-established relationships with or whomever you decide to enter into relationships with in the future. According to reciprocal determinism, not only will your relationships influence you, but you will also shape others.

We have looked at various ways you can claim your education, both in and out of the classroom, academically and socially. Our hope is that you will stake a more assertive claim and that you continue to evaluate the extent to which you are driving your educational process.

FIRST-YEAR DIARIES:
ADJUSTMENT REFLECTIONS

Adjusting to Campus Involvement ~ Kyle

A success that I felt I had this semester was being actively involved in campus life. I didn't sit in my room and wait for things to come to me. Rather, I took the initiative and was rewarded by being elected to the Executive Board of the Media Production Club for my remaining semesters at college.

Adjusting to the Syllabus ~ Alison

Through the "professor and student contract," teachers and learners can share expectations on specific course outcomes and consequently improve the learning process. Also, the process of using the class syllabus requires students to be actively engaged with the professors, asking questions and looking for answers. I found this suggestion to be both simple and practical, and I decided to apply it during this semester. I carefully analyzed the syllabus of each class I took and paid attention to the guiding questions some of them included. It really helped me a lot to understand the goals and objectives of each course, how the homework and quizzes were going to be assessed and relevant topics the class was going to cover. For example, the math syllabus said that there were going to be 12 pop quizzes throughout the semester, so I was ready for that. But the majority of the students who had not read the syllabus had an unpleasant surprise with the first pop quiz the professor gave.

Adjusting to Claiming an Education ~ Jimmie

I'll admit that during the first month and a half I was just receiving an education. I had a lot of different things going on when I first got to campus, and instead of making education my first priority; it got moved to the back. I was going to class, doing my homework, but I wasn't applying myself. In class I wouldn't really pay attention to what was being said. I wouldn't do my homework until the night before it was due. By the time midterm grades came out I had dug myself a big hole. Besides one class, all the rest of my grades were C's or D's. I knew I had to buckle down from then on. I chose to take the sole responsibility for my education. I got a tutor for one of my hardest classes. I began to actively take notes during class. I also tried to do my homework the night it was assigned instead of putting it off until the night before it was due. By claiming my education my grades improved from midterms.

DISCUSSION QUESTIONS

1. Are you currently a primarily active learner or passive learner? What leads you to draw this conclusion about yourself?

2. What specific actions can you take to gain membership into a scholarly community? What does it mean to be an active participant in one's education?

3. What is the relationship between campus resources and active learning?

4. You've likely received a number of course syllabi fairly recently. What do these documents have in common? Of what importance will these documents be in the remaining weeks of the semester?

5. Did your expectations regarding one or more of your classes change after having read the syllabus? How so/not?

6. Describe the ways in which you have demonstrated intellectual curiosity in the last week or so. Are you satisfied with the extent to which you have done so?

7. When have you engaged in automatic thinking? Why did you do so? What were the consequences?

8. Describe your previous collaborative experiences. Did you find them beneficial? What did you learn? What challenges do you face? Would you do anything differently the next time you collaborate?

9. What specific steps are you taking to claim your education?

10. Define what responsibility means to you. To what extent does Rich's definition of responsibility reflect your own?

ACTIVITIES

1.1 Identify a term or concept you heard or read about this week, and use this entry to ask questions to which you seek answers. Ask classmates, professors, staff members, friends, and/or family what they know about the term or concept. Perform a search on the Internet. Search the library's databases. Log your search—as well as your findings—in a journal entry or essay.

1.2 After completing the first assignment in one of your classes, visit the office hours of your professor. To demonstrate your intellectual curiosity, engage in a conversation about a question you had while completing the reading, what you'd like to accomplish through taking this class, or your professor's current research interests.

1.3 Use the services of one of the many campus resources available at your institution (e.g., the campus library or tutoring center). Write a journal entry or short essay about your experience utilizing that resource. What did you expect before you arrived? How did the actual visit correspond to your expectations? Were you satisfied with the outcome? How so/not?

1.4 Over the course of the next week or so, compile a list of terms with which you are not familiar. These terms may come from readings, lectures, class discussion, or TV, for that matter. Now that you have a list, seek out explanations/definitions for these words or phrases. What does this exercise tell you about your education? Are you intellectually curious?

1.5 This activity requires you to research first-year experience (FYE) courses at other institutions. Create a thesis (e.g., "FYE courses have grown in number exponentially in the last 10 years." Or, "most FYE courses focus on the same thing, namely, helping students develop college-level study skills.") and support your findings with evidence from three sources.

1.6 Examine the policies in place for committing plagiarism at your institution, information that can likely be found in your student handbook. How is plagiarism defined? What are the consequences of such an act? Are you satisfied with the explanation(s) offered?

1.7 Generate a list of your expectations of your professors prior to attending your first classes. Now compare these expectations to your observations after attending classes. What strikes you about this comparison?

1.8 Attend a campus organizational fair. What clubs and/or organizations would you be interested in joining? What would be your motivation for doing so? How would getting involved in this way possibly help you in ways you may not have thought of?

1.9 Rich's definition of responsibility acts as great advice for how you might think about conducting yourself during your first year. Take each of the eight pieces of advice and describe at least one example of how you might put the advice into action.

REFERENCES

Beckman, M. (1990). Collaborative learning. *College Teaching, 38*(4), 128–133.

Burke, K. (1973). *The philosophy of literary form* (3rd ed.). Berkeley, CA: University of California Press.

Foss, S., Foss, K., & Trapp, R. (1991). *Contemporary perspectives on rhetoric* (2nd ed.). Prospect Heights, IL: Waveland Press.

Friedman, V. J., & Lipshitz, R. (1992). Teaching people to shift cognitive gears: Overcoming resistance on the road to model II. *Journal of Applied Behavioral Research, 28*(1), 118–136.

Louis, M. R., & Sutton, R. I. (1991). Switching cognitive gears: From habits of mind to active thinking. *Human Relations, 44*(1), 55–76.

Lunsford, A. (2002). *The everyday writer* (2nd ed.). Boston, MA: St. Martin's Press.

Maki, P. (2002). Moving from paperwork to pedagogy: Channeling intellectual curiosity into a commitment to assessment [Electronic version]. *American Association for Higher Education Bulletin, 54*(9), 3–5.

Mischel, W. (1976). *Introduction to personality* (2nd ed.). Austin, TX: Holt, Rinehart and Winston.

Pervin, L. A., & John, O. P. (1997). *Personality theory and research* (7th ed.). New York, NY: Wiley.

Raudsepp, E. (1984). Effective teamwork. *Manage, 35,* 18–22.

Rich, A. (1977). Claiming an education. Speech delivered to the students of Douglass College, Rutgers University, New Brunswick, NJ.

Additional Readings for Students

Academic Honesty/Plagiarism

Ashworth, P., & Bannister, P. (1997). Guilty in whose eyes? University students' perceptions of cheating and plagiarism in academic work and assessment. *Studies in Higher Education, 22*(2), 187–204.

Gillian, S. (2002, July 15). It's a bird, it's a plane, it's plagiarism buster! *Newsweek,* p. 12.

McCabe, D. L., & Drinan, P. (1999). Toward a culture of academic integrity. *Chronicle of Higher Education, 46*(8), B7.

McCabe, D. L., & Trevino, L. K. (2002). Honesty and honor codes. *Academe, 88*(1), 37–42.

Online tool helps universities, colleges fight plagiarism. (2003, January). *College Week, 15*(12), 18.

Roig, M. (1997). Can undergraduate students determine whether text has been plagiarized? *Psychological Record, 47*(1), 113–123.

Smith, J. N., Nolan, R. F., & Dai, Y. (1998). Faculty perception of student academic honesty. *College Student Journal, 32*(2), 305–311.

Stebelman, S. (1998). Cybercheating: Dishonesty goes digital. *American Libraries,* 48–50.

Additional Readings for Faculty

Academic Honesty/Plagiarism

Howard, R. M. (2002, January). Don't police plagiarism: Just teach! Available from www.eddigest.com.

Roig, M. (2001). Plagiarism and paraphrasing criteria of college and university professors. *Ethics & Behavior, 11*(3), 307–323.

Academic Expectations

Center for Educational Policy Research. (2003). *Understanding university success: A project of the Association of American Universities and the Pew Charitable Trusts.* Eugene, OR: Author.

Active/Passive Learning

Rubin, L., & Hebert, C. (1998). Model for active learning. *College Teaching, 46*(1), 26–31.

First-Year Success Courses

Gottfredson, D. C., Marciniak, E. M., Birdseye, A. T., & Gottfredson, G. D. (1995). Increasing teacher expectations for student achievement. *Journal of Educational Research, 68*(3), 155–163.

Jalongo, M. R., Twiest, M. T., & Gerlach, G. J. (1996). *The college learner.* Upper Saddle River, NJ: Prentice Hall.

Perry, R. P., & Penner, K. S. (1990). Enhancing academic achievement in college students through attributional retraining and instruction. *Journal of Educational Psychology, 82*(2), 262–271.

Reynolds, J., & Werner, S. C. (1994). An alternative paradigm for college reading and study skills courses. *Journal of Reading, 37*(4), 272–277.

Simmers-Wolpow, R., Farrell, D. P., & Tonjes, M. J. (1991). Implementing a secondary reading/study skills program across disciplines.*Journal of Reading, 34*(8), 590–594.

Wratcher, M. A. (1991). Freshman academic adjustment at a competitive university. *College Student Journal, 25*(2) 170–177.

CHAPTER TWO

Developing Academic Self-Concept

In This Chapter

Adjust Your Mindset

- What kind of student are you?
- How will your family affect your college experience?
- How will you relate to your roommate(s) and/or classmate(s)?
- How do you present yourself in cyberspace?
- What type of relationship will you develop with your institution?
- What exactly does change and transformation mean for you?

Adjust Your Strategies

- What steps can you take to assess your academic strengths and challenges?
- How will you choose the types friendships and relationships that will support your efforts to achieve academic and personal success?
- What criteria will you use to determine whether you have presented yourself in a positive light in cyberspace?
- What will you do to find out about the wide variety of resources that are available on your campus?

S elf-concept is a sizable part of your personality. Essentially, **self-concept** encompasses all of our thoughts and feelings (Maslow, 1970). If someone asked you the question, "Who are you?" and you responded by describing some of your thoughts and feelings, you would be providing them with some insight into your self-concept. What is of particular interest to personality psychologists is how people develop their self-concepts and how it contributes to and organizes their experiences (Pervin & John, 1997). Your self-concept is important to consider because personality psychologists have discovered that our awareness of ourselves influences our experiences and research suggests that how we feel about ourselves affects our behavior in many situations. Well, most of you are experiencing a relatively novel situation; you are new college students. If what personality psychologists have discovered is true, then you may want to begin to reflect on how you feel about yourself and how those feelings might affect how you will behave as a new college student.

Examining questions like "Who am I?" and "How do I feel about myself?" is not as easy a task as it may initially seem. Yet now that you are in the midst of your first year of college, you may want to consider these questions seriously. "Who am I and how is my sense of self contributing to and organizing my experiences at college thus far?" Investigating these questions will help you determine how you are likely to relate to this new academic environment. To help you focus your thinking, you may want to specifically consider "Who am I as a student and how will that affect my behavior in the wide variety of new situations in which I will find myself here at college?" In other words, what is my **academic self-concept**?

If self-concept encompasses all of your thoughts and feelings, then your academic self-concept would include all of your thoughts and feelings that might affect you as a student. Interior thoughts like, "I'd rather make friends than strive for a solid A average; I have never been good at math; I do better when I am under pressure," for example, will all affect your performance as a student.

In thinking about your academic self-concept, you will want to start by considering how your academic self-concept developed. For example, what might your **academic autobiography** look like? That is, what type of student were you in elementary school? Middle school? High school? How exactly did your academic self-concept evolve through your years of schooling? How do these early learning experiences shape your academic self-concept in college? As long as you are a student, your academic self-concept will likely continue to develop and ideally even transform during college.

Reflecting on your past experiences in school is only one of the many ways to think about your developing academic self-concept. Personality psychologists contend that environmental factors like your family and other close personal relationships influence who you are and how you behave. The environment of your college campus and your living situation, for example, are factors that will affect you as a student. Aside from your

Student Portrait

Maxwell: "I started getting good grades in elementary school and didn't want to stop. My parents were always proud of me when I brought home a good report card, and I liked that. After first grade, I pretty much brought home a perfect report card every term."

academic autobiography, also consider how such factors like family, friends, and work colleagues influence the type of student you are and how you have been conducting yourself in college. Essentially, thinking about your family's influence on your academic self-concept is an exercise in thinking about where you've been—your past. Investigating your

EXHIBIT 2.1   *Student being influenced*

current close personal relationships will help you figure out what's happening in the here and now, the present.

Your academic self-concept will develop and transform over the course of your college career whether or not you are keenly aware of it. It is a good idea for you to establish an accurate perception of those factors, both positive and negative, that are likely to influence your academic self-concept. Recall the idea of reciprocal determinism. Mischel explains how we all possess "great potential for good or ill" as we actively influence the environment, but that we are also influenced by the environment and those with whom we choose to form relationships. As you read the rest of this chapter, keep his words and the idea of reciprocity in mind. How will you contribute to the shaping of your relationships and your institution, and how will they, in turn, influence you?

RELATING TO YOUR FAMILY AND CULTURE: HOW YOUR ACADEMIC SELF-CONCEPT HAS BEEN DEVELOPING UP TO NOW

You may be thinking, "Family? How is my family a part of my academic self-concept?" What about the student who is living away from home for the first time? He or she may think, "My family's not even here. How could they possibly influence what I am doing? Anyhow, one reason I came to college in the first place is because I wanted to have a new experience and live away from my family. Isn't that the point?"

Many students do believe that one of the benefits of college is escaping from the constraints of family, and surely those students do experience a great sense of freedom during the first week or two they are away from home. Indeed, some students think of college as a getaway vehicle from their families. Regardless, whether we like it or not, our family's influence drives us wherever we go.

Of course, not all students live on campus, away from their families. Students who commute may still live with their families. Adult learners coming back to school face the challenges of possibly being parents while taking classes. Regardless of the situation, none of us can escape the profound influence of our families.

Whether you live on or off campus, with a family of your own, or all alone, your family has and will continue to affect your academic self-concept. Erin, a college junior, for example, recalls part of her academic autobiography when her family situation during high school affected her motivation:

> My brother John was born when I was in the eighth grade. My stepsister Rochelle moved back in when I was in the tenth grade. My mother believes that I reached a new level of laziness in the tenth grade, which she thinks may be partially because she couldn't focus all her attention on making sure I did my homework every night.

Now consider Tricia who wanted to go away for school because, as she puts it, "Sometimes my mother drives me crazy." Tricia thought about taking a semester off after high school and starting college in January. When she approached her parents with this idea, her father emphatically said, "Yeah, OK. Not!" Tricia felt like her family placed too many unreasonable expectations on her. She was a straight A student in high school. For her family, the next natural step was for her to attend college immediately after high school. She felt so burdened by her family's expectations that during her senior year of high school she spoke to a counselor to see if she could delay attending college right away. The counselor told her that instead of figuring out what would make her happy, she was attempting to please her family and satisfy their expectations of her. Tricia knew for sure that she did not want to attend college right away, although she did know college *would* be the thing for her at some point in her life. She felt like she didn't want to go to school the following September, but her parents forced her, as she says, to "change her mind."

Now Tricia is embroiled in her first semester. Her past experience surrounding the decision-making process to come to college naturally influences her thoughts and feelings about college now. Essentially, the doubt and confusion concerning whether to attend college continues to affect her academic self-concept. Although Tricia did decide to attend college, she is a reluctant participant in the experience. By her own admission, the final decision to go to school ultimately was made to please her parents. If Tricia's heart is not in the endeavor of pursuing a college education, how might this forced choice affect the way she approaches her first-year experience? At this point, what recourse does she have?

For Tricia's family, it seems that a college education is compulsory; that is, it is required. For most of us, our kindergarten through twelfth-grade educational experience was compulsory. When it comes time for college, we have a choice, don't we? Apparently, for some families, college is just a natural progression in the educational process; it's just what you are supposed to do after high school.

On the opposite end of the spectrum, viewing college as a natural step after high school may not necessarily be the stance all families take. Some students might begin their careers immediately following high school and work for several years before they decide attending college is an option for them. They may start college for the first time in their mid to late twenties, for example. For other students, they are the first members of their families to attend college. For them, there could have been either an absence of that expectation to attend college or a heightened expectation that they would attend college. Their families may have felt that going to college wasn't necessarily the best decision, even though these potential college students really wanted to attend. Perhaps working after high school would make more sense, for instance. In these families, the ones who decide they'll be the first in their family to attend college may be considered either rebels or pioneers; they are first-generation college students. Not only must these students learn what college entails without family to help fill in some of the blanks, some must stay motivated despite family who discourage them from achieving their academic goals.

Richard Rodriguez (1981), a well-known first-generation college student, in an essay entitled "The Achievement of Desire," writes extensively about his family's influence on his educational experience and how that influence affected his academic self-concept. Even though you may not be the first person in your family to attend college, Rodriguez's experience shows that your education will likely change your family relationships:

> Quiet at home, I sat with my papers for hours each night. I never forgot that schooling had irretrievably changed my family's life. That knowledge, however, did not weaken ambition. Instead, it strengthened resolve. Those times, I remembered the loss of my past with regret, I quickly reminded myself of all the things my teachers could give me (They could make me an educated man.). I tightened my grip on pencils and books. I evaded nostalgia. Tried hard to forget. But one does not forget by trying to forget. One only remembers too well that education had changed my family's life. (p. 208)

You may be wondering why Rodriguez had such strong feelings about his education changing his family's life (If so, great. You are displaying intellectual curiosity!). To understand his point of view fully, you'll need to look closely at his background or where he's been, just as you'll have to examine your own background. In the "Achievement of Desire," Rodriguez looks at one particular factor that influenced the type of student he was. He discusses how his Mexican American heritage affected him as a student. A bilingual student, he describes how, in the second grade, he'd come home from school and correct his parents' grammar mistakes. He recounts an incident in which he proudly announces to his family that his teacher recognized that he was losing all traces of a Spanish accent. For him, this was a sign of academic achievement and success. He discusses these experiences as a way to determine how far his schooling had moved him away from his past. He emphasizes that as a student it was difficult to move between two environments, home and the classroom, because they were at cultural extremes. Do you think his family would feel the same way about him losing his accent as he does? Would they see the loss of his accent as an achievement?

For yet other families, the expectation is not only that children attend college, but also that they achieve success beyond what their parents achieved. Take Kay, for example, who feels this pressure as she begins her college experience:

> Like my mother's a lawyer, and I don't want to be a lawyer, so she hasn't influenced me in that way. My father's an accountant, and I hate math. I don't know what I want to be . . . successful. Both my parents are successful. That's what I get from

that, and like each generation has to surpass the other generation. I have friends
from other third world countries that have the same problem as to where their parents
have reached the peak. We can't . . . so we just have to produce at the same level.

Here, we see Kay grappling with the definition of success and achievement
in her family. She is struggling with an aspect of the American dream, the
idea that each generation must surpass the previous generation. Her definition of what it means to be successful will certainly affect her behavior in,
and attitude about, college, thus impacting her academic self-concept.

Have you ever stopped to consider the culture of your family of origin
and how that may influence your academic self-concept? How does your
family define success and achievement, and how might that, in turn, influence your academic self-concept? Students like Erin, Tricia, and Kay often
struggle with these questions and don't realize that the answers are closely
connected to how their academic self-concepts are formed. Rodriguez rec-
ognizes the connection, accepting the premise that education will produce
change and transformation. What exactly does change and transformation
mean for you?

Education is transformative, meaning that education, and more specifically, college, will change your life. On one level, the meaning of this statement is rather obvious; you should certainly expect the courses you'll be
taking in the years to come will change the way you think and alter your
academic self-concept. You should anticipate that the things you are learning out of the classroom will have at least as much of an effect on you as
what you learn in the classroom. You'll learn much about yourself and others; and you probably wouldn't be surprised to hear that many graduates
think they are very different people than those that first walked onto campus. While you are here, you may want to resist any urge you feel to remain
situated in the familiar, in what is most comfortable for you. Allow your
education to be transformative. Allow yourself to experience different perspectives and learn from those individuals who are, well, not like you.

RELATING TO YOUR NEW PEERS

P ersonality psychologists explain that little can be understood about a
person's self-concept without understanding it in relationship to a
group of peers to which the person belongs.

You will meet those who are different from you all over your college
campus. These individuals are now your peers. You are taking classes, eating in the cafeteria, attending sporting events, and participating in clubs
and organizations with your peers. You may even work with some of your
peers on or off campus. If you are a residential student, you are likely living with your peers.

The way in which you relate to your new peers will affect your academic self-concept and whether you will achieve academic success. Consider Kirsten who, during her first two years of college, was always an

average student. She regularly told herself, "I would rather do average and have fun than be a 4.0 student and have no life." She explains how this has been her operating philosophy for as long as she can remember. She found herself believing this theory until the end of the fall semester of her junior year in college. At that point, a new person moved into her suite who had never lived with her before. She played soccer, went out a lot, and had fun, but—surprisingly to Kirsten—she excelled in school as well. Kirsten's new roommate achieved a 3.75 grade-point average and made Kirsten realize that her motto may not hold true after all. She explains, "I believe that I thought it was all right to be average because my friends' grades were also average or below average. I would tell my parents that I was doing fine because I was doing better than or the same as so-and-so."

The new peer in Kirsten's life challenged her belief system and academic self-concept, motivating her to do better. The point here is that you should tune in to the ways in which your peers influence your attitudes about yourself and your schoolwork. In this case, the influence had a positive impact on academic self-concept. In the next example, the effect is not so positive.

Ted commuted to campus with a friend of his, Hamid. Neither Hamid nor Ted was very focused on being successful at college. Ted often talked Hamid out of attending class, convincing him to participate in one of many alternate activities. Eating, working out, and criticizing studious peers were all more fun than actually going to class. Both spent the better part of their first semester in college skipping classes and being ignorant of the relationship between their actions and their academic self-concept. Hamid eventually dropped out of college as a result of his poor grades.

As you are establishing friendships in this new environment, ask yourself whether these relationships are contributing to your growth as a student. In the case of Kirsten and Hamid, a single relationship had an enormous impact on their academic self-concept. For other students, a single relationship could have less of an impact. The overall impact of relationships with your friends—whether that means one close friend or thirty teammates— should be contributing to growth. You'll want to consider this as well when you are establishing and maintaining more intimate relationships.

Jono met a girl named Lindsey who changed his attitude toward many things in school. As he remembers, "She calmed me down and I realized that I started truly to fall in love for the first time." Lindsey strongly influenced many of Jono's decisions. "Lindsey helped me take my academics more seriously again because she was much more diligent and had a better work ethic." It is not unusual when you enter into an intimate relationship to adopt some of the behaviors and attitudes of your significant other. In Jono's case, he was fortunate that Lindsey was such a positive influence. Tim had quite a different experience.

Tim, a junior transfer student, reflects back upon his less-than-successful sophomore year. What it comes down to, he believes, is a strained relationship with his longtime girlfriend. His transfer from a community college to a four-year school meant moving away from this person who he'd known for almost two years. The long-distance relationship proved difficult. Conversations on the phone were frequent but unsatisfying and very expensive. They would see each other on weekends when Tim made the long journey back home, but these visits meant, inevitably, that the two would have to part yet again. Their experiences and interests were diverging, and they began to acknowledge this reality more with each passing week.

This scenario impacted Tim's ability—or, more accurately, his desire or motivation—to succeed academically. He often found himself thinking about his girlfriend, and this kept him from concentrating on papers, exams, reading, and lectures. He wondered whether he'd made the right decision to continue his education. Tim and his girlfriend finally decided to part ways, that it would be best for the both of them to stop seeing each other and focus more on their separate futures.

Intimate relationships can have a profound effect on how people behave. When people are in love, for example, they don't always make logical decisions. Although it is ideal to suggest our feelings are under our control, clearly with Tim, this wasn't always the case. It took him a while to become aware that making the trek home each weekend was taking time away from his schoolwork. Initially, he was unable to see how the relationship was having negative effects on his new college experience. Although Tim really wanted to put his girlfriend out of his mind, he often wasn't able to do so. Instead, he would obsess over her and his decision to transfer, making him unable to focus on school.

It may be easy to think you can keep your intimate relationships and your schoolwork in perspective. You may dismiss the idea that you would ever allow an intimate relationship to interfere with your academic goals, but it is perhaps more realistic to say that this is a possibility because such a perspective allows you to develop a critical awareness of how an intimate relationship *could* affect your academic self-concept. In addition to intimate relationships that may affect your college experience, other types of relationships also influence your academics. These relationships might include old friends from home, new acquaintances, and friends you've met during your first semester, and your faculty members. Maintaining old friendships and establishing new relationships has been made somewhat easier with the Internet, although we'll later discuss the potential for distraction there as well. Students who have a critical awareness of how different types of relationships are formed and sustained and how these can affect their academic self-concepts are more likely to have positive experiences in college.

RELATING IN CYBERSPACE

J ust as peer relationships can affect you academically, so too can your efforts at initiating such relationships. Establishing connections with peers is increasingly being done online because students have easy access to a number of popular sites that allow them to meet peers on the Internet.

Many first-time college students welcome the opportunity to reinvent themselves, and the prospect of doing so in cyberspace is appealing for many. Your cyber-identity may faithfully adhere to your self-perceptions or, to varying degrees, may be a fictional representation. The cyber-self may be more or less outgoing, studious, or independent than the student who actually lives and breathes.

Some of the more popular sites where students can create an identity profile and proceed to network with others in a particular community include Facebook and MySpace. One recent study cites steady growth in the percentage of Americans maintaining a personal profile on social networking sites: from twenty-four percent in 2008 to thirty-four percent in 2009 to forty-eight percent in 2010. In 2010, for those ages eighteen–twenty-four, seventy-seven percent had a personal profile on a social networking site. Two years ago, only fifty-four percent had a profile (Webster, 2010). A separate study (Massimini and Peterson, 2009) found that students' use of such sites increased the likelihood that they'd be late to class, lose sleep, and have less direct communication with others, all factors contributing to an increase in stress—not something college students need. This research also pointed out that the increase in stress often resulted in returning directly to the online social networking activities that were contributing to the problem to begin with. A student named Mark reflects on his experience with technology:

> After a shower, I came out to the common room where I saw six of my roommates on the couch watching television. Not only were they watching television, but also they all had their laptops out surfing the internet. I then thought about how ridiculous they looked. What would past generations think about six able bodied men, sitting on a couch inside on a nice day, engulfed in mindless wondering of the internet and TV? It kind of put some things into perspective that maybe I was spending too much time on the computer and watching TV.

At the end of this chapter, you'll find the thoughts of another student, Brendan Gauthier, of Boston University (2009), regarding his own Facebook addiction. This problem deserves consideration, as these increasingly common, time-consuming activities have a direct impact on academic success.

Online networking sites such as Myspace and Facebook call for users to represent themselves digitally through text, video, photographs, and audio. Even the links you provide to other sources, including the friends listed in your Facebook profile, help observers learn more about you. What does your Facebook profile say about you? If outsiders were looking at your profile, what do you think these observers would see? How do you think they would describe you? What assumptions might they make about you based on your profile?

In the last few years, the media has alerted students, their parents, faculty, and college administrators to the potentially damaging effects of these electronic profiles. Michael Hirschorn (2007) of the *Atlantic Monthly* explains that networking sites like Facebook are intended to link individuals of "geographic or affiliate proximity," and recent articles in the media point to employers' use of the sites to link to potential employees, job candidates. Although it isn't clear whether this is a legal or even ethical activity, what is clear is that these check-ups are taking place. According to a recent article in the *Chronicle of Higher Education* (Read, 2007) referencing a University of Dayton study, "40 percent of companies say they would at least consider perusing Facebook profiles before making hiring decisions." One thing they may be looking for is whether the lifestyle characterized in these profiles are a good match for the organization's core values (Finder, 2006, p. 16). As a result, you may want to use your profile to document some aspects of your collegiate and/or work experience that potential employers may find impressive, in effect creating a portfolio.

Although online networking sites do create a forum for developing a larger, more involved, frequently updated group of friends, remember that your profile may have an audience beyond the one you originally imagined. You will have to think clearly about how you want to present yourself to acquaintances, friends, faculty, and as mentioned, even potential employers. How you present yourself is all part of your self-concept.

There are other means by which students are creating a virtual presence and communicating with each other, such as Twitter. Though Twitter isn't currently as popular as sites such as Facebook, usage has grown from less than one percent of the U.S. population to seven percent from 2008 to 2010 (Webster, 2010).

You will find that student-faculty e-mail messages are quite common. E-mailing professors to ask a question about an upcoming research project, inquire about office hour availability, or let her or him know about an impending absence is almost a daily occurrence. When doing so, keep some things in mind. For one thing, your professor likely has many students. Although they may get to know these students by name, it isn't likely they'll know them by e-mail address. You'll want to always identify yourself within the body of the e-mail. It is also generally a good idea to use the e-mail account provided you by the college or university; avoid using playful e-mail addresses that are more appropriate for friends and acquaintances such as egotistical@aol.com.

This is one of several courtesies you may offer. Your message should also be written in formal English (not texting/instant message lingo), use an appropriate tone, and be clear and concise about what is being asked and/or stated. Finally, send a thank-you message once professors have responded to your messages. Remember that e-mail creates a potentially permanent record and should be treated accordingly.

There are some subjects for which e-mail is not usually appropriate. A recent *New York Times* article cites a number of examples of inappropriate student to faculty e-mails: "One student skipped class and then sent the professor an e-mail message asking for copies of her teaching notes. Another did not like her grade and wrote a petulant message to the professor. Another explained she was late for a Monday class because she was

FAREWELL, FACEBOOK

A COM Sophomore's Reasons for Quitting

BY BRENDAN GAUTHIER (COM'11)

I've been clean for three weeks. Every now and again, I feel the familiar urge. Grinding my nails into my desk, I force myself to focus on my schoolwork. Resisting temptation is difficult. After all, my fix—Facebook—is just a few clicks away.

But I don't give in. I've logged out of Facebook, indefinitely.

I began thinking about deactivating my Facebook account last semester. I couldn't justify the amount of time I was spending—no, wasting—on it. Why was I looking through my friend's roommate's girlfriend's sorority sister's photo albums? I didn't even know this person, yet I could tell you what she did last weekend.

So, three weeks ago, I decided to cut the cord—the Ethernet cord. The results were immediate. On my first Facebook-free day, I cleaned my room, did laundry, and finished my homework—all before my 11 a.m. class. The hole that Facebook left in my schedule quickly filled with more important priorities.

My fingers still want to type the Facebook URL when I open my Web browser. Training my muscles to do otherwise was an intense rehabilitation process: Facebook had become a natural extension of my body. To keep myself from falling off the wagon, I visit the *New York Times* Web site. In fact, I've become a news junkie, certainly an appropriate vice for a photojournalism major.

My friends don't understand. A few are impressed, but most are just perplexed. It was as if deactivating my Facebook account would also deactivate my social life.

It's true that most BU organizations advertise their events on Facebook, and without an account, I no longer receive a steady stream of invitations to auditions, concerts, dance shows, and fundraisers. But all of these groups have Web sites or e-mail lists, which are just as effective.

One friend compared my abandoning Facebook to moving far away. "I won't see you around the Facebook neighborhood anymore," he said.

His comparison is not without merit. With its myriad networks, Facebook is like a town with many neighborhoods. And within these neighborhoods are gatherings, also known as Facebook events, and organizations, or Facebook groups. "Facebookville" even has its own postal system, Facebook messaging, and direct line of communication, Facebook chat.

My friends' responses, both positive and negative, made me wonder about the larger realms of social communication. Since when did society decide it was not only okay, but expected, for us to bare our hearts and souls on a few gigabytes of the World Wide Web?

I can't deny the benefits of Facebook. It has been my sole means of communication with friends from home. But when did we decide that writing, "Hey! How's school?" on a friend's wall was the same as having an extended conversation with her?

And if Facebook were an effective means of communication, then why was I "friends" with more than 300 people? I wouldn't even acknowledge some of my Facebook friends if I ran into them on Comm Ave. I've been introduced to some of them in person, and acted as if I hadn't already looked through 237 of their tagged photos.

At what point are we willing to sacrifice real friendships for convenience? Since giving up Facebook, I've called my high school friends, and our conversations are much more gratifying than three words on our wall-to-wall.

My recent Facebook-free stint has also made me wonder how generations before ours got through college. A mere 10 years ago, hardly anyone our age owned a laptop, let alone a cell phone. And they survived just fine without Facebook.

I guess I am just a stickler for the old days. I still love traditional mail, and I refuse to replace my camera with a digital model.

Going a few days without Facebook might not be for everyone, but I recommend giving it a try. It's an enlightening experience—despite the withdrawal symptoms.

Source: Gauthier, B. (2009). Farewell, Facebook. Retrieved from BU Today's Web site: http://www.bu.edu/today/node/8281

recovering from drinking too much at a wild weekend party" (Glater, 2006, p. A1). Not only are there issues of respect to consider, but matters of privacy as well. For privacy reasons, for example, many professors do not offer grade-related information via e-mail. Also, if you have a sensitive subject to discuss, it would probably be better to do so in person during office hours than through a text or e-mail message. Your physical presence demonstrates the significance of the matter, and the opportunity for non-verbal cues can assist both you and your professor in communicating as clearly as possible.

Another reason you might consider e-mailing your professors is to solicit feedback on your work in progress. Succinct questions are some-what commonplace and are easily responded to, but sending a ten-page draft for commentary is a separate matter. If you would like your professor's feedback on a draft, it would be best to discuss beforehand whether (1) he or she is willing to do so, (2) this should take place in person during office hours, and (3) if e-mailed attachments are acceptable, what type of feedback should be expected. If your professor does allow students to submit drafts for feedback prior to the submission deadline, you'll want to do so early enough to allow for a response as well as your own use of the feedback. E-mailing your professor the day before the paper is due for some last-minute feedback usually isn't a good idea.

Finally, e-learning sites such as Blackboard offer means for students to access course materials—and classmates as well as instructors—between class meetings. Use of these tools is at times woven into courses, particularly those taught all or partly online, and at times is at the discretion of the student. Just like the campus resources we'll be discussing shortly, your usage of these tools will be driven heavily by your academic self-concept. If, for example, you are planning to do only the work that will be checked by instructors because this is how you learned to get by in the past, you may well miss out on the numerous benefits of e-learning.

RELATING TO YOUR NEW ENVIRONMENT

J ust as you have been asked to give some thought to how your family has affected your developing academic self-concept, how your peers influence you as a student, and how cyberspace may affect the way you conduct relationships, it will be helpful for you to give some thought to how your relationship with your college or university will evolve. You probably have not considered the idea that you are beginning a relationship with your college or university, but, just like establishing a new friendship, you will have to put time and effort into getting to know your new environment. The amount of time and effort you choose to put into the relationship with your institution will contribute to the overall quality of that association. Again, like with a new friendship, you will have to determine to what level you want to bring the relationship. Will you put forth minimal effort, thus having a superficial bond, or will you make and take the time to get to know your institution intimately and reap the benefits of a close, personal bond? Remember, the beginning of a relationship is not always easy. There is always uncertainty when new, but working through this can be extremely rewarding.

In this new college environment, you are facing lots of unknowns. You do not have to face these uncertainties alone. Making friends with **campus resources**, departments, people, and programs that support students outside of the classroom can help you become more comfortable within your new environment. Taking charge of confronting uncertainties and the feelings that go along with them by utilizing campus resources will have positive effects on your academic self-concept and will likely strengthen your relationship with your college or university.

Just how different is this new environment? Well, for one thing, it has a language all its own. When you first arrived to campus, you may have felt like you were on another planet hearing unfamiliar terminology like "GPA," "prerequisite," "bursar," "provost," and "syllabus." Fortunately, there are individuals on campus who can help you interpret this new language.

In most colleges and universities, advisors can help you navigate through new terminology. Seek out their advice at the advisement center or counseling office. In addition to these professionals, a more seasoned student also could prove helpful as you are becoming part of this new academic community. An administrator or faculty advisor would offer yet another perspective.

Just as there are expectations placed on you by faculty, such as asking you to take an active role in establishing relationships with faculty members (those people with whom you will primarily interact in the classroom), there will also be expectations placed on you in the larger context of the college or university. The central assumption made by staff and administration at many institutions is that you will establish a relationship with your institution outside of the classroom, that you will be involved and enthusiastically engaged.

Establishing such a relationship means getting involved, taking initiative, and getting more out of your degree than what you learn through taking courses. What these actions entail is that you become an active member of the campus community, by making friends with all the resources that will enable you to develop a positive academic self-concept.

Establishing a relationship with your institution requires you to learn more about the environment you are in and to consider your position within it. Practically, this means becoming more familiar with the college or university staff and student body by participating in college life, for instance.

Participation in college life can certainly contribute to a more positive academic self-concept. According to Richard Light (2001), a professor at Harvard who has done extensive work on assessment and student success,

Those students who make connections between what goes on inside and outside the classroom report a more satisfying college experience. The students who find some way to connect their interest in music, for example, either with coursework or with an extracurricular, volunteer activity or both report a qualitatively different overall experience. (p. 14)

Taking part in an organization like the Make-a-Wish Foundation, for example, will likely affect your academic self-concept. You may develop a keener appreciation of accounting after seeing how important it is to keep track of funds in a philanthropic organization. You may decide to take a management course based on your experience working with other volunteers. You may decide to take a course in elementary education after your experiences with the children you helped. You may conclude that you need to develop a better system for organizing time and resources. In this case, you may decide to attend a time management workshop offered by your campus learning center.

Making connections with what goes on inside and outside of the classroom necessitates getting involved with a variety of activities, which will be found both on and off campus. Making connections and getting involved requires a keen sense of how much time you can afford to spend on each activity and still excel in your coursework. Consider your school, family, and work responsibilities. You will soon find out fitting it all in is possible with careful, deliberate planning.

Your involvement with clubs and organizations on campus will affect your academic self-concept. Your participation in the many programs available on campus will have similar effects. Like with the time management workshop, it would certainly be worth your time to establish relationships with the services available on your campus by familiarizing yourself with the locations of, and services provided by the numerous departments on campus. The counseling office, career services center, registration office, financial aid office, health services department, residence life office, faculty and staff advisors, and public safety department are among the many departments you are likely to have contact with while on campus. It may surprise you, for example, to discover the career services center has programming for first-year students to help you explore career opportunities. You may also want to learn more about the student senate and the many other student clubs and organizations. What if Tim had used services provided by his college counseling office while he was going through that difficult time with the long-distance relationship? Using the counseling services on his campus would have assisted him in handling the stress he was feeling.

How do you find out what is available, whether, say, your campus has counseling services? Well, the passive learner would wait for a brochure or flyer to appear in the campus mailbox. An active learner would examine the student handbook and campus directory, visit offices to meet members of the staff, read newsletters and brochures, browse department websites, and talk to other students.

One student, Andy, reported how he wished he had known that his housing office or office of residence life could have helped him with a difficult roommate situation. He assumed for his entire first semester that he just had to live with the bad circumstances. His roommate, Sean, was big on parties. Andy didn't mind having fun occasionally, but he felt Sean had gotten out of control.

Things were fine at the beginning because Sean's partying was confined to weekends. Eventually, however, Sean started drinking just about every night. Andy felt like he could never talk to Sean because he was either drunk or hungover most of the time. Sean also discovered pot at school. The big joke on their hallway was that Sean would regularly "wake and bake." Before he climbed out of the top bunk in the morning, he would do a few bong hits. At first it seemed funny, but then Sean starting missing classes and work. He would ask Andy to fill him in on notes he missed in the classes they took together and to wake him up in the morning. Andy felt like he had enough to do to take care of himself and keep up with his own work. He was getting tired of acting like Sean's caretaker. When Andy confronted Sean about two-thirds of the way through first semester, they had a huge argument that ended with them not speaking to one another. Other people they knew on their hallway took sides. It was an awful situation that Andy had no idea how to resolve.

If only Andy had known that difficult roommate situations can unfortunately be a common occurrence on college campuses. That is precisely where establishing a relationship with your resident assistant and/or housing or residence life office can be extremely helpful. The housing office plays a key role in helping students confront and resolve conflicts with roommates before they get out of hand.

Other students may find that attending their local community college means being reintroduced to old acquaintances from high school, some welcome and some not. As one student put it, his heart sunk when he got closer to the student union and recognized a group of students he'd gone to high school with sitting on the front steps, welcoming him with a nickname he was quite unfond of and reminding him of the identity he wanted to forget now that he was in college. He thought to himself, "How am I supposed to recreate myself here when these people will bring me back to the 'old' me every day?"

In such a situation, it's important for the student to remember that he is the key agent, the person most in control of who he'll become and consequently, how these prior acquaintances and others will perceive him. Here, again, campus resources can help. If your habits and behaviors change, it is likely you won't come into regular contact with these acquaintances. Getting work done between classes at the library and meeting new people with similar goals and interests during club meetings or tutoring sessions will go a long way to establishing a positive academic self-concept.

By gaining familiarity early on, you will be able to use resources more efficiently: affecting change, getting questions answered, and resolving issues. The extent to which you utilize the resources available to you will affect your academic self-concept.

You may never have stopped to consider how your family, friends, and the way you enter into relationships will influence your academic achievement and educational choices. It's extremely important for you to think about your decision to come to college and whether it is the right choice for you. To be successful in college, you must clarify for yourself if this is what you really want and then ask yourself whether you are doing what is necessary to achieve that goal. Thinking about how your family influenced you to make your educational choices will help you begin the process of formulating your academic self-concept.

As you develop and/or maintain relationships with your peers, you will want to consider the ways in which these relationships are affecting you academically. This critical awareness should be accompanied by the appropriate action(s). If certain relationships prove damaging—limiting your study time, distracting you during class, and so on—talk to the people involved and, if that is unproductive, consider ending the relationship.

Finally, as we've argued here, the extent to which you familiarize yourself with and use campus resources will affect your academic self-concept. There are many programs and services on your campus; find out which are available and how they can benefit you so you can maximize their utility.

FIRST-YEAR DIARIES:
ADJUSTMENT REFLECTIONS

Adjusting to New Friendships ~ Kyle

Some of my successes this semester were that I was able to make great friends and fit into a group where I feel absolutely comfortable. Having that support system in place, whether it is to have fun or to bounce thoughts off of is a key component to make it through whatever choices one makes in life.

Adjusting to the Social Life ~ Jason

Coming out of my shell in my social life has been an extremely big success for me. I have met a lot of great people and they helped me open up more to people that I am not familiar with. Thus, I have learned to become more outgoing and more open with people that I never knew in the beginning of the semester.

Adjusting to Outside Expectations ~ Sandra

The beginning of the school year was stressful. I had to perform well in all of my roles, and there were a lot of people expecting a lot from me. First, I have my family who is expecting me to graduate with honors. They have high expectations because I am the oldest of five siblings and my parents want me to be the best example for my siblings to follow. Then, there are two people who have generously offered to pay for some of my education. They have high expectations of me because they want to see me succeed in the future. I have a boss who relies on me for a lot of his daily tasks. And then, I have my husband who is usually waiting for me to go home and have dinner ready for him.

DISCUSSION QUESTIONS

1. What is your family's definition of academic achievement and success? How does your own definition compare to theirs?
2. Rodriguez says that his "education irretrievably changed [his] family's life." What does he mean? Do you agree? Do you anticipate that your education will affect your relationships with family and friends? How will these changes affect your academic self-concept?
3. Reflecting on the past four or five years, how did you contribute to the shaping of your school and/or community? How, in turn, did your school and/or community shape you?
4. Reflecting on the past four or five years, what contributions have you made to your personal relationships? How have these relationships shaped you?
5. Do you remember Kirsten's motto: "I'd rather do average and have fun than be a 4.0 student and have no life"? Kirsten calls this her "operating philosophy." How might this operating philosophy guide her behavior during her first semester at college?
6. According to Sarah, "motivated and optimistic people help uplift others." Looking back on relationships you've had over the last few years, how would you describe the people with whom you surround yourself?
7. How have you begun to establish a relationship with your college or university? How can you develop this relationship in a manner that will have positive effects on your academic self-concept?
8. You read about a difficult roommate situation in the chapter that required discussion to resolve the conflict. When you experience conflict in your relationships, what steps do you take to resolve them? How effective is your approach? Can it be improved on?
9. Describe your academic self-concept. Based on your description, predict how you think you will do this semester. What grades do you think you will earn for each class? With what types of activities can you see yourself getting involved?
10. Describe a student with an ideal academic self-concept. What characteristics or qualities would she or he possess?
11. Your Facebook profile is an exercise in self-presentation. How have you presented yourself to the outside world? What does your profile reveal about your personality? Is this the persona you want to project?

ACTIVITIES

2.1 Richard Light's findings show that "Those students that make connections between what goes on outside and inside the classroom report a more satisfying college experience." Generate a list of courses and activities that you can imagine would allow for such a connection. Use your college catalog and student handbook as references for this activity.

2.2 Create an academic autobiography tracing your learning experiences from kindergarten through the twelfth grade. Your autobiography can be a lab report, narrative, formal essay, Web site, video, or any other appropriate form. A research technique often used by personality psychologists (e.g., Pervin & John, 1997) will be helpful in framing your thinking. The acronym for this technique is "LOTS:"

> *L:* Life record data (This includes information gathered from report cards and teacher comments.)
>
> *O:* Observer data (This includes information from family, friends, and teachers relating to how these individuals view you as a student. This is typically gathered through an interview.)
>
> *T:* Test data (This includes information like SAT scores, ACT scores, and other standardized test scores.)
>
> *S:* Self-report data (This includes information relating to how you see yourself as a student.)

2.3 Two psychologists, C. R. Snyder and S. J. Lopez (2007), ask that you consider the effects of Internet-related activity on your ability to get course work completed and to concentrate while doing so. They ask:

> Have you ever wondered how much your screen time (time in front of the television, surfing the Internet, instant messaging) affects your ability to immerse yourself in your schoolwork? Take a break from all screen time (except academic use of computers) for two days, and determine whether your ability to concentrate increases or decreases. At what points was it difficult and why? What did you get accomplished that you normally would not have? Thoroughly describe your "dry out" experience.

2.4 Choose three campus resources to visit this week. Select one that presented the most poignant information and create a poster that represents what you learned or an advertisement for the campus resource.

2.5 Select at least one activity to get involved with this semester. What does it take to get involved in the activity? How will you be able to connect this activity with your coursework?

2.6 Interview someone you just met—a roommate, classmate, professor, adviser, tutor—to discover her or his initial impressions of you as a student. Is this how you see yourself? How can you account for any differences?

2.7 Construct a mock e-mail to one of your faculty members. Explain to your professor why you missed class (you may choose the reason) and that you are seeking information about what was covered the day you were absent.

2.8 Examine your current Facebook profile. Consider multiple audiences looking at your profile including faculty and administrators from your institution, and current and future employers. Recreate your Facebook profile with a broader audience in mind.

REFERENCES

Finder, A. (2006). Guess who's looking at your web page? *New York Times Upfront, 139*(2), 16–17.

Hirschorn, M. (2007, April). The Web 2.0 bubble. *Atlantic Monthly, 299*(3). Retrieved April 12, 2007, from http://www.theatlantic.com/doc/200704/social-networking

Gauthier, Brendan. (2009, February 9). Farewell, Facebook. *BU Today: Campus Life*. Retrieved April 3, 2010, from http://www.bu.edu/today

Glater, J. (2006, February 21). To: Professor@University.edu. Subject: Why it's all about me. *New York Times,* p. A1.

Light, R. (2001). *Making the most out of college: Students speak their minds*. Cambridge, MA: Harvard University Press.

Maslow, A. H. (1970). *Motivational personality* (2nd ed.). New York, NY: Harper & Row.

Massimini, M., & Peterson, M. (2009). Information and Communication Technology: Affects on U.S. College Students. *Cyberpsychology: Journal of Psychosocial Research on Cyberspace, 3*(1). Retrieved May 21, 2010, from http://www.cyberpsychology.eu

Pervin, L. A., & John, O. P. (1997). *Personality theory and research* (7th ed.). New York: Wiley.

Read, B. (2007). Online. *Chronicle of Higher Education, 53*(19), A29.

Rodriguez, R. (1981). The achievement of desire. In G. Colombo, R. Cullen, & B. Lisle (Eds.), *Re-reading America: Cultural contexts for critical thinking and writing* (pp. 202–216). Boston, MA: Bedford/St. Martin's.

Snyder, C. R., & S. J. Lopez. (2007). *Positive psychology: The Scientific and practical explorations of human strengths*. California: Sage Publications.

Webster, T. (2010). *Twitter usage in America 2010: The Edison research/arbitron internet and multimedia study*. Retrieved May 2, 2010, from http://www.edisonresearch.com/twitter_ usage_ 2010.php

Additional Readings for Students

Leadership

Cassl, R. N. (1999). Examining the basic principles for effective leadership: A scientifically-based structure. *College Student Journal, 33*(2), 288–302.

Sharpe, R. (2002, November 20). "As leaders, women rule." Retrieved June 21, 2007, from www.businessweek.com/2000/00_47/b3708145.htm

Service Learning

Gujarathi, M. R., & McQuade, R. J. (2002). Service-learning in business schools: A case study in an intermediate accounting course. *Journal of Education for Business, 77*(3), 144–151.

Socialization and Roommates

Hardy, E., Orzek, A., & Heistad, S. (1984). Learning to live with others: A program to prevent problems in living situations. *Journal of Counseling and Development, 63,* 110–113.

Ross, S. E., Niebling, B. C., & Heckert, T. M. (1999). Sources of stress among college students. *College Student Journal, 33*(2), 312–318.

Scott, K. (1998). Roommate roulette. *Career World, 26*(6), 13–16.

Twenge, J. M. (2001, July). College students and the web of anxiety. *Chronicle of Higher Education, 47*(44), B14.

Additional Readings for Faculty

Service Learning

Harkavy, I., & Romer, D. (1999). Service learning as an integrated strategy. *Liberal Education, 85*(3), 14–20.

Ferrari, J. R., & Jason, L. A. (1996). Integrating research and community service: Incorporating research skills into service learning experiences. *College Student Journal, 30*(4), 444–452.

Socialization and Roommates

Bennett, M. J. (1993, Fall). Sharing the vision: Moving beyond tolerance. *School Safety,* pp. 4–10.

Gates, G. S. (2000). The socialization of feelings in undergraduate education: A study of emotional management. *College Student Journal, 34*(4), 485–505.

Hardy, E., Orzek, A., & Heistad, S. (1984). Learning to live with others: A program to prevent problems in living situations. *Journal of Counseling and Development, 63,* 110–113.

Koehler, G. (1991). Teaching stress management at the college level: Theories and practical applications. *Wellness Perspectives, 8*(1), 19–29.

Prentice Hall. (Producer). (2003). *Stress management and communication in a diverse world* [Motion picture]. (Available from Prentice Hall, Upper Saddle River, NJ 07458)

Walker, R., & Frazier, A. (1993). The effect of a stress management educational program on the knowledge, attitude, behavior, and stress level of college students. *Wellness Perspectives, 10*(1), 52–61.

CHAPTER THREE

Reconceiving Diversity

In This Chapter

Adjust Your Mindset

- Why is it important to study diversity?

- What differentiates you from your classmates and faculty?

- What is your perspective on diversity?

- Is it possible to formulate a universal definition of diversity?

- How is the topic of diversity addressed on your campus?

- How does diversity on your college campus compare to your other experiences of diversity?

- How do you think diversity will affect your college experience?

- Which subjects do you consider too sensitive to discuss in a classroom setting?

Adjust Your Strategies

- How might the different diversity perspectives affect your behavior?

- How would you formulate a universal definition of diversity?

- What are the diverse populations on your campus? How do you know?

- What clubs, organizations, activities, and campus departments play a role in diversity education on your campus? What do they do? Where are they located?

- Are there any programs, services, or systems set up on your campus to address bias incidents and hate crimes?

he concept of reciprocal determinism identifies a relationship between individuals and their environment: individuals have the power to shape their environment, but the environment can also affect individuals' behavior. You are asked to consider how you might be influenced by the new environment at your college or university, yet at the same time, encouraged to engage actively with the new environment and claim your education. Consider the wide variety of influences in your new environment, such as friendships and culture and how they might affect your college experience and academic self-concept. It is important to analyze how these factors affect your academic self-concept and the ways in which they may organize and shape your experiences.

This chapter focuses on one particular aspect of your new environment: the *diversity* of your college campus. Experiencing the diversity of a college campus can have a significant impact on your self-concept and worldview. The scope and nature of that impact will be affected by your openness and willingness to allow your new environment to inspire you to learn, change, and grow.

As you read this chapter, you will likely discover that studying diversity raises more questions for you than it answers. Instead of waiting for answers in this text or from your instructor, view yourself as an active participant in the ongoing conversations taking place on your campus and make your own contributions to them. At this point, chances are you have heard a conversation or two on campus about the importance of understanding, appreciating, or studying diversity. How is the topic of diversity addressed on your campus? We hope to encourage you to join in this conversation.

Before you make your contributions, though, it might be helpful to think about your conceptions of diversity before you arrived on your campus. Was diversity a subject of discussion at your high school? At your current or prior place of employment? At home? With friends? If so, what contributions did your teachers, fellow students, work colleagues, family, friends and others make to this conversation? Were differences respected? Was interaction among different groups encouraged? Did you have an opportunity to learn about and from those not like you?

As you work toward understanding how diversity will affect your college experience, you might find yourself challenging some previously held truths as you come to learn more about students of different backgrounds, developing a deeper understanding and awareness of those not like you. A first-year Latina student from Harvard offers some insight to the question of the impact of diversity on her learning, referring to the awareness just mentioned as the removal of a veil:

> Learning from diversity depends so much on being a reflective student. I feel like the first eighteen years of my life there has been a veil. Coming to college has taken off that veil. It takes your ideals and forces you to look back and reconsider them. That's how this education affects my life. It affects how I treat people and how I think about my relationship with those people. I learn a lot from this real-world experience. (Light, 2001, pp. 145–146)

Notice that she refers to college as the "real world," with diversity a vital component, perhaps the factor that makes it real. Although she doesn't say so explicitly in this passage, this student seems to have had a different experience with diversity in college than she did in high school; it is, perhaps, the gap between these experiences that encourages her reflection. You may find this to be the case for you as well.

Diversity in College

How does your home, community, and previous educational experiences with diversity differ from what you are currently encountering on your college campus? That likely depends, to an extent, on your frame of reference. For instance, your high school may have been more or less diverse than your current institution. It is inevitable, however, that in college you will be asked to interact with others, including those of various cultures, religious beliefs, sexual orientations, ages, and physical abilities, in ways you didn't—or at least to the same extent—previously. Some of these situations will be social in nature, others academic or work related. All are opportunities to learn from others with alternate ways of looking at things.

The student who described her experience as a removal of a veil indicated that her experience with diversity affected how she treated people and how she thinks about her relationships with them. You will likely have the opportunity to interact with people who are different from you, and ideally, you will think deeply about those relationships to learn from them. Such an interaction might involve a traditional age student working collaboratively in an introduction to economics course with an older, returning student. In another situation, a student with no military experience may find herself discussing Mark Twain's short story "War Prayer" with an Iraqi war veteran.

A student named Sarah formed a close relationship with someone from a different culture. Sarah explains how one of the closest, most meaningful relationships she has is with her college roommate, Twee:

> About a year ago, I moved into a new suite on campus, and Twee was a transfer student who moved into the room at the same time. Twee is originally from Vietnam and has only been in the United States for about four years. When I first met her, I thought she was very nice but didn't think we had enough in common to become close friends. I have realized that you never know who you will become friends with until you give a person a chance. My first impressions are not very trustworthy, and once I got to know Twee, I realized what an awesome person she is. We are now great friends, and I have learned a lot from her. I am so glad she is my roommate and friend.

Sarah has a great deal of insight into her relationship with Twee. Her detailed account of her friendship provides an apt illustration of how such relationships can profoundly contribute to and organize our experiences, key components of academic self-concept:

> I have received a lot from my friendship with Twee. For one thing, she has given me hope in people in general. I yearn to be around honest, friendly, and insightful people, and she is definitely one of them. Meeting her has helped me realize that there are a lot of uplifting people out there; you just have to find them. As a roommate she has been so considerate. She is always around to lend a helping hand, and will stop what she is doing to help me if I am in need. She is an optimistic person, and having her around helps keep me optimistic also. I had a rough time during my sophomore year because I was living with people who tended to be very negative and unmotivated. Being around Twee is great for me; motivated and optimistic people help uplift others.

Sarah goes on to explain the two-sided nature of her relationship with Twee, saying how she hopes Twee views her as a great friend also. She states that when she first met Twee, everything about living on campus, and a lot about American culture, was brand new to her. She says, "I have been sort of a liaison for her because I have helped her adjust and adapt to this new experience. I teach her a lot about American culture and have helped her better understand why and how elements of it work." Sarah introduced Twee to people who she knew and tried to make her feel comfortable at school. Sarah explains how she hopes that she has been a helpful, caring, considerate, and genuine friend to Twee. In Sarah's words, "I hope that she learns a lot from me, because I have learned a lot from her."

In this new environment, you may not only have the opportunity to establish close friendships with those from different cultures, but you may also interact with different types of people in the classroom, perhaps through working on a group project. You may find that working in such a group toward a shared goal means reconsidering viewpoints—and perhaps even beliefs—as the group works toward consensus, possibly culminating in a final product, such as a group paper or presentation. In college, professors expect final group products to represent the work of all group members; a strong product results from the productive labors of all parties involved. Although it may have been possible in high school or the workplace to take on a so-called group project individually, compensating for those who weren't involving themselves adequately, or perhaps eliminating the need to work to consensus by limiting the discussion to a single voice, this strategy will not be effective in college. One goal of group projects is for students to develop their collaborative abilities—instead of working through or around differences in opinion and perspective, to produce a stronger presentation or paper *because* these various perspectives have been considered.

In addition to negotiating different perspectives in group work situations, expect to discuss sensitive topics during class discussions, in both face-to-face and online environments such as WebCT and Blackboard. Sensitive topics, such as a discussion of religion or affirmative action, can result in some *productive tension,* possibly causing students to reevaluate their own ideas. These situations require employing active listening strategies, respecting those whose values, attitudes, backgrounds, and beliefs differ from your own.

Synthesizing conversations he had with undergraduate students at Harvard University, Richard Light (2001) notes the importance of open-mindedness, a *tone of goodwill* (p. 135). He defines this concept as "an eagerness to meet and engage with people who look different from oneself and come from different backgrounds" (p. 135). Harvard students thought such a welcoming tone was important so "students can quickly get beyond the trivialities of 'how different we look,' and begin to interact and to learn from one another" (p. 136). This tone of goodwill, then, becomes a crucial value shared by the newly formed community. The students share other, related values as well. Light explains, "Each assumes other students are here because they treasure the value of a good education. Worked hard to get here. Expect to have their thinking challenged in class. Expect to contribute in class" (p. 141).

To ensure that this tone is conveyed to other students, it is important to engage in self-reflection in regard to self-presentation in a class environment. Bucher (2004) asks students to consider the way they communicate with others in the classroom, taking on the role of ethnographer. He asks students, "How might your body gestures influence how your message comes across to others? How do you react to lectures, discussions, and group work in class?" (p. 154). Consider how you respond during a discussion to ideas with which you disagree. Do your responses encourage further thought and discussion? Or do you reply in a manner that serves to diminish the disagreeable thought—or its originator? Do you give sufficient and genuine consideration to such ideas and the argument(s) behind them? Remember that debate is crucial in a democracy, and honest debate means entertaining opposing views and oftentimes making concessions to reach a workable agreement. Such self-reflexivity is another way to understand and develop your academic self-concept.

The conversations you have outside of the classroom with the diverse members of your college community can be equally enlightening (and challenging!). In college you may find yourself spending more time interacting with individuals of different ages, marital status, sexual orientation, religion, aptitude, socio-economic status, or race; again, their values, attitudes, and priorities—even their methods of communication—may be influenced by these variables.

Consider students of different ages. One student is an adult learner, a thirty-six-year-old single mother who works a full-time job. The other student is an eighteen-year-old living at home with her parents. Both students decide to attend a time management workshop because they are feeling overwhelmed with their busy schedules. When the adult student is asked what's making her feel overwhelmed, she replies, "Well, I have so much reading to do tonight, but before I do that, I need to go grocery shopping, make dinner for my children, give them baths, and put them to bed. By that time it's nearly nine P.M., and I'm exhausted. I have to get up at five a.m. for work tomorrow. When will I get this reading done?" Upon hearing the older student's story, the eighteen-year-old student suddenly feels less overwhelmed. The workshop ends at five P.M. All she has to do is eat the meal her father has prepared and get her reading done before class at noon tomorrow. She has no other commitments. The older student's story provides the younger with a new perspective on what "busy" means.

Of course, students aren't the only diverse population on a college or university campus. Your professors will have different backgrounds, and you'll be challenged to interact productively with a wide variety of people. You may, for example, have bilingual faculty who speak English with an accent with which you aren't familiar. You may hear some students speaking in a derogatory manner toward such individuals, an act of discrimination termed *linguicism,* and you might consider reminding these students that we *all* have accents (Bucher, 2004, p. 148). It isn't reasonable, after all, to expect everyone at an institution to sound the same.

Extending this example a bit further, we can see the need for goodwill mentioned by Light's students and demonstrated by Sarah and Twee in their roommate relationship. In terms of accents, the reality is that countless Englishes are spoken throughout the world. Acknowledging this reality means assuming responsibility for developing our ability to comprehend those various Englishes. You will find that your ability to comprehend bilingual faculty increases over the time you spend listening to and speaking with these individuals, that is, if you are open minded and willing to learn. The reason that communication is difficult is that you likely have had little experience communicating with individuals who speak the particular Englishes in question. College gives you the opportunity to develop your skills in this area.

Exposure to different Englishes and accents will not be the only way you are challenged to think about diversity. Besides language differences, what other types of differences will you encounter in college? Are all differences considered components of diversity? That depends on how diversity is defined.

THE DIFFICULTY OF DEFINING DIVERSITY

One of the difficulties of studying diversity is defining it. A technical definition found in the *American Heritage Dictionary* is variety; diversity refers to the quality of being different. This explanation fails to explain the significance of the term in our current educational context when we consider that these differences have, historically, affected relations of power. Another complication is that people's reactions to differences have changed over time. Respecting diversity means more than being on a campus with people different from you in a number of ways. It also means examining the way in which you interact with others who are different, and how they interact with *you.*

One college professor recently asked students in one of her courses to offer their definitions of diversity. Although some students considered geography or physical characteristics and others saw diversity as *culturally situated,* their definitions did have certain features in common. Examine them closely to identify the pattern:

1. Different backgrounds getting along together
2. Each aspect of every person that makes us different and creates a community
3. Everything that is different that makes up a person and his or her environment
4. The acceptance of various backgrounds and cultures
5. Each person is different from one another no matter where they are from, even within the same town or country
6. Different minds with one goal; acceptance of individuals coming from different faiths and backgrounds
7. Cultural, racial, religious, economic, or any variety of sociocultural elements that make each and every individual unique
8. Individuals from different backgrounds accepting others, not judging anyone and having open minds
9. Knowledge and awareness of differences—physically, intellectually, and emotionally
10. The acceptance, recognition, and understanding of all people regardless of race, religion, and sexual orientation
11. Differences

Closely examine definitions 1, 2, 3, 5, 8, and 11. What do you notice? These definitions seem to encompass general differences without any reference to the dimensions of race, gender, religion, social class, or sexual orientation, for instance.

Similarly, after surveying 462 first-year college students on the first day of classes, Himley (2007) and her colleagues found that 242, or fifty-two percent, thought diversity referred to any type of difference. Different ideas, differences between plants and animals, and differences among groups were examples provided by students. She called the types of differences her students referred to *benign variation* (p. 454).

Consider definition 5: each person is different from one another no matter where they are from, even within the same town or country. On the surface, the idea that two individuals are different if they come from the same town does indeed seem benign. Let's take two close friends from Boones Mill, Virginia, a very small town. These individuals are white males; they have known each other since they were small children. What benign differences might exist between these two young men? To do so, let's situate the example in a historical context. What if the year was 1864 when our country was embroiled in civil war? What potential differences might there be between these two individuals given the location of the state where they live? Perhaps one friend was fighting for the Union and the other was a Confederate. Let's bring our two young men into 2007. What if one was gay and the other straight? Might that difference have a significant impact on how others in the town relate to each individual? What if one was from a wealthy family and the other poor? One Muslim and another Jewish?

Himley (2007) argues that the study of diversity should involve consideration of *historical and political context,* and a significant number of the students she surveyed agreed. Forty percent understood diversity as embedded within a historical context and a struggle for *social justice* (p. 455). For them diversity was about addressing social injustice and oppression in the world. Himley argues that for students who see diversity as merely benign differences, there doesn't seem to exist a performative view of diversity: the idea that diversity is a "kind of action, a kind of effort, often institutional, to bring different kinds of people together for a positive purpose" (p. 454).

What *is* diversity then? Is it simply individual, group, or cultural differences? Does discussing diversity as merely group, individual, or cultural differences diminish the importance of examining diversity in terms of social justice? Does a benign individual difference such as one person has brown hair while another has black hair have the same implications as exploring differences between men and women, blacks and whites, rich and poor, and gay and straight? Should the study of diversity be grounded in a historical, social, and political context, leading to the "action" Himley (2007) suggests?

DEFINING DIVERSITY

Diversity has been defined in many ways, some emphasizing the need for people of different ages, ethnicities, genders, and sexual orientations to function more productively together than would be possible separately. Other definitions focus on the need for all individuals to be treated respectfully, emphasizing the influence individuals have on each other and relations of power.

Definitions of diversity also differ in how they suggest we respond to differences. Some promote acceptance of others who are different, and this idea is complicated by the notion that we wield the power to decide whether to accept others or not, that those different from the majority must be granted approval. Some definitions promote tolerance, suggesting we should do our best to tolerate those who are different, at best a transparent gesture. Still others see diversity as something to be managed toward a productive end; here the business model is at work with people's utility taking precedence over relationships and feelings. Finally, some definitions of diversity see the goal as fostering an inclusive environment, one that seeks out and appreciates difference, flourishing from an enriched perspective. Of course, some definitions combine these concepts to form hybrid understandings of the term.

One definition of diversity focuses on individuals' perceptions of freedom; in other words, how individuals perceive their relative freedom to function within an environment where others are aware of differences that exist among and within individuals and groups.

For instance, consider gender. How would you answer the question, "Are you male or female?" Let's say you answer, "I am female." Imagine you are in a psychology class discussing how gender affects human development. Your professor explains that research suggests boys tend to play in large groups with very little discussion, whereas girls play in smaller groups, typically with one friend. This idea challenges your individual experience. As a child, you played in large groups and were raised with the idea that girls and boys are the same. In this class your ideas of gender equity are tested. You learn that women earn eighty cents for every dollar that men earn in the same job. What you thought about gender equity changes, and thus your feelings about being female are influenced. As a result, you reevaluate your self-concept. Being female serves as a reference point to what it means to be male. Does the statistic that women tend to earn less than men for "equal jobs" represent a benign difference between males and females, or is this an issue of social justice?

THE DOWNSIDE OF DIFFERENCE

The statistic that raises the controversy of "equal pay for equal jobs" illuminates that the difference of gender creates inequity, aptly illustrating the social justice perspective of diversity. In addition, the statistic supports the idea that differences do indeed make a real difference: in this case, in earning potential. Aspects of your identity such as your gender, race, ethnicity, sexual orientation, and religion may have profound effects on what you experience and how you are treated on college campuses. According to *Teaching Tolerance,* a project of the Southern Poverty Law Center:

- Every year more than half a million college students are targets of bias-driven slurs or physical assaults.

- Every day at least one hate crime occurs on a college campus.

- Every minute a college student somewhere sees or hears racist, sexist, homophobic or otherwise biased words or images (Willoughby, 2005, p. 1).

A **bias-incident** is an action that is motivated by a person's real or perceived race, religion, national origin, ethnicity, sexual orientation, disability or gender. **A hate crime** is a criminal act including physical assault or vandalism when the victims are targets because of their real or perceived race, religion, national origin, ethnicity, sexual orientation, disability or gender. You may be surprised that bias incidents or hate crimes would occur on your college campus. Unfortunately, the fact is that these types of incidences happen on campuses all over the country. At Manchester University in Indiana, for example, a student sent threatening e-mail messages to minority and international students, opening with the line, "your time is up." At the college the University of Oregon, a packet of racist material with derogatory remarks about blacks, Jews, gays, and lesbians was mailed to the student government office. At Brown University in Rhode Island, a black senior was beaten by three white students who tell her she is a "quota" and doesn't belong (Willoughby, 2005).

What would you do if you saw a member of your campus community scrawling anti-Semitic graffiti on a locker or heard someone say, "Go home slant-eyes!" Would you stand up? Would you do anything?

Robert Sternberg (1985, 1990), a Yale Psychologist, argues that a wise person would most likely take action. In his **balance theory of wisdom**, he says a wise person goes through a process of moral decision-making. First, the individual, when faced with a real-life situation, balances interests and responses to environmental contexts in relation to wisdom (achievement of the common good). In this situation, to achieve the common good would be to stand up against the bias incident in an effort to help create an environment where all members of the campus community feel included and respected. Many colleges and universities take creating an inclusive environment and challenging violations to civility very seriously. Not only do these campuses have student pledges or codes of conduct to help cultivate such environments, but they also have a hotline system set up to help students report such incidences. Bryant University, for example, pledges to be a community in which diversity is not only accepted but is "aggressively pursued" and where "high standards of civility are set and violations are challenged."

Of course there are many students who possess the mindset that bias incidences and hate crimes are wrong, but are immobilized when it comes to standing up against an occurrence if they witness one on their own campus. Taking action requires *courage*. According to positive psychologists, courage, like wisdom, is a universal virtue. When researchers study individuals' views of courage, they find considerable variation. Some perceive it as an attitude while others see it as a behavior like saving someone's life. Others claim that courage involves a risk (Snyder & Lopez, 2007).

O'Byrne (2000) identifies the type of courage required to take action against bias incidents and hate crimes as **moral courage**. Moral courage is the behavioral expression of authenticity in the face of the discomfort of dissension, disapproval, or rejection (e.g., an abolitionist helping to free slaves). Students may be challenged to display moral courage in order to create campus communities where all members are appreciated and respected.

The Southern Poverty Law Center spent two years investigating bias incidents and hate crimes on college campuses. After examining hundreds of cases involving thousands of students, they concluded that, although administrators, faculty, and staff are vital in the response to these incidences on campuses, the student activist makes the most difference (Willoughby, 2005). They implore students: "Your voice, your action, your input matter. Because things improve only when you take action. Because each student has the power to make a difference. And because apathy, in some ways, is as dangerous as hate" (Willoughby, 2005, p. 1).

Compare the Southern Poverty Law Center's plea urging students to become activists to Himley's views on diversity. The performative view contends that diversity is a kind of effort or action. Himley argues that for students who see diversity as merely "benign" differences, a performative view of diversity doesn't seem to exist. The benign view, then, may very well breed apathy. On the other hand, possessing the mindset that diversity is about addressing social injustice and oppression in the world may propel students to display moral courage, take action, and bring different kinds of people together for a positive purpose" (Himley, 2007, p. 454). In short, this perspective may motivate students to delve into diversity.

DELVING INTO DIVERSITY

To delve is to search deeply. This chapter has suggested that you delve into your self-concept to consider who you are in relationship to the different people with whom you interact. Delving into diversity requires that you look at diversity from three perspectives and consider how your identity influences your alignment with each:

- *The benign difference perspective:* Diversity is any type of difference such as the difference between plants and animals.

- *The social justice perspective:* Diversity is embedded within a historical context and a struggle for social justice. This definition is concerned with equity relative to race, gender, ethnicity, religious affiliation, and sexual orientation.

- *The performative view perspective:* Diversity is a "kind of action, a kind of effort, often institutional, to bring different kinds of people together for a positive purpose" (Himley, 2007, p. 454).

Delving into diversity also requires that you consider yourself and your campus community relative to these three perspectives, linking your understanding of diversity to your self-concept. Understand the benign differences that exist between you and your classmates, and you and your professors. Now consider answering the question "Who am I?" considering your race, gender, ethnicity, religious affiliation, and sexual orientation. How might this impact how you relate to other individuals? Other groups? Do you approach your interactions with a "tone of goodwill"? Will delving into diversity motivate you to take the performative approach? Will you become a student activist, display moral courage, and take action? What can you do on your campus to "bring different kinds of people together for a positive purpose?" (Himley, 2007, p. 454). What follows is a student who embodies the performative view of diversity through poetry:

What Is Diversity?
Whether it's in the workplace or a university
The term is always accompanied with adversity
What Is Diversity?
We've tried educating ignorant thoughts from the start
But embracing diversity truly comes from the heart
What Is Diversity?
Something we will accomplish sooner or later
The tougher the challenge makes the accomplishment greater
What Is Diversity?
Past history shows us that we need it
If you don't learn from the past you are doomed to repeat it
What Is Diversity?
It's deeper than just physical characteristics
And the essence is greater than national statistics
What Is Diversity?
A struggle we've been fighting for years
For some who cares
For others it's worth tears
What Is Diversity?
He left us with a dream before he went to his grave
For this fight we call diversity his life he gave
What Is Diversity?
It should represent a society
Which reflects a variety
Of cultures and races
People born in foreign places
What Is Diversity?
Embracing a culture different of your own
Living among people of a different skin tone
What Is Diversity?
One's nationality is not how they should be referenced
Nor should they be judged on their sexual preference
What Is Diversity?
Trying foods that have a different texture or taste
We shouldn't need a month to celebrate a gender or race
What Is Diversity?
A community of people from different geographical zones
Because part of diversity is exploring the unknown
What Is Diversity?
Acceptance of those that fought for civil rights
And those that light candles for 8 days and 8 nights
What Is Diversity?
Understanding that February is not for blacks to rejoice
But the chance for the world to hear an oppressed voice
From persons whose achievements were once a mystery
It shouldn't be Black but U.S. history

What Is Diversity?
Celebration of christmas, kwanzaa, and also hannukah
You can wear your turban or kufi but respect the yarmulke
What Is Diversity?
Praying to Buddha but respect for the man on the cross
Understanding why his life was lost
What Is Diversity?
Whether a red dot on your forehead or a cross in ashes
Should never be the reason for cultural clashes
What Is Diversity?
Black white and everything in between
Martin Luther King we are living your dream
What Is Diversity?
Don't talk about it be it
It's a look it's a feel you'll know it when you see it
That Is Diversity!

Lorenzo Perry (2007)

FIRST-YEAR DIARIES:
ADJUSTMENT REFLECTIONS

Adjusting to a Diverse Community ~ Ryan

Before coming to college, diversity was a rarely talked about subject in any school I had ever attended. To be honest I was ashamed of this. It was as if diversity was an ugly subject that no one wanted to talk about. It was a refreshing surprise when the first day I walked onto campus here that there was a banner in the student union that said something to do with diversity. Until I attended college I was not aware of all that diversity truly meant and what further helped was the class exercise we did on diversity and discrimination. When I had to sit down and examine if I had been discriminated against in my life, and I realized that I had, it made me understand diversity even more and it made the issue hit home even more.

Adjusting to Diverse Roommates ~ Caitlin

During my first semester, I was able to experience the diversity of the campus. I am a white student. Two of my roommates were from minority groups. Their group of friends, who spent a lot of time in my room, also came from a wide-variety of backgrounds. The places where they came from ranged from Jamaica and Haiti to Cambodia. Living with others in close quarters was a difficult adjustment, made especially so when your roommates are of a different race. By interacting with them through the course of the semester, my eyes were open to a wide variety of cultures and I developed a respect for diversity.

DISCUSSION QUESTIONS

1. Have you experienced people judging you based on your physical characteristics, behaviors, and/or choices? If so, how did you respond or react? If not, how do you imagine this experience would affect the people judged? How might others perceive you as different?
2. How is the topic of diversity addressed on your campus? In what ways is diversity different in college as opposed to high school?
3. What differentiates you from your classmates and faculty? How do you anticipate that these differences will affect your college experience?
4. Why is diversity an important area of study?

ACTIVITIES

3.1 Conduct your own research to find a definition of diversity. Where does this definition fit given the categories established in this chapter? Is the definition adequate?

3.2 List the benign differences that exist between you and your classmates, and you and your professors. Now answer the question "Who am I?" considering your race, gender, ethnicity, religious affiliation, and sexual orientation. How might this impact how you relate to other individuals on campus? Other groups?

3.3 Do you approach your interactions with a "tone of goodwill"? Take the performative approach. What can you do on your campus to "bring different kinds of people together for a positive purpose?" (Himley, 2007, p. 454).

3.4 During the next week of class, concentrate on students' participation during class discussion. How are disagreements dealt with? Do students listen attentively and/or take notes while other students are speaking? What did you learn from your fellow students this week?

3.5 The following poem demonstrates the complexity of defining diversity. Which of the perspectives outlined in this chapter, namely benign, social justice, and performative, are at work in the poem? Which sections best illustrate this and how?

REFERENCES

Bucher, R. D. (2004). *Diversity consciousness: Opening our minds to people, cultures, and opportunities* (2nd ed.). Upper Saddle River, NJ: Prentice Hall.

Himley, M. (2007, February). Response to Phillip Marzluf. *Diversity Writing: Natural Languages, Authentic Voices, CCC* 58:3b, 449–463.

Light, R. J.(2001). *Making the most out of college: Students speak their minds.* Cambridge, MA: Harvard University Press.

O'Byrne, K. K., Lopez, S. J., & Petersen, S. (2000, August). *Building a theory of courage: A precursor to change?* Paper presented at the 108th Annual Convention of the American Psychological Association. Washington, D.C.

Perry, L. (2007). *What is diversity?* Unpublished manuscript, Bryant University, Smithfield, RI.

Snyder, C. R., & S. J. Lopez. (2007). *Positive psychology: The scientific and practical explorations of human strengths.* California: Sage Publications. Sternberg, R. (1985). Implicit theories of intelligence, creativity and wisdom. *Journal of Personality and Social Psychology, 49,* 607–627.

Sternberg, R. (1990). A balance theory of wisdom. *Review of General Psychology, 2,* 347–365.

Additional Readings for Students

Diversity

Bollinger, L. C. (2003, January 27). Diversity is essential. *Newsweek,* pp. 32–35.

Brotherton, P. (2001). Standing up for diversity. *Black Issues in Higher Education,* 19(17), 26–30.

Crockett, R. O. (2003, January 27). Memo to the Supreme Court: "Diversity is good business." *Business Week,* pp. 96–97.

Cullinan, C. C. (2002). Finding racism where you least expect it. *Chronicle of Higher Education,* 48(38), B13–14.

Dervarics, C. (2002). University, corporate leaders urge United States to focus on diversity. *Black Issues in Higher Education,* 18(25), 9.

Lance, L. M. (2002). Acceptance of diversity in human sexuality: Will the strategy reducing homophobia also reduce discomfort of cross-dressing? *College Student Journal,* 36(4), 598–603.

Marcus, D. L. (2000, May 1). Strangers on a strange campus. *U.S. News & World Report,* 128(17), 55–56.

Morgan, R. (2002). Beyond Howard Stern. *Chronicle of Higher Education,* 48(36), A8.

Taylor, S., Jr. (2003). Do we want another 100 years of racial preferences? *National Journal,* 35(5), 335–337.

Trosset, C. (1998). Obstacles to open discussion and critical thinking. *Change,* 30(5), 44–50.

Wolfe, A. (2002). Faith and diversity in American religion. *Chronicle of Higher Education,* 48(22), B7–11.

Additional Readings for Faculty

Diversity

Clark, L. (2001). Students as constructors of their cultural heritage. *College Teaching,* 49(1), 19.

Grimes, S. K. (1995). Targeting academic programs to student diversity utilizing learning styles and learning-study strategies. *Journal of College Student Development,* 36(5), 422–430.

Wood, T. E., & Sherman, M. J. (2001). Is campus racial diversity correlated with educational benefits? *Academic Questions,* 14(3), 72–88.

CHAPTER FOUR

Planning, Prioritizing, and Procrastination

In This Chapter

Adjust Your Mindset

- What are your academic goals?

- What would it mean for you to be successful in college? Do you possess the motivation necessary to achieve this success?

- How will your ability to manage your time affect your academic success?

- What demands will the various aspects of college life place on your time?

Adjust Your Strategies

- How will you do to prioritize your academic goals?

- What are the exact behaviors that contribute to college success? Do you possess the motivation to enact the behaviors deemed necessary to achieve this success?

- Which of your behaviors may present challenges to your ability to manage your time effectively?

- What strategies will you use to determine a healthy balance for meeting the demands of the various aspects of college life?

- Are you a procrastinator? If so, what type of procrastinator are you?

TIME MANAGEMENT AND ACADEMIC GOAL SETTING

[M] any of you have come to college from high school environments where your teachers and administrators planned and prioritized how you would use your time during the course of a six-hour school day and throughout the school year. These people planned how much time you would spend in your classes, and, within those classes, teachers prioritized your learning activities. Many first-year students who are recent high school graduates get excited at the prospect of going from six hours per day in a highly structured learning environment like high school to a more free and flexible schedule in college. After all, in college, full-time students are only expected to be in the classroom an average of three or four hours per day.

The change in the structure of the learning environment creates an illusion, for some first-year students, that school will require a minimal time commitment. They think, "Wow, this is great! I'm only going to be in school a few hours a day. I'll have tons of time to have fun with friends and family, make some money and get my work done." Students with this mindset fail to recognize that time is more limited than they may realize. Like other limited resources, you simply cannot afford to waste time. There are only twenty-four hours in a day, seven days in a week, and about fifteen weeks in a college semester. You have heard the expression "time flies," and so too will your first semester at college. You will likely be surprised at how much you will be expected to accomplish within this limited time frame. Consequently, in college, you will have to do both short-range ("How will I use my time today?") and long-range ("How will I map out my semester?") planning, prioritizing, and goal setting. In other words, you will have to look to the future and plan ahead. The good news is that predicting how you are going to use your time effectively is a learned skill called **time management**.

TIME MANAGEMENT AND COLLEGE SUCCESS

[P] sychologists have studied time management practices extensively and have concluded that effective time management practices have a significant influence on college achievement. Consider that intellectual and educational achievement takes time. College students have to complete a large number of tasks in a short period of time. Given this situation, college students tend to feel overloaded and stressed, leading them to consider how they might manage their time more effectively. Researchers report that close to seventy percent of college students want to manage their time more effectively (Britton & Tesser, 1991).

Britton and Tesser (1991) studied the effect of time management practices on college grades. They observed, "People with modest abilities can accrue substantial lifetime achievements if they focus their abilities effectively on achievable goals in a limited

Students are expected to multitask and satisfy the demands of four or five different professors, and grades in large part, are a factor of their ability to do so.

domain over a lengthy period of time. In contrast, some persons of high ability who do not select, prioritize and monitor their goals, sub-goals, and tasks, and who therefore seem disorganized, accomplish relatively little" (p. 406). College grades depend on managing the completion of a variety of tasks with varying deadlines. Students are expected to multitask and satisfy the demands of their coursework for four or five different professors, and students' grades are, in large part, a factor of their ability to do so.

Britton and Tesser (1991) found that well-developed time management practices positively influence college grades. In fact, in their study, the effects of time management were independent of Scholastic Aptitude Test (SAT) scores, and even a stronger influence than SAT scores on grade-point average during the first year of college. What does this mean to you? Well, think of your SAT scores and/or high school grades as a reflection of your abilities. You need to channel the abilities that allowed you to be accepted into college productively; otherwise, those abilities will only bring you so far. The key is to "focus those abilities effectively on achievable goals" (Britton & Tesser, 1991, p. 406). That's where sound time management practices come in.

Student Portrait

Ann: "I think I lucked out because I got a real good floor when I moved here. I like a lot of people on my floor, and I think a lot of people in my classes are nice people, too. I've definitely met a lot of good friends here. I'm also on the rugby team, so in that aspect I don't have a lot of time. Kind of a rigorous schedule, but it's something I adapted to. I just plan everything out really carefully. I guess it's working so far."

SELF-REGULATING YOUR OWN LEARNING

The question, then, is "What are sound time management practices, and how and when do I implement them?" Naturally, in college, you'll need to spend considerable time outside of class reading and studying. That is not to say you won't have time to relax and have some fun, but you must balance your time effectively considering the demands on you to work, socialize, relax, and study, among other activities. You may also, for example, be involved with volunteer work or care for family. This balancing act is difficult because you may think that schoolwork demands an average of just three hours per day, failing to include time needed for coursework outside of class. You will have to **self-regulate** your own learning. Unlike in high school where you may have had teachers and parents helping manage your reading and studying time, in college this process is *your* sole responsibility.

You may be surprised to learn that when professors structure their courses, they do so with the expectation that students will spend an average of two to three hours studying outside of class for every hour spent in the classroom. If you have five classes, then, at approximately three hours per week, the expectation is that you'll be doing out-of-class work for thirty to forty-five hours per week. You can see why many people consider college a full-time job (where the currency earned is knowledge and sense).

Many students, such as Kirsten, when they consider the demands on their time, immediately consider such demands unreasonable: "There just aren't enough hours in the day. How can I spend that much time on schoolwork and still have a life?" Rest assured, if you manage your time effectively, you can have both a fulfilling college life and a handle on your schoolwork.

Consider the 8-8-8 Formula

There are twenty-four hours in a day. Let's say the average human adult needs eight hours of sleep per night, give or take. You would like eight hours of leisure time, spent by yourself or with others. You may need to use this time to work outside or within the home. That leaves eight hours remaining. If you spend three of those hours in class, you have five left for out-of-class work, in other words eight hours of schoolwork. That is the **8-8-8 formula**.

Now, take those five hours per day for out-of-class work and multiply that by five, as you'll be doing this for each of the days in the week. That gets you to twenty-five hours of schoolwork. On the weekends, you'll have to find another five to twenty hours for studying, so you can reach that thirty to forty-five hours per week expectation. Think of thirty hours as the minimum and forty-five hours as a maximum. Of course, this assumes a full-time student schedule. Adjustments can be made for a part-time course load. Achieving a balance is crucial for many students needing to work full-time or nearly-full-time in order to pay for their college courses. Those with families to support have to carefully consider where their time will be allocated each day.

The purpose of the 8-8-8 formula is to show you there *is* enough time in the day if you are prepared to manage your time. There will be times when you will need to do more studying and forgo some of your leisure time. These time commitments will change depending on the demands of your classes and the time of the semester. During midterms and finals, for example, you may be working forty-five hours per week outside of class. You may want to stockpile your course-work hours during the week and take weekends off from studying. You may want to reserve your leisure hours for the weekends. The possibilities of how you will plan and organize your time are endless.

You will have to tailor your time management practices to your personality, lifestyle choices, and college activities. It's all up to you, and a positive attitude counts! It is likely, in fact, that you'll begin to blur the lines between leisure, work, family, and study time. While at first you may only read novels and plays assigned in your literature courses, you may find the reading genuinely interesting and enjoyable. Study time and leisure time may blend at times. Similarly, there may be opportunities for you to draw upon work or family experiences in the classroom (and vice-versa).

Cutting into Your Leisure Time: Making Difficult Choices

You may observe that the 8-8-8 formula is rather straightforward and, on the surface, doesn't necessarily account for unique situations in which students may find themselves. What if students have to work twenty hours per week or are student athletes, for example? Where would they find the time in the 8-8-8 formula to use for such activities that are not clearly outlined by the formula? Well, these students would be faced with having to make some difficult decisions. Let's say a varsity tennis player has team practices from three to six P.M. every day or another student has a job on campus that takes up four hours daily. From where within the 8-8-8 formula would they borrow these hours?

EXHIBIT 4.1	8-8-8 Formula

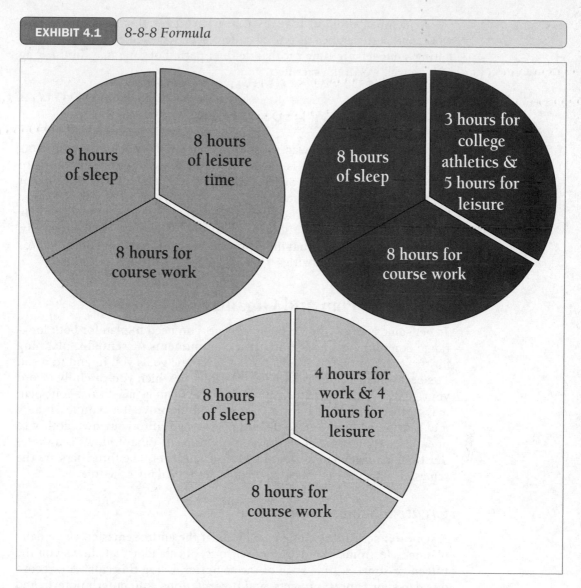

Most experts on sleep would likely agree that taking time from healthy sleep habits and operating in sleep deprivation mode would not be the best solution. Sleep deprivation results in lower tolerance toward fighting off infection, for instance. With the pace of a college semester, you can't afford to get sick. Imagine having to make up missed work and, at the same time, keep up with current assignments if you had to take time off for an illness. That would be challenging.

How about borrowing from those eight hours dedicated to classes and schoolwork? That may work during some weeks but overall likely is not the best solution. Unfortunately, what none of us like to do is dip into our leisure time, but participating in a demanding activity like a varsity sport or having to work out of financial necessity may require doing so.

Remember, though, that there is a payoff for this dedication, hard work, and perseverance. A typical college semester is fifteen weeks, so forfeiting some leisure time for that distinct period of time may, in the long run, be well worth the sacrifice.

How to Manage Your Time

N ow that you are aware of the importance of managing your time while at college, it is time to look at some practical methods of doing so. These methods are discussed as they relate to the *three major roadblocks to successful studying*, identified by Alan Lakein (1973), a Harvard MBA graduate who coined the term *time management*, namely the lack of (1) planning and organization, (2) a proper place to study, and (3) responsible behavior—procrastination, wasting time, and/or running away from priorities.

Be Sure to Plan and Organize

To get some control of your life in college, you need to plan for both long-range commitments and short-term commitments. Essentially, planning for these commitments means setting academic goals you intend to meet. The best way to do this is to make schedules in which you carefully record your goals, try the schedules out, and revise them as necessary. Your plan may not work perfectly at first, but you can improve it as you learn how much studying you need to do and gain insight into your own ability to organize and meet the goals you set for yourself. What follows is a **three-tier time management system** for college students. The three tiers are the semester schedule, the weekly schedule, and the daily schedule.

Create a Semester Schedule

A **semester schedule** will help you look at the entire semester. Use a daily planner, electronic planner, or other form of calendar that shows you the fifteen-or-so week time span of the semester. Using this calendar, record due dates for papers, projects, and presentations, and enter midterm and final exam information into the appropriate dates and times.

Doing so will help you think about the total amount of work you are required to do to be successful in your courses. To complete a semester schedule, you will need to look closely at your course outlines and syllabi. This is a beneficial exercise for two reasons. First, you will be more aware of the work expected in each particular course. Equally or even more important, however, is that you will see where work overlaps across courses. You will undoubtedly, for example, have weeks when you have a paper due in more than one class as well as an exam. Because much of this information is available to you from the start, you can plan weeks in advance, have a less stressful time getting things done, and do a better job in the process.

Now that you've entered this important information in your calendar, you are ready to consider how much time it will take you to prepare for each of these papers, projects, and exams. After all, you don't expect to start working on a project or studying for an exam the day before your work will be collected, do you? Such last-minute work is typically of poor quality and results in an anxious student dissatisfied with the experience. Cramming for an exam usually results in a subpar performance; the more serious effect, however, is that cramming results in short-term retention of just some of the information. Assuming you are at college to learn and retain information, such study techniques should be avoided. To avoid putting yourself in this situation, estimate the amount of time you will need to spend on particular assignments. Establish deadlines for finishing each one, and enter the dates on your calendar. The key is to be as specific as possible and generous with your time allotments.

Let's use a biology midterm exam as an example. How might you work backward from the date of this exam so you aren't waiting until the last minute to cram? Let's say four weeks of material must be digested before the exam. You could try studying for the exam during this entire four-week period. Doing so might involve placing notes in your daily planner to "Review biology notes" for days between classes. You might also include notes to "Take chapter self-test" each Friday. Continual review and self-testing would allow you to get your questions answered—whether through consulting the textbook or asking your professor during class or in office hours. When you break up large projects, such as a lengthy written assignment, into smaller and more manageable units, enter mini deadlines in your semester calendar.

Many institutions now offer a free calendar function to students via the campus intranet. This function allows you to input your semester schedule online (perhaps even directly through a PDA or properly equipped cell-phone) with easy access to the events going on around campus. Consider taking advantage of such a resource if it is available.

Exhibit 4.2 is part of a semester schedule created by Kendra, a first-year student. Has Kendra used the advice offered thus far? How could her semester schedule be improved?

Create a Weekly Schedule

Many students are shocked into good study habits when they see how much good study time they aren't using. If you feel you must find more study time, try making a **weekly schedule** to see how much of your time is available for study.

Write in fixed commitments such as classes, labs, job hours, and child-care pick-up times. Then list times for life support; these would include eating, sleeping, grooming, and transportation.

Next, tentatively block out large spaces of time for studying. Within those times, schedule your highest priority subjects when you usually feel the most alert. This time of day will vary

EXHIBIT 4.2	*Sample Semester Schedule*

MONDAY	TUESDAY	WEDNESDAY
1 Felicity's 18th! Meetings: Dr. Hasseler—3 p.m. Father Joe—3:30 p.m. Poetry reading—7 p.m. S.A.I.L.—7 p.m.—Papitto	**2** Proposal Due—Psych Business Exam! Finance Assoc.—4:30 p.m. ΔΣΠ—7 p.m.—Papitto	**3** Room inspection—6 p.m. Article summaries— Microeconomics Tutor training—ACE—3 p.m.

8 Columbus Day—No classes!
 	
Research for Psych.
  1) find sources
  2) begin notes (25 cards)
	9 No Liberal Arts Seminar
	
	Ch. 7—Psychology
	
	Business meets in library
	
	Finance Association—4:30 p.m.
		10 Chp. 21—Microeconomics
		
		Tutor Training—ACE—3 p.m.
		
		Confirmation class—4:45 p.m.

15 Take-home exam issued in
Microeconomics—Due Friday
 	
Psych. Research (25 cards)
 	
ΔΣΠ—Elections
 	
S.A.I.L.—7 p.m.—Papitto
	16 Ch. 9—Psych.
	
	Ch. 14—Business
	
	Overview & planning document
	     due—Business
	
	Finance Assoc.—4:30 p.m.
		17 Economics Exam
		     Due 10-19
		
		Tutor training—ACE—3 p.m.
		
		Confirmation class—4:45 p.m.

22 Psych. research—complete ΔΣΠ S.A.I.L.—7 p.m.—Papitto	**23** Ch. 11—Psych BNA #3 Due ⎫ ⎬ Business B.P. Day ⎭ Finance Assoc.—4:30 p.m.	**24** Ch. 24—Microeconomics Dinner w/Marcus @ 6:30 p.m. Tutor Training—ACE—3 p.m. Confirmation Class—4:45 p.m.

with individuals. Some people are more alert at night; others do their best work early in the day.

Be sure to plan time for fun and relaxation. You cannot work every minute, so be fair to yourself by scheduling definite times for recreation. Don't feel guilty about using this time for fun! Soon you will see that scheduling time for fun and relaxation is a vital component to following through on your schedule.

Exhibit 4.3 shows Kendra's weekly schedule. The grid she has used is easy to duplicate; consider using this or a similar format to construct your own weekly schedule.

EXHIBIT 4.3	Sample Weekly Schedule

SCHEDULE FOR THE WEEK OF: October 1 to October 5

	MONDAY	TUESDAY	WEDNESDAY	THURSDAY	FRIDAY
8:00		Psychology 8:00–9:15		Psychology 8:00–9:15	
:15					
:30					
:45	Breakfast 8:30–9:00		Breakfast 8:30–9:00		Breakfast 8:30–9:00
9:00	Math Reasoning 9:00–9:50		Math Reasoning 9:00–9:50		Math Reasoning 9:00–9:50
:15					
:30		Breakfast 9:15–10:00		College Relations Office 9:30–11:00	
:45					
10:00	Homework 9:50–11:30				Homework 9:50–11:30
:15		Homework 10:00–11:00	College Relations Office 10:00–12:00		
:30					
:45					
11:00		Hon. Intro. To Business 11:00–12:15		Hon. Intro. To Business 11:00–12:15	
:15					
:30	Lunch 11:30–12:00				Lunch 11:30–12:50
:45					
12:00	Microeconomics 12:00–12:50		Microeconomics 12:00–1:15		
:15					
:30		Hon. Liberal Arts Seminar 12:30–1:45		Hon. Liberal Arts Seminar 12:30–1:45	
:45					
1:00	College Relations Office 1:00–2:30				College Relations Office 1:00–4:00
:15			Homework 1:15–6:00		
:30					
:45		Homework 1:45–4:30		Lunch 1:45–2:15	
2:00					
:15				Homework 2:15–6:30	
:30					
:45					
3:00	Homework 3:00–6:00				
:15					
:30					
:45					
4:00					
:15					Homework 4:00–6:00
:30		Finance Association 4:30–6:00			
:45					
5:00					
:15					
:30					
:45					
6:00	Dinner 6:00–7:00	Dinner 6:00–6:30	Dinner 6:00–6:30		Dinner 6:00–6:30
:15					
:30		Homework 6:30–10:00	Homework 6:30–10:00	Personal Productivity Software 6:30–8:30	Homework 6:30–10:00
:45					
7:00	SAIL Students Advancing in Leadership 7:00–9:00				
:15					
:30					
:45					
8:00					
:15					
:30				Dinner 8:30–9:00	
:45					
9:00	Homework 9:00–10:00			Homework 9:00–10:00	
:15					
:30					
:45					
10:00					

Create Daily Schedules/To-Do Lists

Planning for an entire semester and looking at when you'll do course-work during a typical week are important activities in time management. Eventually, though, you'll need to do this work, taking it one day at a time. A daily **to-do list** will help you achieve the goals set down in the two schedules. You can make weekly and daily to-do lists on your weekly schedule on a separate sheet of paper or via an electronic organizer that contains date book and to-do list functions.

Remember to refer to your semester and weekly schedules to prioritize your lists. You'll probably want to carry your to-do list with you so you don't lose track of what you need to accomplish each day. After all, you'll be answering to yourself in regard to this list. It is up to you to meet the deadlines you've set for yourself. Focus on completing your priorities first, crossing off tasks as soon as you finish them. Exhibit 4.4 is a sample to-do list. Has this student seemed to prioritize her time? How might this list help or hinder her time management?

Typing or writing things out in this manner not only forces you to plan your time, but also, in effect, causes you to make a promise to yourself to *do* what you have written down. Adherence to the schedules and lists you've created is critical; here again, your attitude is important. You must have the drive to implement your plan and the perseverance to follow it daily. Don't let your manager's offer of an extra shift or an impromptu party in your residence hall extinguish your plan to read macroeconomics and *Macbeth* Thursday night.

Plan for a Suitable Place to Study

Along with planning your time, you need to *plan carefully for a suitable place or places to study*. Studying at home (including a residence hall) can be problematic; there are too many distractions: friends and family coming in and out of your room, televisions and radios blaring, facebook and video games, to mention a few. It would be better to study in a quiet place, preferably with a desk and chair, and a place to spread out your books and papers. You need adequate light and a comfortable temperature for optimum productivity.

The most important thing about your study place is that you use it for study only. If you go there, you should automatically be able to use your habitual pattern of studying to help you start work immediately without a long warm-up period. Use this study space for your large blocks of study time. You may need other study places; these could be used for shorter study periods such as time between classes.

There are many places where you can *take advantage of shorter spans of study time*. You can listen to a tape as you drive or walk to class as a way to review lectures or other study material. You might take advantage of an empty classroom or couch in a low-traffic location as a place to review your notes before your next class. You may have time in between classes or while

EXHIBIT 4.4	*Sample To-Do List*

THINGS TO DO: Week of: 10–1 to 10–5

Monday

Math Reasoning 1—Math project—Due Wed.

Microeconomics—Article summaries

Meetings—Prof. Hasseler—3 p.m.

*Monday: 10-01-2001

Father Joe—3:30 p.m.

Ch. 19—455–460, Notes

Other Stuff—Intro to Business Test Tomorrow

Psych. paper proposal for tomorrow

Poetry Reading—7 p.m.—MRC4

Tuesday

Psychology—Test Thursday

Intro. To Business—Test Today

Liberal Arts Seminar—No Class Today!—

   Read pgs. 1–75 Black Picket Fences (Thurs.)

Other Stuff—Microeconomics: Finish notes, Ch. 19

Finish Math Project

Wednesday

Math Reasoning 1—Hw #9: 1–4—

   #2, 9, 17, 40, 47

Read pgs. 52–54 Do #1–5—#9, 19

   pgs. 55–58 Do #6

Microeconomics—Ch. 20—Notes,

   pgs. 482–490, Article Summaries

Other Stuff—Read pgs. 76–152—Black Picket Fences

      Psych. Exam tomorrow!

      Business Plan brainstorming

Thursday

Psychology—Exam Today!—create outline for paper

Intro. To Business—Ch. 13—pgs. 381–395

Liberal Arts Seminar—finish Black Picket Fences

   for next Thursday

Other Stuff—Microeconomics: Finish Ch. 20,

   Notes, and Article Summaries

Friday

Math Reasoning 1—Hw #10: 2–1—

   #6, 7, 26, 28, 35, 38, 42, 45

*Friday: Call ACE for appt. next Tuesday

Microeconomics—Project

Other Stuff—Rough draft of mid—term

Saturday/Sunday

waiting for a scheduled meeting. If you plan ahead by making study guides for review, or if you select a textbook section you need to read, you can accomplish a great deal of routine work while waiting in a number of places.

Managing your time well so you may read and study has been mentioned over and over again. Nevertheless, many students confess that they don't know exactly how to study or, as the weeks of their first semester fly by, they realize that the study habits they used in high school simply aren't working in college. Not to worry, learning college-level study strategies are addressed at length in this text. For now, know that it's important to be sure you have set enough time aside for studying.

Learn to Avoid Procrastination

After you have scheduled your study time and found a suitable place to study, you may still run into the third roadblock: putting off completing tasks, despite the fact you've designated them as top priority.

In his book, *How to Get Control of Your Time and Your Life*, Alan Lakein (1973) states that, even if you set up high-priority activities, you may have difficulty completing them for several reasons. First, you *procrastinate*; that is, you do not start or work on your important project because it seems too complex, difficult, time consuming, and overwhelming. Instead, you work on some lower priority items because you can see immediate results.

To avoid procrastinating on a research paper, for instance, you can take steps toward starting immediately by spending some time thinking about the assignment and writing down some ideas, talking with your instructor about the topic, or spending a few minutes looking for sources of information in the library. These activities help you get started and break up the task into smaller, more manageable pieces.

After you begin your project, you will still need to keep yourself on track and following through. Lakein (1973) suggests a number of activities that will help you get back on track: (1) getting more information, perhaps by talking to your instructor or by reading more sources; (2) setting a next step—this will keep you involved; (3) taking rest breaks and work breaks; (4) setting a deadline: committing yourself to a series of actions at definite times; (5) giving yourself a pep talk; (6) not letting fear or lack of self-confidence stop you; (7) learning to stress benefits and rewarding yourself for a period of good work; and (8) being aware of when you are running away from your priority activity. He also offers a list of some escapes to avoid, such as indulging yourself with something you like to do instead of working, socializing, reading irrelevant material, doing something that you could delegate to others, running away—such as going out shopping and daydreaming.

These are great suggestions, but why is it that many of us find it extremely difficult to reach the goals we've set for ourselves? It's fine to create plans and schedules (e.g., the semester and weekly schedules, and daily to-do lists) and carefully and deliberately to record academic goals, yet it sometimes seems impossible to *attain* the goals. Why is this?

BEHAVIOR MANAGEMENT, MOTIVATION, AND PROCRASTINATION

I nextricably linked to time management and academic goal setting are the concepts of behavior management, motivation, and procrastination. Many students with good intentions heed the advice of creating semester schedules, daily schedules, and to-do lists, thus designing elaborate time management systems for themselves. Nevertheless, they still have difficulty meeting the academic goals reflected on the schedules. As a result, they become frustrated and feel their system isn't working. Why is this?

Consider this scenario. Arielle has her day planned out to the tee. After her classes comes tennis practice from three to five P.M. She will relax for thirty minutes, go to dinner with her roommate, and then off to the study lounge to read biology from 6:30–7:30 P.M. The remainder of her study session until ten P.M. will be spent doing a reflection paper for her literature class. Clearly, Arielle is in control of her *time*. Reflect on what happens next.

From 6:30–10:00 P.M., Arielle's intention is to get a biology chapter read and a literature paper written. While she is reading about photosynthesis, her instant message beeps. She stops reading for a moment and discovers that her aunt, a neighbor from home, and a few of her friends are on-line. She spends twenty minutes instant messaging. She returns to biology, but soon her cell phone rings. It's her boyfriend. They chat for a bit, but she tells him she has to hang up and focus on her reading. Moments later, she gets a Facebook message. How exciting! Her best friend has posted the pictures from last week's luau. She begins to watch the 150 picture slideshow, reliving the experience. After realizing it is 9:30 P.M., she closes her biology text in aggravation. She now must skip the reading so that she can get to work on the paper, as it is due tomorrow.

Arielle might believe she knows how to manage her time as each time block was planned out very precisely from 6:30–10:00 P.M.; however, what Arielle did *not* do is manage her *behavior* very well during this time frame. Students who find themselves in similar situations will fare better in completing academic goals if they change their mindsets from thinking in terms of managing their time to managing their behavior. For most, the distinction between time management and **behavior management** is an important one.

Managing behavior is a question of self-regulation. Arielle has important decisions to make, such as, "While I am studying, would it be wise to disrupt my plan if my cell phone rings?" What is helpful when faced with these decisions is to think about *wants* versus *needs*. Arielle may have *wanted* to see the pictures from the luau, but did she *need* to do so at that very moment? Instead, Arielle could have thought about using viewing the luau pictures as a reward for reaching her academic goal, "After I finish my biology chapter, then I'll look at the pictures." This mindset is characterized by a little self-discipline: work first, leisure after.

One of the reasons behavior management presents challenges for new college students is the difficulty of figuring out exactly how to allocate their time. In tuning into the idea of behavior management, new students will have to consider **time on task**. Again, it may not be that you don't know *how* to manage your time. What might be producing frustration is an inability to predict time on task accurately in your new learning environment.

Back to Arielle. It is now 9:30 P.M., and she still needs to write a reflection paper for her literature class. Similar assignments in high school would typically take Arielle about two hours to complete. As she goes about tackling the assignment, she realizes that she has to reread, "From Social Class and the Hidden Curriculum of Work." She thinks to herself, "What does this title even mean?" Rereading the essay carefully enough to write about it takes Arielle two and a half hours! At 11:30 P.M., she hasn't even begun to compose her draft. Tired and defeated, she thinks, "This time management strategy stinks! It's obviously not working for me........aargh."

Arielle's situation clearly illustrates that even the most organized students with the best intentions may experience frustration with time management practices when they begin college. In order to overcome their frustrations, they will need to make adjustments to both their mindsets and strategies. Arielle was able to motivate herself to the point where she planned how she would use her time, and she even clearly set the academic goals she wanted to achieve. Managing her behavior was what interfered. Other students may never quite reach the point Arielle did. Many just don't follow through and use their schedules at all, even though they made them. They just can't seem to get motivated. Why is this? What *is* motivation exactly?

According to psychologists, motivation is "the need or desire that serves to energize behavior and direct it toward a goal" (Myers, 2002, p. 335). For our purposes, let's think about goals in terms of academic demands: going to classes, taking notes, reading, starting and completing projects, writing papers, and studying for tests and exams. Let's think of motivation in terms of reaching these goals to the best of your ability. Some individuals have the need to succeed. Others are less driven. One psychologist described the "need to succeed" as **achievement motivation** or the desire for significant accomplishment, for mastering skills or ideas, for control, and for rapidly attaining a high standard (Murray, 1938).

People who have the need to succeed in college, or other endeavors for that matter, have some traits in common. They enjoy moderately difficult tasks where success is attainable, yet attributable to their skills and effort; they are persistent, eager, and self-disciplined (Myers, 2002). Ultimately, whether you decide to engage in the pursuit of achievement in college depends, to an extent, on your attitude, the extent to which you are prepared to claim your education, and how you look at and tackle your academic goals. All you need, then, is a positive attitude, right? Not exactly. In addition to having a positive attitude along with the need and/or desire to do the right thing, you need to follow through. Like with Arielle, good intentions and a positive attitude don't always translate into the desired behavior.

Procrastination and Motivation

Many college students claim they are particularly motivated to get their schoolwork done when they are under pressure. These students say, "I do my best work when I am under pressure, like the night before my paper is due." This is a common credo of the procrastinator. Just as motivation is related to time and behavior management, so is procrastination.

Think of **motivation** as an expression of your attitude toward achievement and **procrastination** as a behavior. **Procrastination** is putting off *doing* something until a future time or needlessly postponing or delaying doing something. If you have the attitude that you can't get motivated until you are under pressure, then you certainly will needlessly postpone or delay doing that paper until the night before it is due. In a sense, when students tell themselves they work best under pressure, they are giving themselves permission to procrastinate. In reality, they are deceiving themselves.

Procrastination Has Consequences

There is a deceptive component to procrastination. When you procrastinate, you put yourself in the position of lying to yourself and others. Many professors will tell you that students lie to them when it comes time to take a test or turn in a paper or project. At these times, it seems an inordinate number of relatives are dying, cars are having mechanical problems, and computers are crashing. Is it merely a coincidence that natural deaths, dead car batteries, and computer viruses are on the rise during exam time or around due dates posted on a syllabus? That is highly doubtful. Such excuses indicate, for the most part, that students have procrastinated and need to lie themselves out of the precarious situations they have created.

Identifying a lie you've told to another person is a lot easier than figuring out when you are lying to yourself. Experts estimate that most people lie at least twenty-five times in a single day! It may be obvious when you've lied to someone else, but how many of those twenty-five times are you lying to yourself? One of the keys to combating procrastination is having an awareness of your patterns of lying. Experts identify three broad categories for why people lie: to make others feel better about themselves, "No, that outfit doesn't make you look fat"; to boast about ourselves and make ourselves look better, "I didn't even crack that book, and still got an A on the exam"; or to protect ourselves, "I don't feel like studying right now; I'll start after dinner." The third type of lie has the greatest influence on procrastination behavior. We may not feel motivated to study, so to safeguard against having to think about the work that has piled up, we convince ourselves it is OK to begin later, like after dinner. Accepting that most people lie about twenty-five times a day, do you have a sense into what categories your lies fall?

Besides lying, procrastination has other serious consequences. Not surprisingly, procrastinators start studying significantly later, and thereby study fewer hours, than more motivated nonprocrastinators (Lay & Burns, 1991).

The result is obvious. Less time spent studying results in lower grades and less learning. This research is contrary to procrastinators' mantra that they work well under pressure; what they are actually saying is that the work gets done despite having been repeatedly put off. That may be true, but *completing* a set of readings or finishing a research paper does not mean that either was done *well*.

Indeed, the tendency to procrastinate impacts grades negatively. One researcher found that procrastination, like time management practices, has a stronger influence on college grades than high school grades and SAT scores combined (Wesley, 1994). College admissions' offices use SAT scores and high school grades as predictors of student achievement, yet these two indicators typically account for only about thirty percent of the picture when it comes to first-semester college grades. Procrastination behaviors significantly impact college grades beyond the influence of SAT scores and high school record. What this all means is no matter what kind of academic history you bring to college—strong high school grades and respectable SAT scores, for instance—procrastinating ultimately will impede your academic performance.

For college students, procrastination has serious consequences beyond academic performance. A leading expert on procrastination says that health is yet another cost. Marano (2007) discusses research, which found that over the course of a single academic term, procrastinators exhibited evidence of compromised immune systems such as more colds and flus and gastrointestinal problems; these students also had insomnia. The research also pointed out the negative effects of procrastination on relationships. Procrastination may shift the burden of responsibilities onto others, who become resentful. Imagine if you were assigned to work on a group project with a procrastinator? Perhaps one of the most detrimental side effects of procrastination is higher levels of alcohol consumption. Among those who drink, procrastinators drink more. Why? Well, it's actually an avoidant behavior; they replace the activity of academic work with the activity of drinking, which is a maladaptive way of coping with a particular situation (Marano, 2003).

For those whom procrastination leads to impeded academic performance, increased drinking, and other health issues, the habit of procrastination becomes a maladaptive life style. Procrastinators sabotage themselves by saying, "I'll feel more like doing this tomorrow;" they put obstacles in their own paths and actually choose paths that hurt their performance. Leading experts say that some twenty percent of people identify themselves as chronic procrastinators (Marano, 2003). If you think you fall into this statistic, you may want to probe more deeply into this detrimental behavior pattern.

Gaining Control over Procrastination

If you accept the idea that procrastination may lead to a maladaptive lifestyle, then you should be interested in what you can do to combat procrastination. The good news, it can be done, but remember, behavior change takes motivation, energy, and effort. The initial step is to first identify the type of procrastinator you are and then reflect on common procrastination behaviors. In other words, develop a keen awareness of how *you* procrastinate, including any behaviors that produce problems with self-regulation.

Ferrari (qtd. in Marano, 2003) identifies three basic types of procrastinators:

1. Arousal types or thrill seekers wait until the last minute to get that euphoric rush.
2. Avoiders are in denial about their fear of failure or fear of success. In either case, they are concerned with what others think of them and would rather have others think they lack effort than ability.
3. Decisional procrastinators can't make decisions. Not making a decision absolves them of their responsibility for the outcomes of events.

In order to break this maladaptive behavior pattern, you have been advised not only to consider how your patterns of lying may feed into procrastination behavior, but also to identify the type of procrastinator you are. Now reflect on these typical procrastination behaviors. The following list is not exhaustive, but it will surely help you get started identifying your tendencies. Do any of these look familiar? You may want to check off those that apply to you.

1. Waiting until the last minute to do things
2. Waiting until a crisis arises or the semester has ended before taking action
3. Not setting personal deadlines and sticking to them
4. Doing things quickly, but incorrectly, thus having to redo them
5. Spending a lot of time on routine and trivial things
6. Not establishing a daily schedule
7. Failing to prioritize tasks; treating everything as if it was equally important
8. Not saying "no" to requests or invitations
9. Spending time socializing instead of working
10. Reading things unessential to the work at hand
11. Spending too much time on the cell phone
12. Not having clear goals or objectives
13. Seldom asking other people to help; a failure to delegate tasks
14. Failing to listen to or read instructions
15. Trying to do the "perfect" project, paper, and so on
16. Overscheduling, taking on too many commitments, overextending
17. Paper shuffling
18. Not anticipating the emergency situation; a full schedule does not accommodate the unexpected

You may want to hit the panic button at this point. Many students admit they check off every item on the list and feel like lost causes. Don't worry. Nearly every human being procrastinates; it's a matter of degree. **Delaying gratification** or restraining our impulses can be challenging. It's far easier to put fun first. Self-disciplined people do, however, find ways to put work first and then have fun. Remember, those with high achievement motivation are self-disciplined. Freud's Theory of Personality may shed some light on why some human beings have difficulty delaying gratification while others are more able to put work before fun.

According to Freud, there are three parts to the personality: the id, ego, and superego. He contends that for those who exhibit healthy personality traits and habits (as opposed to maladaptive ones), the three parts of the personality are balanced or in equilibrium. The first part of the personality is the **id**. That's the part of us that wants to have fun. He identified it as the pleasure seeking part of the personality. Don't we all want to eat, drink, and be merry? Well, it's OK to have fun, but in moderation. Think about how you feel when you have eaten too much. What about drinking too much? It's no coincidence that embedded in the word idiot is *id*. Certainly, you have seen those who have had one too many cocktails act like idiots? Be realistic: it's ok to have a good time, in moderation, but after you have reached your academic goals. This brings us to the next part of the personality: the **ego**.

Freud says the ego's job is to gratify the id safely. That is, the id is the part of the personality that seeks instant gratification, and may have difficulty delaying satisfaction. The ego's job then, is to help the id be realistic: the reality part of the personality. What might have Arielle's ego said to her id? It might have gone something like this:

> *Listen up id! You have been looking at those luau pictures for over a half hour while you are supposed to be doing your biology reading. What's up with that? Get out of Facebook. Finish your reading, and then look at the pictures.*

How Freud might describe procrastination is that Arielle's ego was simply too weak to stand up to the pressure of her id. When procrastination happens, the id is in control of the behavior. Those who are chronic, die-hard procrastinators have underdeveloped egos.

You may conceptualize it in another way. Think of your id as luring you away from your priorities and responsibilities, whereas the ego is saying, "Do your work." The id retorts, "Nah, I'll have plenty of time to do it later." Should you complete your academic goals now or later? Who is right? The id or the ego? That depends on your values, morals, and your sense of integrity and responsibility. What encompasses your values and morals is the third part of your personality: the **superego**. While no one is perfect, the superego is the context in which the id and ego function. Your superego defines for you what the ideal student would do. The superego strives for perfection. What constitutes the best habits for academic achievement? How should you behave in this situation? Your parents, community, society, and culture shape those answers for you, thus developing your superego: the perfection part of the personality. How would your family react if your id was always winning, and you were treating your college experience as one long vacation? You might get a little anxious thinking this way. Indeed, Freud says that yet another consequence of procrastination is anxiety. As you examine the list of procrastinatory behaviors, many of us do these things some of the time. For others, these become habits that create anxiety. How can you kick the habit?

Ask yourself these questions: What am I currently putting off doing? What have I procrastinated about in the past? Does a pattern emerge? Are there certain types of tasks I tend to put off? How will I be aware that I am procrastinating? Do I engage in **replacement activities,** in other words, activities other than those I should be doing?

Identify Your Replacement Activities

As mentioned, there are maladaptive activities that replace your priorities, like drinking too much. Other replacement activities aren't so serious and detrimental. Most are quite easy to identify; these usually include the obvious like watching too much TV, playing video games, text messaging, or hanging out with friends. Students usually have their favorites. Often, however, it is difficult to identify other types of replacement activities because many times they are masked by productivity. For example, you may have to do your laundry, do dishes, clean your room, go to the bank, or mail your monthly bills. All of these tasks are important and necessary, but are they priorities relative to your studies?

Take Jack, for example. After a rough morning of class, he decides on an early workout. He has a big philosophy exam tomorrow and thinks working out will help him get his brain energized. An hour and a half later, Jack is headed back home, a bit sore, but ready to tackle the five chapters he has put off reading. When he finally gets to his room, though, he sees piles of clothes on his desk and bed. "Can't study in this mess," he thinks, and he begins to get his laundry together for a wash and dry. "This won't take long," he says to himself, "and when I'm done, I'll be able to concentrate on philosophy." The next two hours are spent in the laundry room. Although he realizes that it's getting late, Jack tells himself that he'll get to reading after dinner. When seven o'clock does roll around, Jack begins reading Chapter Eight; the problem is it takes him an hour and a half to get through its forty pages. He decides that he'll do more skimming for the next four chapters. This is faster, for sure, but now he's not certain he understands the material. At two A.M., Jack is beginning to think he won't do so well on his exam. At least he's got clean laundry.

Students often engage in productive activities, like doing laundry, to put off doing more important things, like reading a chapter due the following day. They make themselves feel better because an important task was accomplished, and now they can cross "laundry" off their to-do list. Engaging in these types of activities makes the person feel like they've accomplished something, but, in essence, what they've really done is avoided their top priorities. Students who do this are productive procrastinators. They'll clean their rooms (a noble activity) and one or two hours will go by before they realize they are actually wasting important homework time. This is yet another aspect of the deceptive nature of procrastination and why it can be so hard to identify. Combating procrastination, then, necessitates establishing some effective behavioral patterns and habits.

Try These Anti-Procrastination Strategies

In college, those who manage their time and behavior effectively have the ability to delay gratification and combat procrastination. They are able to do so by abiding by some basic principles, outlined here, some of which have been mentioned previously:

1. *Study in a regular place at a regular time.* Establishing habits of study is extremely important. Knowing when you are going to study, and where, saves a lot of time in making decisions about studying. Locate a study place that is comfortable for you and has few distractions (e.g., family, friends, noise, phone, TV, video games, instant messaging, e-mail, etc.).

2. *Study during your periods of maximum alertness.* Some people are more efficient in the early mornings and others in the afternoon or early evenings. Find out when you are the most effective, and plan to do your studying then, if it's possible. Utilize those periods when you know you can be the most productive.

3. *Limit your blocks of study time to no more than two hours at a time on any one course.* After one and a half to two hours of studying, you begin to tire rapidly and your ability to concentrate diminishes. Taking a break and then switching to studying for another course will provide the change necessary to maintain your efficiency.

4. *Set specific goals for each study unit.* When you record your goals on a schedule, actually write what you are planning to accomplish during the study period. For example, don't just write "do math" or "study" or "read." Instead, put "do math problems 1–10." Be that specific.

5. *Plan enough studying time to do justice to each subject.* Again, most college professors require about two to three hours of work per week per credit in the course. By multiplying your credit load by three, you can get a good idea of the time you should set aside for studying. Of course, if you are a slow reader or have other study deficiencies, you may need to plan more time to maximize your learning potential.

6. *Attempt to complete all assignments as soon as possible after class.* Check over lecture notes while they are still fresh in your mind. Start assignments while the memory of the assignment is still accurate.

7. *Provide for a spaced review.* That is, schedule a regular weekly time period when you will review the work in each of your courses and be sure you are up to date. This review should be cumulative, covering briefly all

the work done thus far in the semester. Studies show that consistent cumulative reviewing over the course of a semester has a far greater impact on memory and retention than the cramming method.

8. *Plan a schedule of balanced activities.* As suggested in the 8-8-8 formula, be sure to include time for social activities when you construct a weekly study schedule. Seeing that you have some fun things to look forward to will motivate you to study. Build in rewards for yourself for a job well done.

9. *Trade time—don't steal it.* When unexpected events arise that take up time you had planned to study, decide immediately where you can find the time to make up the study missed and adjust your schedule for that week.

These anti-procrastination strategies should sound like sensible suggestions, but what if you can't get yourself to try them? If this is the case, you are probably a **die-hard procrastinator**: You tend to get stuck in a rut to the point where you are completely immobilized. One way to figure out if you fall into the category of die-hard procrastinator is to ask yourself if you typically use your snooze alarm in the morning. Think about it; those who use snooze alarms are procrastinating waking up! Let's face it. If you procrastinate getting out of bed, you meet the criteria. You are a die-hard procrastinator. Luckily, Dr. David D. Burns (1992) knows well the psyches of diehards. He wrote an essay entitled, "Stop Putting it Off!: A Five-Step Plan to Get Even the Most Die-Hard Procrastinator Moving Again," in his book *The Feeling Good Handbook*.

In his essay, Burns explains that many of us find ourselves procrastinating from time to time. He cites a survey conducted by Esther Rothblum and colleagues of 342 students at the University of Vermont; nearly half admitted they procrastinated on writing term papers. The study found that, "Though the reasons varied, the most frequent explanation was fear of failure" (Burns, 1992, p. 87), a characteristic of the avoidant type of procrastinator. How can this possibly make sense? Why would people who fear failing put off doing their work? Instead, you would think they'd overcompensate and work extra hard in an attempt to be productive.

Think of it this way. Jason perceives writing a term paper to be an arduous task. He doesn't know how to begin, so rather than tackling the job, he avoids it. Indeed, there is an avoidance component to procrastination. Every time he thinks about starting the paper, he gets a little anxious because he is unsure where to start. His anxiety fuels the fear of failure. As a college student, he feels it is his job to know how to write a term paper. He avoids asking for help because he doesn't want to be "found out." What if the professor realizes he has no idea how to do the necessary research for him to get the required sources for his term paper? This thought just adds to the anxiety. Every time he thinks about the assignment, he becomes more and more nervous and afraid that he won't be able to do well on the paper. He then says to himself, "I'll just deal with this later. I have plenty of time before my term paper is due."

Anxiety, that feeling of being unsettled, but unsure why, is difficult to handle, and as established, procrastination produces this feeling. Instead of facing our fears head on, we tend to avoid the source of our anxiety—in this case, the dreaded term paper. Freud proposed we use what he called **defense mechanisms**, a way to distort reality to reduce our anxiety. A defense mechanism frequently employed by students on college campuses is **rationalization**, which occurs when we justify our undesirable behaviors with excuses (Myers, 2002). Jason justifies not beginning his term paper because he rationalizes he has "plenty of time." Essentially, he distorts reality to ward off the anxiety created by not knowing how to get the paper started. As each week passes by, he allows himself less and less time to accomplish the task. He keeps telling himself that time is on his side. He never considers the idea that the term paper was assigned during the first week of the semester because the professor knew an acceptable term paper would take an entire semester to complete. The reality is Jason *doesn't* have plenty of time to complete his term paper.

Kirsten demonstrated that she was also quite adept at rationalization when she said, "I would rather do average and have fun than be a 4.0 student and have no life." Students use rationalization to give themselves permission to behave and act in certain ways. Jason tells himself time is on his side to permit himself to continue putting off the task of working on his term paper, whereas Kirsten convinces herself that 4.0 students don't have fun, so she can continue being average instead of working to her potential.

If you employ the defense mechanism of rationalization as a means of giving yourself permission to continue your procrastination behaviors, as die-hard procrastinators tend to do, then you'll want to pay close attention to Burns's five-step plan:

> 1. *Expect difficulties.* Those who procrastinate often assume that successful people achieve their goals without frustration, self-doubt and failure. This is unrealistic. Highly productive people know that life is frustrating. They *assume* they'll encounter obstacles; when they do, they persevere until they overcome them. (Burns, 1992, p. 88)

Jason, for example, assumed that as a college student he should already know how to do research for a term paper. He saw not knowing how to conduct research as an obstacle he couldn't readily overcome. He never entertained the idea that some of his classmates might feel the same way. Instead of procrastinating, though, it is likely the successful students in Jason's class persevered and overcame this obstacle. Perhaps they visited the professor during office hour; maybe they went to a reference librarian and asked for assistance or visited their college's writing or tutoring center; they may have even asked upper-class students how they dealt with the same term paper.

> 2. *Do a cost-benefit analysis.* When you're ducking an important task, weigh the advantages of procrastinating against the disadvantages. (p. 88)

Marcia admits to putting off just about everything, including making it to all of her classes. She describes herself as "lazy" and bored with schoolwork. Rather than studying, she explains, "Even if I know an exam is approaching within a week or that reading regularly would be a good idea for a class, I refuse to do the work. On nights I have a paper due or an exam in class the next day, you can usually find me in my bedroom reorganizing my closet, making my bed, or vacuuming my floor. If I have done all of those things recently, I will lie down and watch TV, do the dishes, or clean the bathroom." Instead of going to class, sometimes Marcia continues her cleaning binges or wanders around, talking to friends.

Marcia tells herself she's lazy and bored with schoolwork, essentially using this rationalization to avoid studying for a test. Clearly, Marcia is not a lazy person. Cleaning and organizing takes a great deal of work and energy. For Marcia, cleaning is her replacement activity, but why can't she direct that same energy toward her schoolwork? Frustrated with her procrastinatory behavior, Marcia decides to do a cost-benefit analysis regarding her behavior. It turns out that Marcia was procrastinating by doing more than just spring cleaning.

Marcia first lists the advantages of her procrastination: "It makes me feel like I've accomplished something when I clean and organize":

Benefit: A neat closet makes it much easier to find an outfit to wear.
Benefit: A clean bathroom makes me feel more at home, less stressed.
Benefit: Watching TV helps me escape the pressures of school.
Benefit: There has to be space on my desk for me to study there.

Marcia came up with three disadvantages:

Cost: All of this cleaning is hurting my grades.
Cost: I'm not as stress free as I thought I'd be.
Cost: I'm not getting along with my roommate because she feels like she can't relax in our room.

When she listed the advantages of procrastinating, Maria discovered she wasn't as lazy as she'd convinced herself she was; this realization led to a reduction in her procrastinatory behavior. She no longer believed her own excuses for not doing her work. The time she was spending cleaning could be better used on her studies.

If you conduct your own cost-benefit analysis, you may learn there are good reasons why you avoid doing something. If this is the case, you may need to reevaluate your goals.

   3. *Little steps for big feats.* Most procrastinators tell themselves, "I'll wait until I'm more in the mood." Let's face it: You're never going to *feel* like studying, reading or beginning a term paper. Sometimes you simply have to prime the pump to get yourself going.

   One way to do this is to break your job into steps that can be accomplished bit by bit. Get into the here and now, and don't worry about everything you have to do in the future. Life exists on one minute at a time, so all you have to do at any given time is one minute's worth of work. That's not so hard, is it? (p. 89)

Take that 300 pages you have to read this week and spread it over five days. Now take that sixty pages per day and break it into three reading sessions. You could read twenty pages in the morning, twenty in the afternoon, and twenty at night. That doesn't seem as overwhelming, does it?

    4. *Time out negative thoughts.* When you're avoiding a task, it may be because you're feeding yourself unrealistic, negative messages. By writing them down, you have a chance of dispelling them. (p. 89)

    5. *Give yourself credit.* Once you've begun a job you've been avoiding, it's important to give yourself credit as you go along. A mental reward will boost your motivation. Too often people discount their accomplishments and focus on what they haven't been able to do.

    We usually think of rewards as coming from the outside. A compliment for a job well done feels good. Getting a high grade on a test or making a sale to a difficult customer can be highly motivating. But ultimately, all rewards must come from within. If you never allow yourself to feel satisfied with your efforts, you'll soon find it pointless to try. So, no matter how small the achievement, give yourself credit. Then you can tackle your toughest task. Simply begin now. (p. 90)

In this chapter, we have seen it is crucial to prioritize your time while at college. To achieve success, you'll need to be aware of how your time is spent as well as what you can do to be more efficient. The 8-8-8 formula and three-tiered system presented will allow you to gain some measure of control over your day—and your semester. Remember, though, that procrastination is the enemy of sound time management practices; be conscious of the ways in which you typically procrastinate, and make the effort to avoid these activities.

FIRST-YEAR DIARIES: ADJUSTMENT REFLECTIONS

Adjusting to Using A Planner ~ Ryan, a transfer student

I made a pact with myself before the semester started that my old study habits were not going to work. One of the most helpful skills that I gained was to make a semester calendar. This has helped me immensely keeping my academic life in order and countless times it has saved me. Before this college, I never kept a calendar. I used to remember my assignments and do them one or two days before they were due. You could say I was a great procrastinator. Yet, I also knew I could get away with it at my former schools, but I knew that wouldn't fly here. So by creating a semester calendar it forced me to get things started and finished ahead of time. So no longer was I rushing to finish things which would lead to mistakes and worse grades. I now had a plan of action and it really kept me focused and on track.

Adjusting Your Study Space ~ Kyle

I quickly learned that the rigorous academic program would require more time and effort than my other school. Not to mention a complete overhaul of my studying techniques. The first thing that hit me was that I was no longer able to get the most potential of studying when I try to study in my room. I would need to go to the library or any quiet study lounge.

Adjusting to the 8-8-8 Formula ~ Terry

My goal is to graduate with honors, and I knew I needed to put in extra effort to make that happen. I had to leave behind my procrastination habits get things done early. Being thrown into classes, I started off using all my free time to get work done. I was finishing homework days before it was due, which left free time that I did not know I had. After learning about the 8-8-8 formula, I realized I actually had more time for relaxing than I thought. I ended up working out a routine that allowed me to get work done, have fun with friends, and get enough sleep.

Adjusting to Combating Procrastination ~ Samuel

Procrastination was a problem that had plagued me while at my old school and was something that I had hoped to fix during my time in this course. Unfortunately I never did quite fix my procrastination problem. I took some steps involved in attempting to fix the problem that I had not used before. This semester I started using a planner to write down all of my assignments and when I had tests or papers that were due. This gave me a good idea on the work load that I would have in upcoming weeks and allowed me to gauge when I would be able to enjoy some free time and when I would need to buckle down and do the necessary work for my classes. However, just because I wrote all of that stuff down, did not mean it worked to its full potential. I would often write down all of my assignments and then never look at what I had recorded until the next time I had to open up my planner to write a new assignment. Eventually I just stopped using my planner and honestly forgot I even had it at all unless I went rummaging through my backpack to find my calculator.

DISCUSSION QUESTIONS

1. In the student portrait, students talk about rigorous schedules, budgeting their time, and balancing schoolwork and outside activities. You've been at school for weeks now. How are you balancing the "demanding" college life Ernie mentions? Are you "planning everything out really carefully" like Ann?

2. Describe the academic planning tools you use. How do they compare with the student samples?

3. Which of the antiprocrastination behaviors and habits do you use, if any?

4. Which replacement activities do you typically use when you procrastinate? Why is it important to be aware of these activities?

5. What kinds of things might prevent you from following through if you set up an academic plan?

6. Why is planning and prioritizing an important consideration for college students? How does planning relate to course selection?

7. When do you find it most difficult to prioritize tasks? How do you handle these situations?

8. Speaking from your own experience, describe the consequences of failing to plan adequately.

9. How does motivation relate to procrastination?

10. Describe a time where you were very successful in planning and executing a major project or task. What contributed to your success? How can you transfer these skills to your coursework?

ACTIVITIES

4.1 Create a semester and weekly schedule. How much time do you have to do coursework? Will this be adequate, given what you've learned regarding professors' expectations?

4.2 Exchange your semester schedule with that of one of your classmates. How has your partner broken down large projects/tasks into manageable chunks? Have you done so in your own schedule?

4.3 Create a to-do list. Be sure to put at least ten items on it. Next to each item, estimate the amount of time you think it will take to accomplish the task. Choose a few items from your list to test the accuracy of your time predictions. Go about completing the tasks. How did you do? Were your time predications accurate or unrealistic?

4.4 Choose a study space on campus that meets the criteria outlined in this chapter. Use this new space for at least an hour to do some coursework. Were you more efficient in this new study environment? Why or why not? What have you learned about selecting a study space?

4.5 Recall that the experts estimate the average person lies about twenty-five times a day. Tune in to your behaviors and thoughts. Keep a lie log for a week, diligently recording each time you tell a lie. Given the three broad categories of lies, can you identify the types of lies you tend to tell? To what extent are your lies feeding into procrastination behavior?

4.6 Take each of the five strategies suggested by Burns and apply them over the course of the next week: (a) What difficulties arose that you did not expect? Keep a running list. (b) Create a chart of your personal cost/benefit analysis. (c) Choose a paper or project that is due toward the end of the semester and break that big feat into little steps. (d) What negative thoughts crept into your head? Write them down. Discuss the strategies you implemented to tune out those thoughts. (e) What kinds of rewards did you use to congratulate yourself for a job well done?

REFERENCES

Britton, B. K., & Tesser, A. (1991). Effects of time-management practices on college grades. *Journal of Educational Psychology, 83*(3), 405–410.

Burns, D. D. (1992, January). Stop putting it off! *Reader's Digest*, pp. 87–90.

Lakein, A. (1973). *How to get control of your time and your life*. New York, NY: P.H. Widden.

Lay, C., & Burns, P. (1991). Intentions and behavior in studying for an examination: The role of trust procrastination and its interaction with optimism. *Journal of Social Behavior and Personality, 6*, 605–617.

Marano, H. E. (2003). Procrastination: Ten things to know. *Psychology Today*. Retrieved May 14, 2010, from psychologytoday.com

Murray, H. (1938). *Explorations in Personality*. New York, NY: Oxford University Press (p. 373).

Myers, D. G. (2002). *Exploring psychology*. New York, NY: Worth.

Wesley, J. C. (1994). Effects of ability, high school achievement, and procrastinatory behavior on college performance. *Educational and Psychological Measurement, 54*(2), 404–408.

Additional Readings for Students

Motivation, Procrastination, and Goal Setting

Arenofsky, J. (1999). 10 ways to motivate yourself. *Career World, 28*, 6–12.

Brownlow, S., & Reasinger, R. D. (2000). Putting off until tomorrow what is better done today: Academic procrastination as a function of motivation toward college work. *Journal of Social Behavior and Personality, 15*(5), 15–34.

Fee, R. L., & Tangney, J. P. (2000). Procrastination: A means of avoiding shame or guilt? *Journal of Social Behavior and Personality, 15*(5), 167–184.

Pychyl, T. A., Morin, R. W., & Salmon, B. R. (2000). Procrastination and the planning fallacy: An examination of the study habits of university students. *Journal of Social Behavior and Personality, 15*(5), 135–150.

Senecal, C., Koestner, R., & Vallerand, R. J. (1995). Self-regulation and academic procrastination. *Journal of Social Psychology, 135*(5), 607–619.

Additional Readings for Faculty

Motivation, Procrastination, and Goal Setting

Burns, L. R., Dittmann, K., Nguyen, N., & Mitchelson, J. K. (2000). Academic procrastination, perfectionism, and control: Associations with vigilant and avoidant coping. *Journal of Social Behavior and Personality, 15*(5), 35–46.

Carter, C., & Kravits, S. L. (1996). *Keys to success: How to achieve your goals*. Upper Saddle River, NJ: Prentice Hall.

Cone, A. L., & Owens, S. K. (1991). Academic and locus of control enhancement in a freshman study skills and college adjustment course. *Psychological Reports, 68*, 1211–1217.

Dweck, C. S., & Leggett, E. L. (1988). A social-cognitive approach to motivation and personality. *Psychological Review, 95*(2), 256–273.

Fulk, B. M., & Montgomery-Grymes, D. J. (1994). Strategies to improve student motivation. *Intervention in School & Clinic, 30*(1), 28–34.

Garavalia, L. S., & Gredler, M. E. (2000, December). An exploratory study of academic goal setting, achievement calibration and self-regulated learning. *Journal of Instructional Psychology, 29*(4), 221–231.

Harris, M. D., & Tetrick, L. E. (1993). Cognitive ability and motivational interventions: Their effects on performance outcomes. *Current Psychology, 12*(1), 57–79.

Hess, B., Sherman, M. F., & Goodman, M. (2000). Eveningness predicts academic procrastination: The mediating role of neuroticism. *Journal of Social Behavior and Personality, 15*(5), 61–74.

Janssen, T., & Carton, J. S. (1999). The effects of locus of control and task difficulty on procrastination. *Journal of Genetic Psychology, 160*(4), 436–442.

Jones, C. H., Slate, J. R., & Marini, I. (1995). Locus of control, social interdependence, academic preparation, age, study time, and the study skills of college students. *Research in the Schools, 2*(1), 55–62.

Lasane, T. P., & Jones, J. M. (1999). Temporal orientation and academic goal-setting: The mediating properties of a motivational self. *Journal of Social Behavior and Personality, 14*(1), 14.

Lefcourt, H. M. (Ed.). (1984). *Research with the locus of control construct.* New York, NY: Academic Press.

Orellana-Damacela, L. E., Tindale, R. S., & Suarez-Balcazar, Y. (2000). Decisional and behavioral procrastination: How they relate to self-discrepancies. *Journal of Social Behavior and Personality, 15*(5), 225–238.

Purdue Research Foundation. (1994). Staying focused: Improving motivation and concentration [Motion picture]. West Lafayette, IN: Purdue University Continuing Education.

Trice, A. D. (1985). An academic locus of control scale for college students. *Perceptual and Motor Skills, 61*, 1043–1046.

Wilhite, S. C. (1990). Self-efficacy, locus of control, self-assessment of memory ability, and study activities as predictors of college course achievement. *Journal of Educational Psychology, 82*(4), 696–700.

Time Management

Lakein, A. (1973). *How to get control of your time and your life.* New York: P. H. Widden.

Purdue Research Foundation. (1993). *Academic success skills: Time management* [Motion picture]. West Lafayette, IN: Purdue University Continuing Education.

CHAPTER FIVE

Developing Malleable Mindsets and Metacognitive Skills

In This Chapter

Adjust Your Mindset

- How do you learn best?
- What assumptions do you make about learning? What attitudes do you possess in relation to learning?
- Do you have an internal or external locus of control?
- Are you aware of your metacognitive ability?
- What is critical thinking?
- How can writing promote learning?
- How can you read actively and critically?
- Do you consider writing an opportunity for learning or as a demonstration of what you already know?

Adjust Your Strategies

- For the classes you are taking, identify your instructors' teaching style. Compare it to your learning style. What are the implications?
- How does your locus of control affect the way you use new study strategies?
- How does your conception of intelligence influence the way you use new study strategies?
- How does learning change your brain, and thereby, your behavior and study strategies?
- How can honing critical thinking skills help you solve problems?
- What writing strategies promote learning?
- What strategies promote reading actively and critically?

S tudents enter a transitional period of their lives when they begin college. Experts who study this transition identify a variety of issues students have to deal with, such as separation from family and friends, indecision about their majors or future career goals, new relationships, and perhaps even conflicts with family members (Rabinowitz, 1987; Wratcher, 1991). On top of these adjustment issues, this chapter outlines academic adjustment concerns such as developing study habits and mindsets that are critical to making the grade first semester. Naturally, you should be concerned about earning good grades and achieving academically during your first semester, and good study habits will help you to do so; however, good study habits require more than an understanding of *how* to study (how to take notes, how to read, how to manage your time). You must actually execute these study habits. You must also be motivated and willing to adapt your study habits to each professor's teaching style and expectations. You may sit quietly in one course, taking notes dutifully during daily lectures, and participate in group exercises every week in another.

To be successful in college, you will need to reexamine how you learn best as well as the various factors that influence your own academic achievement. Many students think they already have college-level study skills when they arrive on campus, but they soon discover unexpected obstacles and challenges, particularly regarding work done outside of class.

This chapter offers information regarding how students learn: when reading, writing, talking with others, or thinking for themselves. Equally important, this chapter encourages you to reflect on the study methods you currently employ and to be open to experimenting with new approaches. Attending college involves a process of acculturation. Don't forget everything you ever knew, but the academic demands of college will require you to be open to the idea of trying new study strategies you haven't before and adjust to using and applying them.

The study habits inventory that follows, designed by Craig Jones and John Slate, will help you gauge how your current study habits compare to the study habits used by many successful college students.

STUDY HABITS INVENTORY

Craig Jones and John Slate

INSTRUCTIONS: *Read each statement below; fill in the blank spaces to the left of each numbered item using the following key:*

A = *True; I usually study in this way.*

B = *False; I usually* do not *study in this way.*

Remember, your responses should describe your typical study habits. The inventory will be of value to you only to the extent that you are perfectly honest in answering the questions.

———— 1. I study most subjects with the idea of remembering the material only until the test is over.

———— 2. I try to write down everything my instructor says, as close to word for word as possible.

———— 3. If I am sure I will remember something, I do not write it in my notes even if it seems to be important.

———— 4. I try to complete assigned readings before my instructor discusses them in class.

———— 5. I sometimes skip classes, especially when attendance is not required.

———— 6. When sitting in my classes, I have a tendency to daydream about other things.

———— 7. When taking notes in class, I simply try to get everything down so I do not have to take the time to think about what the material means.

———— 8. When taking notes in class, I abbreviate words and jot down phrases rather than complete sentences.

———— 9. I tend to include a lot of irrelevant or unimportant information in my notes.

———— 10. When I take notes, I try to follow an outline or some other type of organized format.

———— 11. I take notes on odd loose slips of paper instead of in a notebook.

———— 12. I keep the notes for all my classes in the same notebook.

———— 13. As soon as possible after class, I recopy my lecture notes.

———— 14. Except for important quotations and the definitions of technical terms, I copy my notes in my own words rather than the exact words used by my instructor or my textbook.

———— 15. When I have difficulty with my work, I do not hesitate to seek help from my instructor.

———— 16. I put my lecture notes away after an exam and never look at them again.

———— 17. I tape-record lectures instead of taking notes.

———— 18. I have a definite, although reasonably flexible, study schedule with times for studying specific subjects.

———— 19. I spend too much time on loafing, movies, dates, and so forth, that I should be spending on my coursework.

———— 20. I spend too much time on some subjects and not enough on others.

_____ 21. My study periods are too short for me to get "warmed up" and really concentrate on studying.

_____ 22. I usually write reports several days before they are due, so I can correct them if necessary.

_____ 23. I frequently do not get enough sleep and feel sluggish in class or when studying.

_____ 24. I often do not have reports ready on time, or they are done poorly if I am forced to have them in on time.

_____ 25. I do most of my reviewing for a test the night before the examination.

_____ 26. I try to space my study periods so I do not become too tired while studying.

_____ 27. I stick to my study schedule except for very good reasons.

_____ 28. My study time is interrupted frequently by telephone calls, visitors, and other distractions.

_____ 29. I have trouble settling down to work and do not begin studying as soon as I sit down.

_____ 30. I have to wait for the mood to strike me before attempting to study.

_____ 31. I frequently get up, write notes to friends, or look at other people when I should be studying.

_____ 32. I have a tendency to doodle or daydream when I am trying to study.

_____ 33. I often study with a radio/stereo playing or with other people talking in the same room.

_____ 34. I often sit down to study only to find that I do not have the necessary books, notes, or other materials.

_____ 35. I read by indirect (diffused) light rather than by direct light.

_____ 36. To help stay awake while studying, I frequently drink a lot of coffee or other beverages that are high in caffeine.

_____ 37. I often try to make schoolwork more enjoyable by having a beer while studying.

_____ 38. I make a preliminary survey by skimming a chapter before reading it in detail.

_____ 39. I use the headings to make an outline of a chapter before I begin to read it.

_____ 40. Before reading a chapter, I jot down a few questions and a list of key terms to focus my attention while reading.

_____ 41. I pause at logical breaks in my reading, such as the end of a section or chapter, and recite to myself the principal ideas in that section.

_____ 42. Sometimes I discover I have "read" several pages without knowing what was on them.

_____ 43. I take notes after I have completed a reading assignment rather than taking notes as I go along.

_____ 44. I look up in a dictionary the meanings of words I do not understand.

_____ 45. I tend to skip over the boxes, tables, and graphs in a reading assignment.

_____ 46. In studying a textbook, I try to memorize the exact words in the text.

_____ 47. Sometimes I make simple charts or diagrams to show how the facts I am learning are related to each other.

_____ 48. I try to break large amounts of information into small clusters that can be studied separately.

_____ 49. I work out personal examples to illustrate general principles or rules I have learned.

_____ 50. I use the facts I learned in one course to help me understand the material in another course.

_____ 51. I practice using new words by putting them into meaningful sentences.

_____ 52. I use the facts learned in school to help me understand events outside of school.

_____ 53. I try to think critically about new material and not simply accept everything I read.

_____ 54. I frequently test myself to see if I have learned the material I am studying.

_____ 55. I keep a special indexed notebook or card system for recording new words and their meanings.

_____ 56. I review frequently.

_____ 57. I try to do some "overlearning," working beyond the point of immediate recall.

_____ 58. I review previous work before beginning work on an advanced assignment.

_____ 59. If I plan to study with friends, I do not study by myself ahead of time.

_____ 60. Whenever possible, I use the workbook that accompanies a textbook.

_____ 61. I often read too slowly to complete reading assignments on time.

_____ 62. I have to reread material several times before I get the meaning of it.

_____ 63. I have trouble picking out the important points in the material I read.

When you've finished, total your number of matched items using the key provided. Give yourself 1 point for each matched item. Your score will range between 0 and 63. The raw score you receive, divided by 63, indicates the percentage of college-level study skills you are currently using. If, for example, your score is 31, you are using roughly 50% of the study habits that will enable you to be successful in college. This tells you that there is ample room for improvement; you may be operating at only half capacity.

STUDY HABITS INVENTORY ANSWER KEY

1. B	10. A	19. B	28. B	37. B	46. B	55. A
2. B	11. B	20. B	29. B	38. A	47. A	56. A
3. B	12. A	21. B	30. B	39. A	48. A	57. A
4. A	13. A	22. A	31. B	40. A	49. A	58. A
5. B	14. A	23. B	32. B	41. A	50. A	59. B
6. B	15. A	24. B	33. B	42. B	51. A	60. A
7. B	16. B	25. A	34. B	43. B	52. A	61. B
8. A	17. B	26. A	35. A	44. A	53. A	62. B
9. B	18. A	27. A	36. B	45. B	54. A	63. B

Used with permission of Drs. Craig H. Jones and John R. Slate.

WHY SHOULD I CHANGE?

You might be asking, "Why should I change my study habits? I'm in college, so I already know how to study." Take the skill of memorization, for instance. Many students rely solely on this method to learn material for their classes. This method may have resulted in a fair grade-point average in high school, but employing this strategy to prepare for college-level material will not work because professors have different expectations. The application of certain high school study skills, such as memorization, will not yield the same results in a college environment as they did in high school; it is common for college personnel to hear from first-year students, "I don't understand why I received a C on that test, I always got As and Bs in high school" or "I have always been a good writer; I don't understand why I'm having so much trouble in my composition class." Researchers attempt to explain such perspectives of first-year college students.

Some who have examined effective methods of studying at the university level are aware that applying study skills in college should be a response to the different types of requirements of college courses (Thomas, Bol, & Warkentin, 1991). This kind of research indicates that course features between high school and college differ greatly in workload, degree of cognitive challenge, and need for self-direction. As opposed to high school, where teachers help students adapt to the different demands of each class—a **teacher-directed environment**—in college, students are expected to adapt to such variability on their own—in a **student-directed environment**. In this student-directed environment, you will now be expected to identify the most important information in textbooks or what will be on the test. Your professors are not likely to approach you if they suspect you are having difficulty with material, particularly if the roots of your difficulties lie in the area of study skills (Wratcher, 1991). Consequently, to achieve academically, you either must already have or quickly develop the appropriate study skills needed to respond to the change in the learning environment from high school to college. In short, you will have to adjust your mindset and your strategies.

A wide range of skills and strategies have been identified as the study skills needed for making the grade in college. Some researchers describe the necessary study skills as reading, writing, and finding and organizing information (Reynolds & Werner, 1994). Others define time management, listening, note taking, test taking, problem solving, and critical thinking as the necessary skills for college achievement (Anderson & Anderson, 1992). Clearly, a vast repertoire of skills is needed for college success, so this means you will have to figure out which you possess and which need honing.

Academic success in college largely depends on your capacity to self-reflect, to become aware of current mindsets, and to control your own study habits. Regulation of study behaviors is commonly called **metacognition**. Metacognitive strategies allow students to plan, monitor, evaluate, and revise learning strategies whenever they're needed in studying and learning new materials. Students with the ability to self-regulate have at least four things in common. They set goals, develop and adapt diverse methods to strive toward those goals, are motivationally engaged in the process, and are aware metacognitively of their learning decisions, processes, and products that those processes create (Hadwin & Winne, 1996; Turner, 1992; White & Kitchen, 1991).

How can you become metacognitively aware? Well, some type of study skills training is a start, but you'll also need to consider your current attitude(s) toward learning. Students may know what effective study skills are, may make an effort to acquire those study skills, may even achieve competency in the area of study skills after having received study skills training. However, for study skills to have an effect on academic achievement, students must use the study skills they have learned. If students have

Student Portrait

Melodie: "I don't know. I look back at high school now, and it was so easy. It was so incredibly easy. Like if I had to repeat high school again, it would probably be by like the snap of the finger. Now, high school just absolutely did not prepare me for college. I don't know, like coming here is like starting from scratch again. It feels horrible because it's like the majority of the people here are already at that level of education. It seems like everyone else is ready, so I'm kind of stuck with everyone. High school was the same way, but I was used to being above, at the top, whereas now I'm below, so . . . I feel like I'm at the bottom."

developed good study skills, what would prevent them from using their skills, especially if they know doing so will help them earn higher grades?

Experts question student utilization of newly learned study skills. They reason that even if students do learn more effective study skills, whether they will use these skills depends to a large degree on their perception of whether the use of these skills will make a difference (Jones, Slate, & Marini, 1995). Students will say, "I never liked to read or was very good at it. I can't see how using this new type of outlining is going to change that." Or students will say, "Sure, I know I should take notes when I read, but I just can't picture myself taking the time to do it. What difference will it make, anyhow?" Internalizing these beliefs essentially gives students permission to avoid the hard work of changing their old study habits.

For many first-year students, the thought of adding study skills training that challenges them to change their habits seems a burden. What students don't often consider is that ineffective study strategies often take much longer to implement and yield inconsistent or poor results. Taking the time to learn college-level study strategies can literally be a time-saver. The idea that changing study habits is a waste of time is just one of the faulty internalized beliefs that impact whether students are willing to change the way they study.

Researchers have discovered that the willingness to change is a critical component of wisdom. According to Baltes and Staudinger (2000), "Wisdom is the ways and means of planning, managing, and understanding a good life" (Baltes & Staudinger, 2000, p. 124). What would the good life in college constitute? Achieving academic success, perhaps? They go on to identify two criteria that characterize wisdom: factual and procedural knowledge. In essence, wise performance requires expertise.

Factual knowledge is "knowing what." In this case, knowing exactly what college-level study strategies contribute to academic success. Nevertheless, knowing these facts is of little use without executing the behavior that is the product of that knowledge. Ask yourself this critical question: you may know what study strategies contribute to college success, but are you using them?

Procedural knowledge is "knowing how." For instance, developing strategies to deal with problems and overcoming obstacles (like procrastination) that could impede implementing the study habits (Baltes & Staudinger, 2000). Once you learn new study strategies for use at the college level, if you encounter roadblocks while you are attempting to apply them, then what will you do? Evidence suggests that how you answer this may be found in your attitude. You would be wise then, to reflect on your attitudes toward learning.

STUDENT ATTITUDES TOWARD LEARNING

As mentioned, research indicates that teaching first-year students specific study strategies is a worthwhile goal because better study habits in college lead to higher achievement. You may now be convinced that changing your high school study habits is a worthwhile endeavor. Wise students do come around to the realization that their habits must change, and they become open to learning new strategies. Unfortunately, this real-ization oftentimes comes about after their high school study habits fail them. As discussed, of further concern is that once students learn college-level study strategies, not all students use them.

Whether students use new strategies depends on their attitudes. Researchers point out that for students to use their new study skills, the attitudes that influence their use need to be addressed (Jones, Slate, & Marini, 1995). In other words, reflecting on your attitudes toward learning might be of equal importance to learning new college-level study skills. Two particular attitudes have been found to strongly influence whether you will use study skills you have been taught: your locus of control and your attitude toward intelligence.

What Is Your Locus of Control?

Locus of control involves a generalized expectancy that people hold regarding the degree to which they control their fate (Jones, Slate, Marini, & DeWater, 1993). This expectancy is an attitude that influences students' use of academic skills. Some people believe what happens to them is largely determined by personal effort, ability, and initiative; whereas others believe outcomes are largely determined by other people, social structures, luck, or fate. People with an **internal locus of control** feel they have a rea-sonable amount of control over their outcomes. People with an **external locus of control** feel their fate is largely beyond their control. According to Lefcourt (1982), whether people believe they can determine their own fates, within limits, is of critical importance to the way they cope with stress and engage in challenges.

Oftentimes, first-year students see college as novel, ambiguous, and, well, stressful (Cone & Owens, 1991). Dealing with the anxiety of social and academic adjustment issues is not easy. Locus of control can affect the way students adjust to the stresses and challenges of the first semester. If students don't believe that they can control their personal fate within their new surroundings, they can begin to feel alienated from the scholarly envi-ronment. Not only can locus of control influence adjustment to stress, it can also affect whether students get involved in the pursuit of achievement (Lefcourt, 1982).

Locus of control relates here to delayed gratification. For students, the future value of their efforts is not always obvious; what student hasn't wanted to close the textbook and head out-side with friends? Out-of-class work is often repetitive and may interfere with more enjoyable activities. College is a place that offers the opportunity for achievement, and it requires a degree of self-management, conscious effort, and sacrifice to attain future goals. For people who doubt the potential of their efforts, sacrifice is improbable (Lefcourt, 1982).

Locus of control can affect the way students adjust to the stresses and challenges of the first semester.

Locus of control is a complex concept. Whether you have an internal or external locus of control will affect the likelihood of your using college-level study skills. Some studies show that locus of control is the most powerful predictor of whether you will use new study skills. External and internal students differ primarily in terms of both motivation to study and their ability to concentrate on academic work: "Students with an external locus of control were not only less likely to study than students with an internal locus of control, but were also more likely to be distracted from studying once they had begun" (Lefcourt, 1982, p. 60). The results of these studies suggest it is critical for you to look at the motivational and attitudinal variables that affect your use of study skills. If you have an external locus of control, you will need to make a conscious effort to apply the new skills you have learned.

Measure Your Locus of Control with the Trice Academic Locus of Control Scale

As we have discussed, locus of control refers to the degree to which people feel they control their own fate, an attitude that refers to a generalized expectancy about the extent to which reinforcements are under internal or external control. If individuals believe events are controlled by luck, fate, chance, or powerful others, they are called *externals* (external locus of control) as opposed to *internals* (internal locus of control), individuals who believe an event is contingent on their own behavior.

Locus of control plays a mediating role in determining whether students get involved in the pursuit of achievement. A significant correlation has been found between locus of control and grade-point average. By completing the following Trice Academic Locus of Control Scale, you will see how your locus of control correlates with your GPA.

TRICE ACADEMIC LOCUS OF CONTROL SCALE

_____ 1. College grades most often reflect the effort you put into classes.

_____ 2. I came to college because it was expected of me.

_____ 3. I have largely determined my own career goals.

_____ 4. Some people have a knack for writing; others will never write well no matter how hard they try.

_____ 5. At least once I have taken a course because it was easy to get a good grade.

_____ 6. Professors sometimes make an early impression of you and then no matter what you do, you cannot change that impression.

_____ 7. There are some subjects in which I could never do well.

_____ 8. Some students, such as student leaders and athletes, get free rides in college classes.

_____ 9. I sometimes feel there is nothing I can do to improve my situation.

_____ 10. I never feel really hopeless; there is always something I can do to improve my situation.

_____ 11. I would never allow social activities to affect my studies.

_____ 12. There are many more important things for me than getting good grades.

_____ 13. Studying every day is important.

_____ 14. For some courses it is not important to go to class.

_____ 15. I consider myself highly motivated to achieve success in life.

_____ 16. I am a good writer.

_____ 17. Doing work on time is always important to me.

_____ 18. What I learn is more determined by college and course requirements than by what I want to learn.

_____ 19. I have been known to spend a lot of time making decisions that others do not take seriously.

_____ 20. I am easily distracted.

_____ 21. I can be easily talked out of studying.

_____ 22. I get depressed sometimes, and then there is no way I can accomplish what I know I should be doing.

_____ 23. Things will probably go wrong for me some time in the near future.

_____ 24. I keep changing my mind about my career goals.

_____ 25. I feel I will someday make a real contribution to the world if I work hard at it.

_____ 26. There has been at least one instance in school where social activity impaired my academic performance.

_____ 27. I would like to graduate from college, but there are more important things in my life.

_____ 28. I plan well and I stick to my plans.

Total your number of matched items. Give yourself 1 point for each matched item. Your score will range between 0 and 28. As indicated in the table, the scores are significantly correlated with grade-point average. Low LOC scores are associated with higher GPAs, and high LOC scores are associated with lower GPAs. Exhibit 5.1 indicates how scores correlate to GPA.

SCORING KEY

1. F	8. T	15. F	22. T
2. T	9. T	16. F	23. T
3. F	10. F	17. F	24. T
4. T	11. F	18. T	25. F
5. T	12. T	19. F	26. T
6. T	13. F	20. T	27. T
7. T	14. T	21. T	28. F

Source: Trice, A. D. An academic locus of control scale for college students. *Perceptual and Motor Skills,* 1985, 61, 1043–1046. © Perceptual and Motor Skills 1985. Used with permission.

EXHIBIT 5.1   *Study Habits Inventory Scale*

Relationship among Locus of Control, GPA, and Study Habits Inventory

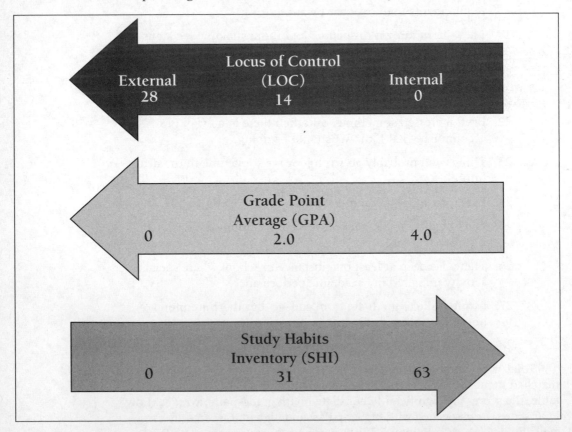

The Relationship Among Locus of Control, Study Habits, and Grade Point Average

Review your score on the Study Habits Inventory (SHI) and compare it to your score on the Trice Locus of Control Scale (LOC). Researchers have established that there is a correlation, that is, a strong relationship, between these two scales and your first semester grade point average (GPA). Students who have *low* scores on the LOC possess an internal locus of control. Internals are more likely to use the college-level study strategies that have been taught to them; therefore, internals tend to have high scores on the SHI. Using college-level study strategies contributes to a higher grade point average (GPA). It's no surprise then, that there is also a correlation between scores on the SHI and GPA. Finally, there is a correlation between LOC and GPA. Internals are more likely to achieve higher GPAs compared to externals. So the reverse is also true. Those students who tend toward externality are less likely to use the study habits that have been taught to them; their scores on the SHI are typically lower, and they are more likely to earn lower GPA compared to their internal counterparts.

THEORIES OF INTELLIGENCE

Dweck's Mindset Theory

Carol Dweck and Ellen Leggett (1988) propose that your **attitude toward intelligence** is another reliable indicator of your use of study habits. They argue that people hold one of two basic viewpoints of intelligence: an entity view or an incremental view. People with an **entity view** believe intelligence is a fixed single ability. Thus ability, not effort, is the key factor that determines performance. People who hold an **incremental view** believe intelligence involves a set of skills that can be improved through effort.

Building on the work of Dweck and Leggett, other researchers have found that college students with an incremental view of intelligence tend to work harder, and thus they exhibit a stronger use of study skills compared with students with an entity view of intelligence (Jones, Slate, Marini, & DeWater, 1993). The research indicates that students with an incremental view engage in more positive academic behaviors than the students with an entity view. More specifically, Jones et al. (1993) found, compared with students with an entity view, students with an incremental view of intelligence give a greater investment in effort. They are more likely to complete reading and written assignments ahead of time, less likely to engage in rote memorization, and less likely to daydream in class (Jones, Slate, Marini, & DeWater, 1993).

Why would our attitudes toward intelligence influence our academic habits and behaviors? Dweck and Leggett (1988) discovered through their research that individuals' views of intelligence create frameworks within which they interpret and react to events, like an upcoming exam. Those with an entity view tend to react with a helpless response, "Why bother to study for my math exam? I've always been bad at math." On the other hand, students who have incremental view are more mastery-oriented tending to seek challenges and persevere in the face of failure, "Given that I failed my last math quiz, I better find a tutor who can help me work through the problems for my upcoming exam." The entity counterpart might say, "I was born bad at math, a tutor can't help me change my genetic make-up!"

Dweck's (2008) more recent theory conceptualizes these two views of intelligence in terms of mindsets. The **fixed mindset** (entity view) believes qualities are carved in stone. She believes some of us are trained in this mindset from an early age; it's the hand you are dealt with that you have to live with. On the other end of the spectrum is the **growth mindset** (incremental view) based on the belief that basic qualities can be cultivated through individual effort. If you possess this mindset, you live your life believing that you can change and grow through application and experience. This belief system conceives of intelligence as a malleable, changeable quality (Dweck, 2008). It's probably not difficult to figure out that research has linked growth mindsets to higher grade point averages, increased use of college-level study strategies, and an internal locus of control. You may be asking, "What if I am external and have an entity view?" The answer is simple. As the theme of this book suggests, you can change; you can adjust your mindsets.

Still, at some point it is natural for students to question their ability to be successful in college. They may ask themselves, "Am I smart enough to be here?" Students' beliefs regarding the nature and strength of their academic abilities will influence whether they will use new study skills. As indicated, you've heard students say things like, "I was born bad at math. No amount of tutoring is going to fix that." You may have even said such things to yourself. This fixed mindset causes them to react to learning challenges by claiming their problems are unsolvable, preventing them from seeking to improve by implementing new skills. This can also work in the reverse, that is, for students who have been successful and would not likely question their abilities.

Students who perceive themselves as strong academically face the traditional issues of college adjustment, and they too might be faced with having to form new learning strategies (Wratcher, 1991). A history of academic success affects the way talented students react to difficulty or failure in college. For example, because talented students are unaccustomed to dealing with academic difficulties, it takes them longer to recognize patterns of academic trouble and to seek assistance. In approaching their studies, talented students tend to be rigid in learning approaches and strategies, and they may possess unrealistic academic goals (Wratcher, 1991). Think about how it wasn't until Colleen's subpar performance on two exams that she was able to begin to break through the rigidity of the index card learning approach. This can be a painful way to learn, but Colleen was able to take something positive from the experience.

The question remains, "Are you smart enough to be here?" The answer is, "That depends." In college, there's a difference between being intelligent and doing intelligent . . . and between having factual knowledge and using procedural knowledge. You could have the highest IQ on campus, but if you are not using your smarts, it won't make a difference; again, this is what distinguishes a fixed mindset from a growth mindset. Take two students of equal ability. One procrastinates and avoids schoolwork and the other is diligent and hardworking. Who will be viewed as more intelligent?

In college, there's a difference between being intelligent and doing intelligent.

There is a perennial debate among scholars over what constitutes or defines intelligence. In the 1960s, personality characteristics and attitudes as they relate to academic achievement and intelligence began to receive attention. This awareness led educators to begin to question our culture's traditional views of intelligence.

Gardner's Theory of Multiple Intelligences

Howard Gardner's (1983) **theory of multiple intelligences (MI theory)** challenges the idea that intelligence is a single capacity that equips a person to deal with various situations. Likely, Gardner would challenge the entity view of intelligence. He argues that people use at least eight autonomous intellectual capacities with their own distinctive ways of thinking. He suggests that people use the **eight intelligences**, which he identifies as linguistic, musical, logical-mathematical, spatial, bodily-kinesthetic, interpersonal, intrapersonal, and naturalist, to approach problems and create products. According to Gardner,

> A human intellectual competence must entail a set of skills of problem solving—enabling an individual to resolve genuine problems or difficulties that he or she encounters and, when appropriate, to create an effective product—and must also entail the potential for finding or creating problems—thereby laying the groundwork for the acquisition of new knowledge. (p. 61)

> **Student Portrait**
>
> **Maria:** "For me as a person, it would make me more comfortable to know I have a social environment to make me more confident in my schoolwork, 'cause I'm not always confident in what I can produce. I think that holds true for a lot of people. You either have to have your confidence in one thing or another, and, if it's your academics, your social can maybe produce around that, or social can produce around your academics."

To enforce his point, Gardner provides an example of a twelve-year old male Puluwat in the Caroline Islands who has mastered sailing. Under the tutelage of master navigators, the boy learns to combine the knowledge of sailing, stars, and geography to find his way around hundreds of islands. The boy exhibits a high level of competence in a challenging field and should, Gardner argues, be viewed as exhibiting intelligent behavior, or "doing intelligent."

The research on student achievement, along with Gardner's (1983) theory of multiple intelligences, has received a great deal of attention in the field of education and sparked endless debates about the factors that contribute to and predict student achievement. It seems apparent from the research of Gardner and others, that besides using the traditional modes of standardized tests of intelligence and aptitude to predict academic achievement, other factors should be considered. Nevertheless, many institutions of higher education still rely on the traditional admissions credentials of high school grades and SAT scores in spite of research that suggests attitudinal and personality factors may be additional reliable criteria for predicting academic achievement. Again, take those two students of equal ability. Their admissions' credentials are virtually identical: same SAT scores, same high school grades. One can't get motivated to do the required work, whereas the other has established a daily routine for studying. In this case, who is more likely to achieve academically?

Goleman's Theory of Emotional Intelligence

Another person who questions how we traditionally look at intelligence is Daniel Goleman (1995). He questions the ways in which intelligence is quantified in our culture, in particular through a shift in interest from intelligence quotient to **emotional intelligence**. Emotional intelligence includes qualities that those who are high achievers share: self-awareness, impulse control, persistence, and self-motivation. A person's belief system, for instance, affects her or his achievement. Goleman's work is based on that of the Stanford psychologist Albert Bandura, who offered insight into a concept called **self-efficacy**, the belief you are capable of producing desired results, such as mastering new skills and achieving personal goals. Simply put, "if you believe you can do it, you can." Think about situations when you feel confident and how you might act compared to situations where you feel insecure. This idea is directly related to what study skills educators say regarding students' beliefs about their own academic abilities, including the relationship between students' loci of control and their study habits (Jones, Slate, Marini, & DeWater, 1993). If you believe the new study habits you have learned will produce desired results, and you recognize this as a result of your own efforts, you will more likely continue to use those new strategies and feel confident about doing so.

APPROACHES TO LEARNING

E ven those students with the most positive attitude toward learning can benefit from thinking more critically about how they learn. The remainder of this chapter gets into various approaches to learning that employ metacognition, reflecting on the ways you come to understand.

It is easy to remain entrenched in old habits, in old ways of thinking and learning. Friedman and Lipshitz (1992) call this "stuckness" **automatic thinking**. They explain that students sometimes are immobilized when trying to learn new information because of past experiences. Learning from experience, which seems to be a natural activity, is a critical skill for individuals and organizations. Experiential learning, however, results in behavior that tends to occur automatically rather than from conscious thought. Friedman and Lipshitz note that the advantage of automatic thinking can become a disadvantage in the face of change or uncertainty. They argue that automatic thinking leads people to rely on what they already know and contributes to the tendency to ignore critical information and rely on standard behavior repertoires when change is required (1992). That is, people continue to do what they feel most comfortable doing even if it isn't working for them; they resist change. Aside from experiential learning, other types of learning require switching to a more conscious reflective mode, and researchers argue that people resist switching to this mode when it's needed the most. This conscious reflective mode is **metacognition**.

Let's take these concepts and apply them to your use of new study strategies. You are stuck in your old study habits that you learned from experience in high school. For four years those habits served you well. You graduated from high school with a B average. Without thinking about it much, you automatically apply those strategies when you get to college. You don't even think about it. Why would you? Your ways always worked in the past, but now you are faced with change and uncertainty. Your automatic thinking causes you to ignore critical information. Like Colleen, you don't get great results using your study habits from high school, but you don't bother to look at how you might change your ways to adapt to the demands of college. You can't move out of your comfort zone, but you have to because you aren't happy with your grades. To figure out how your study habits affect your grades, you need to enter into that reflective mode of thinking. The way to start is to first understand the process of learning, to consider your critical thinking skills, and then to identify your learning style.

The Process of Learning Changes Your Brain

According to experts on brain development, all human brains look more or less alike when we are born. Neurons, the cells that make up your brain and central nervous system, number in the hundreds of millions at this time. Neurons, on their own, however, don't do much; our brains' ability to make sense of the world is a function of how our neurons connect. By the time we are adults, the connections among our neurons are complex and intricate.

Neurons connect to other neurons by extensions called axons. When one neuron's axon connects with another neuron, a synapse develops. Axon connections and growth between neurons continue well into old age. This process is what enables us to see, touch, smell, taste, and hear. This process is what makes humans "never too old to learn to learn something new." The connections between neurons allow perception and thought, and in turn, experience and interaction with the environment solidifies these neural connections (Leamnson, 1999). **Active** engagement with the environment is part of the process of learning. If a learner becomes **passive**, experts contend that the connections between neurons weaken. According to Leamnson (1999), "New axons make connections

EXHIBIT 5.2   *Neuron*

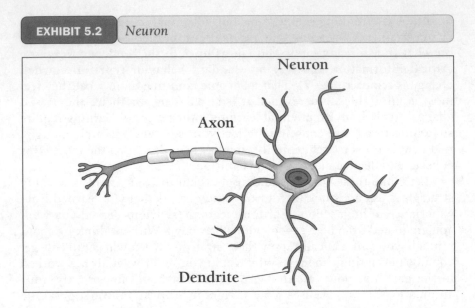

Neuron

Axon

Dendrite

with other neurons, but the connections, or synapses, are initially, quite labile, meaning here that they easily regress if not used" (p. 13). Given the way our brains function, then, when it comes time to solidify information in your mind for later recall, active engagement with the material is what is necessary to strengthen neural connection: practice, practice, practice.

Why is it important to understand the biological process of learning? The point is that learning goes beyond simply using your brain; it actually changes the brain's structure. Experts have discovered that, "learning makes the brain different than it was before, and permanently so" (Leamnson, 1999, p. 14). Humans have the capacity to become different when they learn something new. Learning can even lead to behavioral change. Think of something as simple as burning your hand on a hot stove. Your skin blisters, and you feel pain. The next time you are near the stove, you'll be more aware and careful not to touch it. Learning increases awareness. For example, in recent years, our society has become much more conscious about environmental conservation, and the long-term effects on the environment if individuals don't make an effort to recycle. The result has been a social movement called "going green."

Now let's apply the idea of learning leading to behavior change to the process of developing as a student. Here's how one student, Matt, made sense of his experience when he learned, that **massed practice** (cramming) was not as effective as **spaced practice** or **chunking**; that is, learning material in small parts, ahead of time, allows your brain time to solidify those neural connections:

> I started studying more and more as the semester went on and I now feel like I need to continue that to keep my grades up. I came to the conclusion

that there is simply too much material to just start studying for an exam the night before. Instead, I study about thirty minutes at a time, a couple of days in advance. This helps comprehend the material much better. I found myself more focused when using this strategy, rather than "studying" for two hours and daydreaming for about an hour of that time. I feel as though mid-semester is when I really took responsibility for my work and I also wanted to prove to myself that I could raise my grades. Changing all my habits and cutting down on my job hours helped me to achieve my goals. This, once again, included studying days in advance so I would really understand the material. Since I started practicing them, I can see a big difference in my work. I feel a lot more confident going into exams and about papers that I hand in.

Matt's reflections illustrate that he learned how one approach to studying was not quite as effective as another. As a result, his mindset changed, thereby changing his study strategies. Matt also recognized that perhaps working too many hours wasn't a good idea if he wanted to excel in school. He made a difficult decision and cut down on his job hours. In order for Matt to come to these conclusions and create change, he had to consider his habits, how he learns, and how he thinks. He engaged in the conscious, reflective mode of metacognition: thinking about how he learns and thinks. In short, Matt thought critically about his approaches to learning.

Thinking Critically

Critical thinking " is the art of analyzing and evaluating thinking with a view to improving it" (Paul & Elder, 2009, p. 2). Paul and Elder (2009) contend that our thinking, left unchecked, will be distorted, biased, and uninformed, in other words, shoddy. They go as far to say, "Shoddy thinking is costly, both in money and quality of life" (Paul & Elder, 2009, p. 2). For Matt, their words ring true.

If Matt decided not to cut down on his minimum wage job hours, then the cost may have been failing a class. If his tuition dollars exceeded the amount of money he was earning at his job, failing the class would've resulted in a waste of his money. Working, going to school full-time, and studying inefficiently all contributed to Matt's quality of life. Matt recognized he needed to make a change. He needed to look at alternative ways of approaching his semester. His goal was to improve his grades and his quality of life. In this case, Matt had to think open-mindedly with alternative systems of thought, according to Paul and Elder (2009) one of the five habits of a well cultivated critical thinker:

- Raises vital questions and problems, formulating them clearly and precisely;
- Gathers and assesses relevant information, using abstract ideas to interpret it effectively;

- Comes to well-reasoned conclusions and solutions, testing them against relevant criteria and standards;
- Thinks open-mindedly with alternative systems of thought, recognizing and assessing, as need be, their assumptions, implications, and practical consequences; and
- Communicates effectively with others in figuring out solutions to complex problems (Paul & Elder, 2009, p. 2).

Paul and Elder (2009) have also designed a framework of questions designed to help students and others develop the habits of a well cultivated critical thinker. These questions can also be used when solving problems, writing a paper, designing an activity, and reading assignments. They are called *Questions Using the Elements of Thought*:

Purpose:	What am I trying to accomplish?
	What is my central aim? My purpose?
Questions:	What question am I raising?
	What question am I addressing?
	What information so I need to settle the question?
Information:	What information am I using in coming to that conclusion?
	What experience have I had to support this claim?
	What information do I need to settle the question?
Inferences/ Conclusions:	How did I reach this conclusion?
	If there another way to interpret the information?
Concepts:	What is the main idea here?
	Can I explain this idea?
Assumptions:	What am I taking for granted?
	What assumption has led me to that conclusion?
Implications/ Consequences:	If someone accepted my position, what would be the implication?
	What am I implying?
Points of View:	From what point of view am I looking at this issue?
	Is there another point of view I should consider?

Source: Paul and Elder, 2009, p. 6. Foundation for Critical Thinking, www.criticalthinking.org. Used with permission.

Let's reexamine Matt's dilemma of faulty study strategies and his issue of working too many hours to do justice to his school work. In solving these problems, he utilized components of Paul and Elder's (2009) framework. What was Matt trying to accomplish (purpose)? A more balanced schedule of work and school and more efficient study strategies. What was he taking for granted (assumptions)? Perhaps that cramming would still work for him in college. What information did he need to settle his dilemma (information)? He had to have information regarding whether his supervisor at work would agree to decreasing his hours. When looking at these lists, you might assume that simply following a step-by-step process of working through these questions will lead you to becoming a well culti-vated critical thinker; but if you were, you would recognize that you are an individual. These lists are merely what researchers suggest as guidelines of what the typical habit patterns of critical thinkers. Within these patterns are you, the individual with a particular learning style.

Identify Your Learning Style(s)

Study strategies and critical thinking skills are often taught using a one-size-fits-all approach. In many instances, students are taught one particu-lar way of taking notes, and the assumption is that every person will benefit from applying that particular note-taking technique. **Learning styles theory**, in contrast, addresses the ways in which a person learns best and tailors approaches to learning and studying based on the individ-ual. Study experts like Reynolds and Werner (1994) advocate for an approach that is "learner-centered, where individuals develop personal ways of learning which can be called learning style characteristics. This pattern of personality and environmental factors related to how one learns is called '**learning style**'" (p. 272). For some students, a learner-centered approach is a worthwhile pursuit, and those students need to take the time to develop their own personal ways of learning. Students usually have a preferred way of learning new material, via one or more of several sensory modalities, including auditory, visual, and tactile/kines-thetic. Simply put, people process information using their ears, their eyes, and their sense of touch.

Auditory learners use their ears as the primary mode for learning. They are most likely to remember what they hear and what they say. If they find something difficult to understand, they want to talk it through. Pro-fessors may notice that auditory learners tend not to take as many notes in class as other students do. Auditory learners have a keen ability to remem-ber things without writing them down. When they want to remember something, they use verbal rehearsal techniques. That is, they go over con-cepts by saying them aloud, sometimes several times, because the oral rep-etition implants the information in their minds. These are the students who get heavily involved in class discussions. On the downside, auditory processors may get easily distracted by sound because they attend to all of the noises around them. They are uncomfortable when forced to work qui-etly at their desks for an extended period of time or to study in a quiet room (Guild & Garger, 1986).

Visual learners want to see a picture; they want to actually see the words written down. For example, a visual learner would find handouts, overheads, and PowerPoint slides very helpful in the classroom. These learners tune in to the physical environment. They like to organize their own materials and work spaces. They prefer illustrations, diagrams, and charts to help them understand and remember information. They tend to review and study material by reading over their notes and by recopying and reorganizing them in outline form (Guild & Garger, 1986).

Tactile/kinesthetic learners prefer learning when they are physically involved in what they are studying. These learners want to act out a situation, create a product, or work on a project. They understand and remember best when they physically do something. They may take lots of notes to keep their hands busy, but they may avoid rereading the notes. They learn a new skill by actually trying it, experimenting, and practicing. They learn concepts in history by simulating experiences in the classroom. They become interested in poetry by becoming physically involved in the thoughts expressed. Many of these learners want to be as active as possible during the learning experience (Guild & Garger, 1986).

Mixed modality learners are able to function in more than one modality. Students with mixed modality strengths often have a better chance of success than do those with a single modality strength because they are able to process information in whatever way it is presented (Guild & Garger, 1986).

You may have arrived at college favoring one of the three primary learning styles (auditory, visual, or tactile/kinesthetic). Because study experts say you have a better chance at success if you are mixed modality, you should identify your preferred style and work on developing the other modes.

Many students complain, for instance, that they have trouble learning in classes that rely primarily on PowerPoint presentations for instruction. Part of the problem is that these students likely are not visual processors; perhaps they are either auditory or tactile/kinesthetic processors. They may be yearning for some class discussion or perhaps group exercises. So what should the students do about the situation?

Unfortunately, students often have little or no control over the way in which information is presented in the classroom, which is precisely why mixed modality learners have a better chance of success, they are able to process information in whatever way it is presented. Your challenge is to identify your preferred style and work on strengthening the modes with which you are least comfortable. Because you often have little influence over the ways your professors choose to teach, try enhancing the extent to which you can learn outside of the classroom in various contexts. To do so, formulate study strategies that tap into all three learning modalities. We'll help you do so.

Writing to Learn and Journal Writing Can Help You Better Understand How You Learn

Writing is a metacognitive activity. There is a lot that can be learned about how you think through the process of writing. In fact, although many students say they'd like to learn how to be a better writer, fewer students fully use writing as a learning tool. Writing isn't only a way for you to demonstrate what you know, it is also a way to discover and experiment with ideas, to arrive at an understanding. This view of writing suggests you needn't have things all figured out when you sit down at your blank computer screen. Viewing writing as a means of discovery means you don't always know where your sentences will take you.

Imagine, for example, that you decided to write a paper about the Fox television show, *The Simpsons*. You thought you would focus on Homer and Marge as parents. That would be your topic. Now you need to have something to say about that topic: What do you think of these animated parents? This idea will be your working thesis, maybe something like "Homer and Marge Simpson are terrible parents." Simple enough. You begin to brainstorm, writing down what you can remember about Homer and Marge as parents. You do your best to remember specific episodes and particular events. You are using writing to remember, record, and build on itself.

When you look at what you've come up with, though, you discover that most of your examples don't illustrate the point you originally thought you'd make. It turns out that the events you've been able to recall mainly illustrate that Homer and Marge are typical parents, doing their best and making mistakes along the way. Now what? Should you give up and select another topic? The most logical strategy would be to revise your working thesis so it conforms to your findings, the ideas you've generated through brainstorming. This is an example of how writing—in coordination with reflective thinking—can lead you to think differently. Everything isn't already in your head waiting to be dumped onto 8 × 11 sheets.

The goal of a **reflective journal**, in fact, is to think through ideas by writing about them—to figure things out by putting pen to paper or fingertips to keyboard. Journals allow "students and teachers [to] work together through written language to understand disciplinary content—its problems and its possibilities, and its value, usefulness, and connections to other disciplines and other situations" (Gardner & Fulwiler, 1999, p. vi). The act of keeping a reflective journal involves making regular entries and collecting them together to illustrate your thinking over a period of time, typically a semester. These entries might reveal a linear thought process, but they might also reflect back on earlier entries to challenge, extend, and/or complicate ideas. A journal is not a notebook. It is not a summary of what happened in class or a collection of notes regarding course readings. Professors typically encourage students to use journals to question, disagree, argue, complicate, extend, connect, evaluate, and/or identify the impact of discussions or readings.

Some professors *require* the use of a journal, some *recommend* keeping a journal, and others say nothing about journals at all. Because journals are a way for you to be actively involved in a course, you might consider putting some effort into keeping a journal regardless of whether it is required or recommended. Doing so will help you engage with what you are learning on a personal level, giving you a safe space regularly to ask questions and attempt answers.

The collection of entries that comprise a journal will likely indicate what you feel and/or think about discussions you had in class, what you've read in and outside of class, campus-sponsored or promoted events you've attended, and other such reflective opportunities. If the journal is required, your professor may offer prompts to which your entries are expected to respond. Your professor may even suggest you respond to ideas you voiced earlier, in previous entries; these responses have the potential to show you how your thinking changes over time. You might consider discussing what you believe happened between the two entries that caused you to see things differently (if indeed you do). If keeping a journal is your own choice, you can decide on your own prompts, connecting what you are learning to your own personal experience.

If a journal is required, you will likely be asked to bring your journal with you to at least some class meetings. You may be asked to use the journal in class, to do things like read part of an entry to the class, refer to your journal as you take a quiz, or compose a new entry.

Portfolio Development Is Another Useful Metacognitive Activity

Portfolios, collections of student work, emphasize metacognition, requiring those who keep a portfolio to consider what it will include, to make decisions regarding content, organization, and scope, for example. As with journals, portfolios may be required, recommended, or not mentioned. Depending on the situation, a portfolio can consist of writing, artwork, videotaped presentations, PowerPoint slides, sample databases, websites, and other artifacts. A portfolio might reveal things about your experiences in a course—or in your entire college experience.

Nedra Reynolds (2000), a rhetoric and composition scholar, explains the benefits of writing portfolios, benefits that would certainly apply to other types of portfolios as well: "Through reflective learning, you can focus on your patterns, habits, and preferences as a student and a writer; learn to repeat what works well for you; and develop strategies for addressing or overcoming the parts of writing that frustrate or puzzle you" (p. 1). Although reflection is inherent in the process of compiling a portfolio, your portfolio reader may also want some measure of this reflection, perhaps in the form of a letter, videotaped or audiotaped explanation, painting, or photograph—something that shows what you've learned through putting the portfolio together.

What, for example, made you decide to include those particular artifacts? Why have you arranged them in the order you have? What did you learn about your audience or viewer as you reworked these pieces, and (how) did you accommodate your audience's/viewers' needs? If you are asked to include a reflective component in your portfolio, welcome the opportunity to stand back from your work and look at what you've produced.

Read Actively to Employ Multiple Learning Modalities

Like many students, you have probably experienced something similar to the following scenario: when Antonio sits down to read, he reads several pages, and nothing sinks in at all. He quickly becomes frustrated and gives up on the reading. He then goes to class feeling like a fraud, praying the professor won't notice he didn't do the reading. "Someone else will surely answer the questions," he thinks, "and I'll be able just to hide in the background." Antonio also hopes his professor will cover what he was supposed to read during the lecture, so he'll be able to rely on his class notes for the test. This strategy of avoidance catches up with him eventually because the primary vehicle for learning new material in college, aside from classroom instruction, is reading. Antonio soon discovers that questions on the exam were largely derived from his textbook and class lectures were designed as a backdrop for discussing what he was already supposed to know. The lectures didn't go into nearly as much depth as his textbook. Antonio finds that avoiding reading is significantly affecting his test grades. In addition, it is affecting his class participation grade.

Antonio decides that, for the next test, he is really going to try to make the effort. He looks at the syllabus, and, for this class, he has to read about 350 pages per week. No problem. That's about fifty pages a day, applying the academic goal-setting strategy and breaking up the reading into more manageable increments. With highlighter in hand, Antonio begins to read the first fifty pages. For the first few pages, things seem to be going well. After some time has passed, however, he realizes it's happening again. Things just aren't sinking in, and, as he looks down at the page, he realizes that half the page in the book is now hot pink from all of the highlighting he's been doing. On the bright side, Antonio does remember what he's read from the first three pages. The rest, however, is a blur, and he is a full twenty pages into the fifty he set out to read. Looking at the clock, he sees an hour has passed. How is he going to finish this reading assignment? The frustration and anxiety builds. He doesn't know what to do. He feels like such a slow reader.

Like Antonio, what could be happening when you are reading is that you are on autopilot. Most students have been reading since their early years in elementary school. It is such an over-learned activity that you do it automatically. To read for comprehension, you need to reflect on what you are reading. Instead of doing so, however, many students reach for the highlighter.

What could be happening when you are reading is that you are on autopilot.

Using a highlighter may make you feel better. You can unwittingly fool yourself into believing you are doing something productive about your comprehension. After highlighting, you can visually track your passage through a text; you can see you have proceeded through the chapter. Unfortunately, using a highlighter tends to contribute to passive reading. You could highlight a book while you are stretched out on your bed.

You'll merely end up back on autopilot, swiping different colored ink over lines of text.

Think for a minute about what the inside of a textbook looks like. Grab a textbook and check it out. Notice the format and structure. The main headings and subheadings are in bold print. There are content vocabulary words in italics and/or bold print. There are likely shaded boxes with graphic organizers and important information. What do you know: the textbook authors have already done the highlighting for you! If you are highlighting text beyond what they have, chances are you are focusing on the information at a factual level. You are reading for understanding and memorizing definitions. As we have already discussed, learning at college goes beyond testing for factual recall of information.

One general approach to textbook reading assists students of all learning styles. This approach, **active reading**, crosses over all three learning modalities, which will support your retention of the material. Although there isn't one fixed approach to active reading, the process could go something like this. First, read a passage or paragraph. Use imagery, a visual processing activity, in an attempt to picture what you are reading. To monitor your comprehension—to remain in a reflective thinking mode rather than an automatic thinking mode—summarize the passage in your own words, and question yourself about your level of understanding (auditory processing). In other words, have an ongoing dialogue with the text. Think about acting as an interpreter of textual information. Imagine you have to translate the information from text language into student language. Record your translation. Verify the information from another source; consider the questions your teacher might ask regarding the passage and record those questions (tactile/kinesthetic processing). Change the main headings/topics into questions. The key here is to read purposefully. Learn to read skillfully for such purposes as these:

1. to get the main idea,
2. to get the important details,
3. to answer a specific question,
4. to evaluate what you are reading, and
5. to apply what you are reading.

Not only will applying what you've read take your metacognitive processing to a deeper level and improve your comprehension, but it also will serve you well on tests and quizzes by increasing your memory retention. Look for examples in the textbook that the authors use to illustrate key concepts. Record them. You may also generate your own examples to illustrate these concepts in the text. This activity will help build the information into your own **schema**. In other words, connect the new information you are learning to what you already know. Finally, use margin notes to record your understanding of the textual information, a strategy called *text annotation,* covered in more detail later in this chapter.

It Is Possible to Become a Better Reader

You may feel like this active reading approach won't save you any time at all. You may be thinking to yourself, "Why would I do this? I'm already a slow reader, and this is going to make a bad situation worse." Granted, this approach may initially take a little longer, but, with practice, active reading will become a more efficient way to read. Why? For one thing, active reading yields better comprehension. You may have been reading a little faster before, but what's the point if you weren't remembering what you were reading? Reading more effectively and efficiently means accomplishing more in less time, enhanced learning, and, likely, increased class participation and retention of information.

Think of active reading this way: reading is like running; both require periodic training and practice. As you work on becoming a more effective and efficient reader, at times you will feel discouraged, but don't quit. Work hard and steadily as if training for a marathon. At first, with no practice, you may only be able to run a mile without getting fatigued, but, with daily practice, you build up to five miles, then ten. Similarly, you may only be able to read a few pages actively without getting fatigued. Like the dedicated runner, you persist, keep at it everyday, and eventually build up your endurance. You will eventually become a good reader. Good readers read for a purpose, read thought units rather than words, have many reading rates, evaluate what they read, have a good vocabulary, read varied materials, and enjoy reading.

Certain strategies can improve your reading speed and comprehension. You might try reading at the same times every day. Doing so trains your mind to be in thinking mode at those times and cuts down on the time it takes you to become engaged. Also consider the environment in which you read: avoid places where there are constant distractions, and be sure the area is properly lit. Students often think in terms of slow readers and fast readers, but effective readers are able to alter the rate at which they read and are conscious of this rate. In particular contexts and situations it is necessary to read slowly; for example, in reading Derrida for the first time when reading at an increased rate would mean that little comprehension would be taking place. Effective readers also strive to improve their own vocabulary, the collection of words with which they are familiar. As you come across words you don't know, or don't understand in a particular context, take the appropriate opportunity to discover what the word means. You might even consider keeping a word journal, in which you write your new words and their corresponding definitions. This kinesthetic exercise will help you develop your vocabulary more quickly.

Reading effectively means having an adequate level of comprehension. Just as you should take the time to familiarize yourself with new vocabulary, also take the time to understand difficult concepts and passages. When you've had that experience of reading a paragraph or two or perhaps even a page or more without processing what it is you've read, it could be you've read the words only, not taking the time to see the relationship among the words, their meaning in the sentence. Whether you've zoned out for a period of time or just haven't understood what the author was trying to convey, you need to halt your progress for the time it takes to go back, reread, and reassess those ideas.

When active learning was first discussed, we mentioned that ardent active learners don't wait for class to begin the search for answers. The texts you'll read in college offer clues that can direct you toward such answers, and some of the most helpful clues are called *references* and *endnotes*. Often considered ancillary material, and, consequently, often unread, these resources are included by the author(s) for a reason. They say, in effect, "Here is where you might look for additional information on the subject." References include information regarding a source of information. In this textbook, we've offered parenthetical references to the sources of information used. Here's an example:

> Journals allow "students and teachers [to] work together through written language to understand disciplinary content—its problems and its possibilities, and its value, usefulness, and connections to other disciplines and other situations." (Gardner & Fulwiler, 1999, p. vi)

If you were interested in finding out more about journals, you would look for the full citation on the References page. There you would find all of the information you'd need to acquire the source from the library. Endnotes differ from references in that they offer more than source information. Endnotes, typically found at the end of a chapter or article but before the References page, also offer some additional written commentary regarding a particular idea. This information was deemed to be interesting, although not crucial, for readers, and so was included in an unobtrusive way for the intellectually curious. References and endnotes, then, can help you begin your search for answers; and the texts' references will have their own references and endnotes to help keep your search going, if need be.

We don't always read for the same reasons. A student reads *Sports Illustrated* to get the latest information about a favorite player or team, and such information might be used in a conversation with friends or coworkers, although it might just as well be used for entertainment only. This same student would have a different purpose when reading the classified section of the *Boston Globe,* a chemistry textbook, a stock report, or a short story for a literature class. Your method of reading should fit your purpose. Are you reading to get the main idea? Are you looking for important details? Are you trying to answer a specific question? Are you evaluating what you are reading? Will you be expected to apply the concepts you are reading about? Recreational reading and academic reading require different levels of attention from readers.

You may be interested in learning to read more quickly. We've mentioned that at certain times reading quickly isn't ideal, but there are situations in which an increased rate is appropriate. Learning to read at an increased rate takes practice; you'll need to push yourself to read words more quickly, to skip unnecessary words, to focus on the more important sections, and to look for key ideas.

You might want to practice reading at an increased rate with your favorite magazine or newspaper. This material should be fairly digestible, and your familiarity with the format and layout will make it easier for you to navigate efficiently through the reading. You can also, of course, practice with other reading material. When reading a novel, for instance, try reading an entire chapter at the increased rate.

At times, you'll need to skim a text for a general impression. You might, for example, need to decide whether a book is relevant to the research you have undertaken. The title and/or subtitle has likely led you to this source; now you need to review the table of contents and index to determine whether, and to what extent, the relevant topics are discussed.

Text Annotation Encourages Active Reading

Another way you can actively engage with what you are learning in college is by using text annotation, sometimes called *marginalia*. **Annotating text** means writing analytical, critical, and/or summative notes in response to a written work. This activity involves writing comments, notes, and questions in the margins, essentially establishing a written conversation between reader and text. Text annotation is a great way to stay on task and monitor your comprehension.

Why bother annotating text? For one thing, good readers react to what they read. We want to scream at the narrator in Ellison's "Battle Royal." How can he fall for the electrified rug trick? Doesn't he know he's being used as entertainment? Why doesn't he refuse to fight Tatlock?

We feel for Matt Fowler in Dubus's "Killings." After all, is it that unthinkable that a father would consider avenging his son's murder as Fowler did? Who hasn't watched a news story about an abducted child and thought about what we would do if that was our child? When we think of our own child in this case, we are integrating the information into our schema. Literature forges connections between the fictional characters and the experiences of readers. Indeed, meaning is made as readers view the sequence of words on the page, filling in the blanks, and making pictures in their minds that represent the characters' actions.

Text annotation is a good way for you to react to literary works within, around, and on the work itself. The act of writing a comment or question may help you think through a complex idea. If you think of text annotation as an exploratory exercise, as an interaction with the text or a way to situate yourself around or within it, then this activity produces much more than just notes.

Text annotation can be a great prelude to class discussion. When the professor asks students what they think about a character's actions or an author's thesis, the student who has annotated the text is not only likely to have a response, but he or she is also able quickly to identify the section of the text that prompted the response.

Here's another reason to consider text annotation: if you're anything like the rest of us, you don't memorize everything that you read. For this

Does anyone have questions about the reading?

reason, text annotation also provides a method of recording important elements of a literary work. In addition to reacting to a text, an annotation of "Killings" might very well include a note regarding the place(s) that Matt Fowler seemed to regret his vengeful actions. Such notes enable students to return to the text at a later date and more easily discover useful examples in preparation for an exam or writing a paper.

Text annotation also can be much more helpful than highlighting. Let's face it. Once you've highlighted a chapter in a novel or textbook, all of the highlighted information appears equally important. Nothing distinguishes the significance of certain highlighted information from other highlighted information. In fact, when you look back at that chapter a week or two later, you don't remember why you highlighted what you did. So then what happens? Yes, you've got to reread the highlighted portions, and probably the unhighlighted sections around them, to figure out what you were thinking during your initial reading. *Put down your highlighter*. With a pen in hand, you can identify important elements of a text while at the same time have the ability to identify why you've singled out that word, sentence, or chunk.

The following is a list of suggestions regarding what an annotation might involve:

1. identifying a major theme of the work,
2. questioning the morality of a character's thoughts and/or actions,
3. identifying the central action of the work,
4. noting the organizational pattern(s) exhibited in the work,
5. identifying the author's intended purpose,
6. making connections across works,
7. examining differences across works,
8. identifying with a character,
9. asking a question you can't yet answer,
10. stating the significance of a particular action,
11. noting an event you think is important, and
12. identifying a statement that doesn't seem to fit.

The final component of this chapter is a sample annotated text, shown in Exhibit 5.3. This sample is an annotation of Plato's *Apology,* done by Ashley, a first-year student. Notice how she was able to describe significant passages and concepts, facilitating future references. She also wrote questions in the text at the point where she had them, allowing her to have something to say in class when her professor asks, "Does anyone have questions about the reading?"

This chapter presented you with a variety of college-level study strategies. You were challenged to think about how you learn, practice using these strategies in different contexts, and to develop a sense of when they would—and wouldn't—be effective. This first-year student accepted the

EXHIBIT 5.3   *Sample annotated text*

Impicty charge—

ASHLEY FABRIZIO

religious beliefs — Gods get power & give it to the wise. If you chip it away you chip away at the ideology — no purpose of Gods

APOLOGY

defence

Socrates speech

What trial?

The Apology[1] professes to be a record of the actual speech that Socrates delivered in his own defence at the <u>trial</u>: This makes the question of its historicity more acute than in the dialogues in which the conversations themselves are mostly fictional and the question of historicity is concerned only with how far the theories that Socrates is represented as expressing were those of the historical Socrates. Here, however, we are dealing with a speech that Socrates made as a matter of <u>history</u>. How far is Plato's account accurate? We should always remember that the ancients did not expect historical accuracy in the way we do. On the other hand, Plato makes it clear that he was present at the trial (34a, 38b). Moreover, if, as is generally believed, the Apology was written not long after the event, many Athenians would remember the actual speech, and it would be a poor way to vindicate the <u>Master, which is the</u> obvious intent, to put a completely different speech into his mouth. Some liberties could no doubt be allowed, but the main arguments and the general tone of the defence must surely be faithful to the original. The beauty of language and style is certainly Plato's but the serene spiritual and moral beauty of character belongs to Socrates. It is a powerful combination.

<u>Athenian juries</u> were very large, in this case 501, and they combined the duties of jury and judge as we know them by both convicting and sentencing. Obviously, it would have been virtually impossible for so large a body to discuss various penalties and decide on one. The problem was resolved rather neatly, however, by having <u>the prosecutor</u>, after conviction, <u>assess the penalty he thought appropriate</u>, followed by a <u>counter-assessment by the defendant</u>. The jury would then decide between the two. This procedure generally made for moderation on both sides.

Thus the Apology is in <u>three parts</u>. The first and major part is the main <u>speech</u> (17a – 35a), followed by the <u>counter-assessment</u> (35a – 38c), and finally, <u>last words</u> to the jury (38c – 42a), both to those who voted for the death sentence, and those who voted for acquittal.

literary — Plato
artistic — Socrates

historical accuracy

Who is he?

Courts similar to ours

Choose penalty

3 parts: main speech   counter – assessment   last words to jury

---

1. The word *apology* is a (transliteration) not a translation, of the Greek *apologia* which means defence. There is certainly nothing apologetic about the speech.

(Continued)

EXHIBIT 5.3 *Continued*

[handwritten: audience/jury ↑]

17   I do not know, men of <u>Athens</u>, how my accusers affected you, as for me, I was almost carried away in spite of myself, so persuasively did (they) speak. And yet, hardly anything of what they said is true. Of the many lies they told, one in

b   particular surprised me, namely that you should be careful not to be deceived by an accomplished speaker like me. That they were not ashamed to be immediately proved wrong by the facts, when I show myself not to be an accomplished speaker at all, that I thought was most shameless on their part — unless indeed they call an accomplished speaker the man who speaks the truth. If they mean that, I would agree that I am an (orator,) but not after their manner, for indeed, as I say, practically nothing they said was true. From me you will hear the whole truth, though not, by Zeus, gentlemen, expressed in embroidered and stylized phrases like theirs, but things spoken at random and expressed in the first words that come to mind, for I *put my trust in the justice of what I say,* and let

c   *none of* you *expect anything else.* It would not be fitting at my age, as it might be for a young man, to toy with words when I appear before you. *[handwritten: → means bus]*

    One thing I do ask and beg of you, gentlemen: if you hear me making my defence in the <u>same</u> kind of <u>language as</u> I am accustomed to use in the market place *by the bankers' tables,*[2] where many of you have heard me, and elsewhere, do not be surprised or create a disturbance on that account. The position is this:

d   this is my <u>first appearance</u> in a lawcourt, at the <u>age of seventy</u>; I am therefore simply a stranger to the manner of speaking here. Just as if I were really a stranger, you would certainly excuse me if I spoke in that dialect and manner in which I had been brought up, so too my present request seems a just one, for you to pay

18   no attention to my manner of speech — be it better or worse — but to concentrate your attention on whether what I say is just or not, for the <u>excellence of a judge lies in this, as that of a speaker lies in telling the truth</u> even though it must not

b   sound right, it is true.

    →It is right for me, gentlemen, to defend myself first against the first <u>lying accusations</u> made against me and my first accusers, and then against the <u>later accusations</u> and the later accusers. There have been many who have accused me to you for many years now, and none of their accusations are true. These I fear much more than I fear (Anytus) and his friends, though they too are formidable. These earlier ones, however, are more so, gentlemen; they got hold of most of you from childhood, persuaded you and accused me quite falsely, saying that there is a man called Socrates, a wise man, a student of all things in the sky and below the earth, who makes the worse argument the stronger. Those who spread that rumour, gentlemen, are my dangerous accusers, for their hearers believe that those who study these things do not even believe in the gods. Moreover, these accusers are numerous, and have been at it a <u>long time</u>; also, they spoke to you at an age when you would most readily believe them, some of you being children and adolescents, and they won their case by default, as there was no defence. *[handwritten: Soc has been accused for most of his life.]*

[left margin handwritten notes: who is they?; his words = truth; man be confusing to jury; defending himself 1st; he has been accused from childhood experiences who is Anytus?]

[right margin handwritten notes: SPEAKER; has been accused for years; if they do not believe in god, then why do they believe the accusers?; no morales]

---

2.   The bankers or money-changers had their counters in the market place. It seems that this was a favourite place for gossip.

EXHIBIT 5.3 *Continued*

What is most absurd in all this is that one cannot even know or mention their names unless one of them is a writer of comedies.[3] Those who maliciously and slanderously persuaded you — who also, when persuaded themselves then persuaded others — all those are most difficult to deal with: one cannot bring one of them into court or refute him; one must simply fight with shadows, as it were, in making one's defence, and cross-examine when no one answers. I want you to realize too that my accusers are of two kinds: those who have accused me recently, and the old ones I mention; and to think that I must first defend myself against the latter, for you have also heard their accusations first, and to a much greater extent than the more recent.———> *two accusers: recent & older*

(margin: will 1st defend against older blc heard 1st & heard more) *(d)*

Very well then. I must surely defend myself and attempt to uproot from your minds in so short a time the slander that has resided there so long. I wish this may happen, if it is in any way better for you and me, and that my defence may be successful, but I think this is very difficult and I am fully aware of how difficult it is. Even so, let the matter proceed as the god may wish, but I must obey the law and make my defence.

(margin: addressing jury)

(margin: 19 starting defense)

Let us then take up the case from its beginning. What is the accusation from which arose the slander in which Meletus trusted when he wrote out the charge against me? What did they say when they slandered me? I must, as if they were my actual prosecutors, read the affidavit they would have sworn. It goes something like this: |Socrates is guilty of wrongdoing in that he busies himself studying things in the sky and below the earth; he makes the worse into the stronger argument, and he teaches these same things to others.| You have seen this yourselves in the comedy of Aristophanes, a Socrates swinging about there, saying he was walking on air and talking a lot of other nonsense about things of which I know nothing at all. I do not speak in contempt of such knowledge, if someone is wise in these things — lest Meletus bring more cases against me — but, gentlemen, I have no part in it, and on this point I call upon the majority of you as witnesses. I think it right that all those of you who have heard me conversing, and many of you have, should tell each other if anyone of you has ever

(margin: meletus? b)
(margin: wrote charge c)
(margin: d)
(margin: everyone is a witness)

(margin: being accused of studying too much & having too much knowledge -he was made fun of ideas that he never thought of.)

---

3. This refers in particular to Aristophanes, whose comedy, *The Clouds*, produced in 423 B.C., ridiculed the (imaginary) school of Socrates.

Used with permission of Ashley Fabrizio.

challenge and has begun to develop her text annotation skills. Ashley's positive attitude toward change enabled her to attempt a new study strategy. Her locus of control was primarily internal, allowing her to see she was in large part responsible for how well she would do in each of her classes. You need to decide whether you will accept the challenge to change, in addition to which new study habits you will adopt.

FIRST-YEAR DIARIES:
ADJUSTMENT REFLECTIONS

Adjusting to Text Annotation ~ Ryan

After learning how to annotate a text, my reading life changed drastically. Annotating the text truly helps in remembering the information. Immediately after I learned how to do it, I started to apply these skills and boy has it changed by reading habits. The homework which made us annotate a portion of something we had read for another course really opened my eyes to the helpfulness of this skill. It truly worked. I remembered much more of the text and it made it so much easier at study time to go back and see the main points of the reading. I have made tremendous strides in reading and it has had a direct correlation to my grades and I know that without learning this skill, I would not have seen the same results.

DISCUSSION QUESTIONS

1. In one of the student portraits in this chapter, Melodie reveals that she feels her high school did not prepare her for the rigors of college-level work. How do you think your high school prepared you? She also describes being "at the top" in high school and now she feels like she's "at the bottom" in college. It seems that different high schools prepare students to varying degrees of readiness for college. Why do you think this happens?

2. Describe Colleen's attitudes toward learning from Chapter 1. Consider her locus of control and attitude toward intelligence.

3. In Ernie's student portrait, he expresses doubts about his reading abilities. Do you like to read? How do you feel about your reading load at college? How does your experience compare with Ernie's?

4. Do you believe intelligence is a fixed commodity, that you are born with a certain IQ (an entity view), or do you believe you can increase your intelligence through hard work (an incremental view)? Justify your position.

5. Both Gardner and Goleman challenge the ways in which we think about intelligence in our culture. Of the two theorists, with whom do you agree more? Base your answer on your own experiences.

6. Describe a time where you were stuck in an automatic thinking mode. How were you able to get unstuck? What did you learn from the experience?

7. Choose a current dilemma related to your study strategies that would like to solve or change. Take Paul and Elder's *Questions Using the Elements of Thought*. Which ones would work best to solve the particular problem you chose? How did they help you resolve your dilemma?

8. This chapter discusses different learning styles, including auditory, visual, tactile/kinesthetic, and mixed modality. Which of these styles best characterizes the way in which you learn best? How do you know?

9. Analyze the teaching styles of your professors. Which of the learning styles best coincides with the ways each one teaches?

10. What could text annotation add to your reading experience? Are there any negative consequences of text annotation? If so, do the benefits outweigh the costs?

11. Besides the attitudes outlined in this chapter, what other attitudes can get in the way of student learning? Do you currently possess any of those attitudes?

ACTIVITIES

5.1 Using a reading that has already been assigned, read the text and use text annotation. Write a paragraph or two about the experience, particularly if this is your first attempt at annotation. Did you find you were actively involved in the reading, more so than if you had used a highlighter? What types of notes did you make? How did this activity help you process what you were reading?

5.2 Regardless of whether or not you currently keep a journal, construct a journal entry focused on the way(s) in which you currently read literature and/or textbooks. Describe your reading process to an imaginary student with no college reading experience. Which elements of the process are you most comfortable with and which would you like to change?

5.3 Compose a journal entry that reflects on the entry composed in Activity 5.2. Was this your first journal entry? Was this type of writing different from composing an essay? How so? What did you learn through this process?

5.4 With a group or individually, imagine that you were in a debate about whether intelligence is fixed, the entity view or malleable, the incremental view. Create a list of arguments for both sides of the debate.

5.5 Interview a sophomore and ask him or her to compare the ways in which the student approaches studying in the second year as opposed to the first. What particular differences can he or she identify? Does the student mention any of the study strategies you currently use?

5.6 Create a list of the attitudes you possess that might potentially interfere with your learning. Identify the root of these attitudes (e.g., self-efficacy, past experiences with teachers, family influence, peer pressure, etc.). Generate potential solutions to help you guard against these attitudes creeping in and interfering with your goals.

REFERENCES

Anderson, S. G., & Anderson, C. E. (1992). Study skills made easy. *School Counselor, 39*(5), 382–384.

Baltes, P. B., & Staudinger, U. (2000). Wisdom: A metaheuristic (pragmatic) to orchestrate the mind and virtue toward excellence. *American Psychologist, 55,* 122–136.

Cone, A. L., & Owens, S. K. (1991). Academic and locus of control enhancement in a freshman study skills and college adjustment course. *Psychological Reports, 68,* 1211–1217.

Dweck, C. S., & Leggett, E. L. (1988). A social-cognitive approach to motivation and personality. *Psychological Review, 95*(2), 256–273.

Dweck, C. S. (2008). *Mindset: The New psychology of success.* New York, NY: Ballentine Books.

Friedman, V. J., & Lipshitz, R. (1992). Teaching people to shift cognitive gears: Overcoming resistance on the road to model II. *Journal of Applied Behavioral Research, 28*(1), 118–136.

Gardner, H. (1983). *Frames of mind.* New York, NY: Basic Books.

Gardner, H. (2000). *Intelligence reframed: Multiple intelligences for the 21st century.* New York, NY: Basic Books.

Gardner, S., & Fulwiler, T. (1999). *The journal book: For teachers in technical and professional programs.* Portsmouth, NH: Boynton/Cook.

Goleman, D. (1995). *Emotional intelligence.* New York, NY: Bantam Books.

Guild, P. B., & Garger, S. (1986). *Marching to different drummers.* Alexandria, VA: Association for Supervision and Curriculum Development.

Hadwin, A. F., & Winne, P. H. (1996). Study strategies have meager support. *Journal of Higher Education, 67*(6), 692–715.

Jones, C. H., Slate, J. R., & Marini, I. (1995). Locus of control, social interdependence, academic preparation, age, study time, and the study skills of college students. *Research in the Schools, 2*(1), 55–62.

Jones, C. H., Slate, J. R., Marini, I., & DeWater, B. K. (1993). Academic skills and attitudes toward intelligence. *Journal of College Student Development, 34,* 422–424.

Leamnson, R. (1999). *Thinking About Teaching and Learning.* Sterling, VA: Stylus Publishing, LLC.

Lefcourt, H. M. (Ed.). (1982). *Locus of control: Current trends in theory and research* (2nd ed.). Mahwah, NJ: Erlbaum.

Paul, R., & Elder, L. (2009). *The miniature guide to critical thinking: Concepts and tools* (6th ed.). Dillon Beach, CA: Foundation for Critical Thinking Press.

Rabinowitz, F. E. (1987). A life transition seminar for freshmen college students. *Journal of College Student Personnel, 28,* 282–283.

Reynolds, J., & Werner, S. C. (1994). An alternative paradigm for college reading and study skills courses. *Journal of Reading, 37*(4), 272–277.

Reynolds, N. (2000). *Portfolio keeping: A guide for students.* Boston: St. Martin's Press.

Thomas, J. W., Bol, L., & Warkentin, R. W. (1991). Antecedents of college students' study deficiencies: The relationship between course features and students' study activities. *Higher Education, 22*(3), 275–296.

Turner, G. Y. (1992). College students' self-awareness of study behaviors. *College Student Journal, 26*(1), 129–134.

White, W. F., & Kitchen, S. (1991). Teaching metacognitive awareness to entering college students with developmental lag. *College Student Journal, 25*(4), 521–523.

Wratcher, M. A. (1991). Freshman academic adjustment at a competitive university. *College Student Journal, 25*(2), 170–177.

Additional Readings for Students

Critical Thinking/Problem Solving

Borg, J. R., & Borg, M. O. (2001). Teaching critical thinking in interdisciplinary economics courses. *College Teaching, 49*(1), 20–26.

Cooper, J. L. (1995). Cooperative learning and critical thinking. *Teaching of Psychology, 22*(1), 2–9.

Higbee, J. L., & Thomas, P. V. (1999). Affective and cognitive factors related to mathematics achievement. *Journal of Developmental Education, 23*(1), 8–15.

Inlow, F. H., & Chovan, W. (1993). Another search for the effects of teaching thinking and problem solving skills on college students' performance. *Journal of Instructional Psychology, 20*(3), 215–224.

Macpherson, K. (2002). Problem-solving ability and cognitive maturity in undergraduate students. *Assessment & Evaluation in Higher Education, 27*(1), 5–22.

McBride, R. E., & Reed, J. (1998). Thinking and college athletes—Are they predisposed to critical thinking? *College Student Journal, 32*(3), 443–451.

Moreno, R., & Mayer, R. E. (1999). Gender differences in responding to open-ended problem-solving questions. *Learning & Individual Differences, 11*(4), 355–365.

Trosset, C. (1998). Obstacles to open discussion and critical thinking. *Change, 30*(5),44–50.

Paul, R., & Elder, L. (2009). *The Miniature guide to critical thinking: Concepts and tools* (6th ed.). Dillon Beach, CA. Foundation for Critical Thinking Press. (www.criticalthinking.org)

Vinson, D. (1996). Prepping kids for college: What skills will they need to succeed? [Interview]. *Curriculum Review, 35*(7), 5–6.

Learning Styles

Keri, G. (2002). Male and female college students' learning styles differ: An opportunity for instructional diversification. *College Student Journal, 36*(3), 433–442.

Ladd, P. D., & Ruby, R., Jr. (1999). Learning style and adjustment issues of international students. *Journal of Education for Business, 74*(6), 363–367.

Matthews, D. B., & Hamby, J. V. (1995). A comparison of the learning styles of high school and college/university students. *Clearing House, 68*(4), 257–262.

Schmeck, R. R., & Nguyen, T. (1996). Factors affecting college students' learning styles: Family characteristics which contribute to college students' attitudes toward education and preferences for learning strategies. *College Student Journal, 30*(4), 542–547.

Schroeder, C. C. (1993). New students—new learning styles. *Change, 25*(5), 21–27.

Portfolio Development

Camp, R. (1998). Portfolio reflection: The basis for dialogue. *Clearing House, 72*(1), 10–13.

Additional Readings for Faculty

Critical Thinking/Problem Solving

Alexander, M. S. (1999). The art of teaching students to think critically. *Chronicle of Higher Education, 45*(48), B9–10.

Lindquist-Sandmann, A. (1987). A metacognitive strategy and high school students: Working together. *Journal of Reading, 30*(4), 326–332.

Prentice Hall. (Producer). (2003). *Critical thinking in today's curriculum* [Motion picture]. (Available from Prentice Hall, Upper Saddle River, NJ 07458)

White, W. F., & Kitchen, S. (1991). Teaching metacognitive awareness to entering college students with developmental lag. *College Student Journal, 25*(4), 521–523.

Learning Styles

Cano-Garcia, F., & Hughes, E. H. (2000). Learning and thinking styles: An analysis of their interrelationship and influence on academic achievement. *Educational Psychology, 20*(4), 413–430.

Davidson-Shivers, G. V., Nowlin, B., & Lanouette, M. (2002). Do multimedia lesson structure and learning styles influence undergraduate writing performance? *College Student Journal, 36*(1), 20–32.

Drysdale, M. T. B., Ross, J. L., & Schulz, R. A. (2001). Cognitive learning styles and academic performance in 19 first-year university courses: Successful students versus students at risk. *Journal of Education for Students Placed at Risk, 6*(3), 271–289.

Dunn, R., & Stevenson, J. M. (1997). Teaching diverse college students to study with a learning-styles prescription. *College Student Journal, 31*(3), 333–340.

Matthews, D. B. (1994). An investigation of students' learning styles in various disciplines in colleges and universities. *Journal of Humanistic Education & Development, 33*(2).

McClanaghan, M. E. (2000). A strategy for helping students learn how to learn. *Education, 120*(3), 479–486.

Zhang, L. (2002). Thinking styles: Their relationships with modes of thinking and academic performance. *Educational Psychology, 22*(3), 331–349.

Portfolio Development

Gearhart, M., & Wolf, S. A. (1997). Issues in portfolio assessment: Assessing writing processes from their products. *Educational Assessment, 4*(4), 265–296.

Herman, J. L., Gearhart, G., & Baker, E. L. (1993). Assessing writing portfolios: Issues in the validity and meaning of scores. *Educational Assessment, 1*(3), 201–224.

Paulson, F. L., Paulson, P. R., & Meyer, C. A. (1991). What makes a portfolio a portfolio? *Education Leadership, 48*(5), 60–63.

Rickabaugh, C. A. (1993). The psychology portfolio: Promoting writing and critical thinking about psychology. *Teaching of Psychology, 20*(3), 170–172.

CHAPTER SIX

Developing Communication Skills

In This Chapter

Adjust Your Mindset

- What communication skills will be the most helpful in college?
- What is the relationship between the writing process and the written product?
- Do you plan your time appropriately to put the necessary work into writing a good paper?
- How important is participating in class discussions?
- Do you anticipate the focus for your next class and what your professor will likely discuss?

Adjust Your Strategies

- How can you use feedback from professors to improve your communication skills?
- What does it mean to write a research paper in college?
- What makes an effective in-class presentation?

As a college student, you'll be asked to communicate in various forums, through various mediums, and for various purposes. You'll ask questions in class, write journal entries, talk with faculty during office hours, and may even be elected to the student senate where you'll do some debating and public speaking. You'll instant-message, tweet and e-mail group members about important projects. This chapter addresses three of the ways you'll be asked most frequently to communicate your understanding of material and come to a better understanding of that material, namely through written assignments, class participation, and in-class presentations.

WRITTEN PRODUCTS VERSUS THE WRITING PROCESS

Writing is a process, an action, as well as a product, an object. Although students and teachers alike often focus on the end result of writing, the finished product, numerous activities lead to the creation of a refined, final version. The act of writing—scribbling notes on scrap paper, talking out ideas with a friend, typing a paragraph into a word processor—is a complicated set of activities that writers often take for granted.

To improve the quality of finished written products you produce, you need to make changes in the way in which you go about producing them. Just as you are encouraged to be open to employing new study skills, we also suggest you be open to considering making changes to your writing process. To help you do so, this chapter encourages you to examine the way you currently compose text, helps you evaluate that process, and offers some context-dependent alternatives.

Writing, like studying, is often considered a solitary activity. Many people believe a writer comes up with an idea, writes it down eloquently, and delivers the finished piece to an appreciative audience. Many people, those with a fixed mindset, also believe a fortunate few are born with a talent for writing and the rest of us struggle to *seem* as though we can write. The truth is that good writing usually involves some degree of collaboration and revision, and anyone willing to put in the effort can become a strong writer, a concept aligned with a growth mindset.

Fairly recently, those who specialize in the teaching of writing have begun to challenge the notion there is one writing process that all successful writers utilize. Supporters of what is termed the *post-process movement* contend that not only do different writers have different—and equally valid/useful—processes, but also that writers use countless processes depending on the audience, purpose, and context of the writing they need to do (e.g., Olson, 1999). Instead of writing in the same manner regardless of situation or audience, writers need to be able to modify their writing processes to fit different situations and audiences. Learning to be a better writer, then, means becoming more critically aware of the ways in which you write—another metacognitive activity—and being open to change.

You can write more successfully if you recognize that (1) the writing process takes time because it is often more cyclical than linear and (2) starting early means you can take more time with each activity. Writing well often involves going backward before moving forward. You may decide, for example, that you need to generate additional evidence, an extended explanation, or an additional point after you have written a rough draft. You may decide that the argument you've constructed lacks a logical structure, so you make an outline from your draft and rework your organizational strategy. Just because you've got a version of your paper doesn't mean you can't continue to brainstorm, outline, and scribble.

The writing process, then, is far from a fixed, static set of steps to follow. Writers don't consistently proceed through such a series of steps to arrive at a final, written product; they do, however, engage in certain activities at different times during the writing process. These activities include prewriting, organizing, drafting, and revising, each of which is described in some detail below.

Prewrite to Generate Ideas

At different points in the process of writing, you'll need to generate ideas. You'll want to think about the point you want to make, the reasoning you'll use to support that point, and the evidence you'll provide to support your reasoning. Where do these ideas come from? Well, you might have started thinking about your topic in the classroom, perhaps during class discussion or while listening to a lecture. You've also most likely been doing some reading about your topic. This reading might have initially been limited to your textbook or the novel you were assigned, but your reading might also have involved some library research.

Regardless, you should have some thoughts about the topic you've been assigned, or have chosen, to explore. This exploration can occur through a stage of writing often referred to as *prewriting*, meaning work that comes before writing. This label is a bit misleading because this activity *is* writing, not a detached, disposable precursor to it, and it often occurs at different points throughout the writing process, not only at the beginning.

Prewriting refers to the action of recording ideas with an emphasis on getting ideas in a form you can see or hear. Prewriting is more about *what* you might say than *how* you might say it. The recording of ideas during prewriting might involve one of several different techniques, including brainstorming, freewriting, clustering, and tape recording.

The key to **brainstorming** is to let ideas flow from your mind through your hand onto paper without making judgments as to how to say things perfectly, how to arrange the ideas, or whether or not you *really* want to include a particular idea. Brainstorming is about recording as much of what you are thinking as possible so you can make these judgments later. This, then, should be an energizing and freeing experience because you're simply listing ideas as they come to you, letting the writing generate more and more thought.

An activity very similar to brainstorming is **freewriting**, a kind of prewriting that includes the formulation of sentences and paragraphs instead of the list of ideas that result from brainstorming. Here, too, do not be concerned with how you'll say things. Even though you are creating what look like sentences and paragraphs, the purpose of doing so is to encourage the continual flow of ideas. You can write more freely than you would if you were also concerned with relaying those ideas in grammatically correct form within a well-structured paragraph.

Clustering, also referred to as *branching*, involves a more visual approach. Here ideas are presented graphically as they relate to one another. See Exhibit 6.1 for an example of clustering.

If you feel you can talk out ideas better than you can write, why not take advantage of your verbal abilities? Instead of putting your ideas down in writing, try talking them into a tape or digital voice recorder. With this technique, you can prewrite while driving a car, lying on the couch, or eating breakfast. Once you've recorded your ideas, simply play back the tape and record those ideas that seem most fruitful.

Which of these activities should you engage in when you prewrite? The choice is yours. You may decide to freewrite or you may decide to tape-record. Make your decision after you've engaged in some experimentation; try the different approaches to determine which works best for you. And try them for different types of writing: for different courses, for different professors, for different genres.

Selecting which activity to engage in or what approach to take when you prewrite should be based on your learning style. For instance, visual

| **EXHIBIT 6.1** | *Clustering Ideas on The Simpsons* |

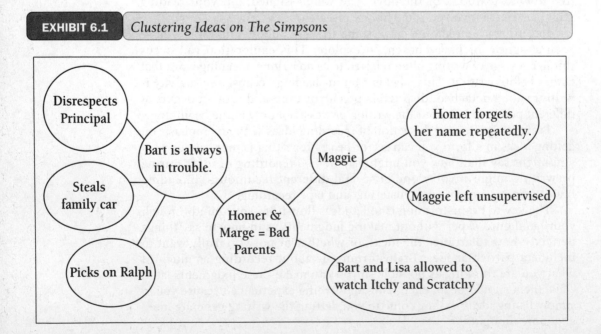

learners may like to brainstorm on a sheet of paper for ideas or prefer clustering as a prewriting activity, so they can see the big picture. Auditory processors may talk with a friend or professor in an effort to generate ideas. Finally, tactile/kinesthetic learners may come up with their best ideas while taking a walk or through the use of manipulatives.

As mentioned, you will be in a better place to make your decisions about how to approach writing after some experimentation. Along with the experimentation, though, comes serious thinking about, and reflecting on, the way in which you write. Thinking about the way you write is yet another metacognitive activity just like thinking about how you learn best. Remember, the most sophisticated learners have that knowledge and control over their own thinking and learning. They are well cultivated critical thinkers.

Organize Your Ideas

Once you've thought about which ideas you want to include, it's time to think about the order in which you want to convey them. This preliminary structure is certainly subject to change as you draft and revise.

It is often helpful for students to create a **logic outline** at some point early on in the writing process. This logic outline is devoid of roman numerals but does help writers think about what they want to accomplish and how they are going to go about achieving these goals. Such an outline includes a **thesis statement**, a sentence that reveals the purpose of the paper, as well as the points the writer will offer in support of that thesis, what will be referred to from here on as **supporting points**.

A logic outline might start out looking something like this:

Thesis: The members of the Simpson family have serious problems relating to one another appropriately.

Supporting Point Number 1: Homer and Marge both neglect their children, particularly Maggie.

Supporting Point Number 2: It is common for Lisa and Bart to assault each other physically.

Supporting Point Number 3: The Simpsons don't have quality conversations at mealtime.

Supporting Point Number 4: Mr. Burns isn't at all fond of Homer.

Supporting Point Number 5: Maggie was once alone in the wilderness for hours.

Creating such an outline will help you present your thoughts in a clear, efficient, and organized way. It will also help you to identify overlapping or irrelevant points. In the example, for instance, supporting point *Number* 4 is irrelevant because Mr. Burns's feelings for Homer don't support the notion that the *family* has problems relating to one another. The example also includes two overlapping supporting points, namely supporting point *Number* 1 and supporting point *Number* 5, because the latter is a specific example of the former. Supporting point *Number* 5, then, could likely be used as a specific example within the section involving Homer and Marge's neglect of their children.

Draft Your Ideas

Many students attempt to begin the writing process at the **drafting stage**. They sit at a blank computer screen and try to compose a focused, well-organized, cohesive, detailed, engaging, grammatically correct draft. They worry about getting the first sentence just right. Not surprisingly, this often results in frustration and limited productivity—commonly referred to as "writer's block."

Drafting, in fact, does not have to begin with the creation of a first sentence or an introductory paragraph. Many writers save that task until the very end of the drafting process, reasoning they can't introduce readers to what will come next when there isn't anything yet there to reference. Drafting can just as easily begin with a supporting point or a paragraph that focuses on a specific example.

If you've created a logic outline, you've got some sentences already: your thesis statement, which is usually found in the introductory paragraph, and your supporting points, each of which can become a topic sentence for a paragraph or the focus of an entire section of your paper. These supporting points should be connected to your thesis via transitional words. These are words that bring your reader from one idea to the next, explaining, in effect, the relationship among sentences and paragraphs.

Using our Simpsons' example, we might imagine the following topic sentence based on supporting point *Number* 2 of our logic outline:

Supporting Point 2: It is common for Lisa and Bart to assault each other physically.

Topic Sentence: Not only is this problem family headed by two neglectful parents, but it also has two preteens who physically assault one another regularly.

The italicized words provide transition from the previous supporting point—Homer and Marge as neglectful of their children—to the next supporting point, Lisa and Bart's physical assaults on each other. Note that this transition also ties back into the idea we are trying to convey in our thesis, specifically, that the Simpson family has problems.

Once you've built this framework, you can drop in evidence to support the claims you've made. In other words, which Simpsons' episodes show Lisa and Bart fighting with each other? What were the circumstances? We'd need to provide sufficient examples to support our contention that these violent exchanges are regular occurrences. The rule here is not to expect your readers to take your word for things. Instead, provide supporting evidence, whether it's mentioning a figure from a corporation's financial statement, referring to a failed marketing experiment, or quoting Hamlet himself.

Revise Each Draft

Once you've written a draft of a paper, letter, or résumé, look it over to see if it needs **revision**. You may make changes because a word, sentence, or paragraph in the writing interferes with the meaning(s) you were trying to convey to your audience. It is a good idea to look for grammar and spelling errors when reviewing a piece of writing, but there are other things to look for as well. Of at least equal importance are unclear and/or underdeveloped ideas that could be interpreted by an audience in ways you didn't intend.

As explained later, different disciplines and writing genres follow somewhat different writing conventions. You will be introduced to some of those differences, and the writing you do in college—and the feedback you receive regarding that writing—will help you understand discipline- and genre-specific writing conventions. Here are some suggestions for revising and editing your work:

1. Read your paper out loud to yourself. This will give you two senses through which to process what you have written. It is often times easier to identify an awkwardly phrased sentence if you hear it spoken. You can also try reading your work out loud to someone else or having that person read your work out loud to you. If you don't have a partner, you might try reading your writing out loud to yourself, perhaps even in front of a mirror. Writing centers are great places to learn more about and practice these techniques; writing centers are discussed later in this chapter.

2. After you've written a draft, wait a while before you revise it. This may mean putting the paper aside for a couple of hours or a few days. Taking a break is a way to bring a fresh perspective to the piece, as long as the breaks don't become a means of procrastinating.

3. Revising does *not* mean relying on the spelling and grammar checkers of word processing programs. Microsoft Word, for example, will let you know which words it thinks you've misspelled and will even offer a suggestion to correct the error. One problem is that Word often identifies correctly spelled words as errors. Another is that the suggestions are often worse than the original; computers can't read, so they do their best to guess which word you meant. And if your spelling was off significantly, the suggestion will be inappropriate, if not comical. Quickly typing "psleing" instead of "spelling," for example, results in Word offering the word "pulsing" as an alternative. The computer wouldn't even notice the problem posed by the sentence reading, "She wanted to go to." The careful student could surely identify these errors, but, oftentimes, students in automatic thinking mode passively accept the computer's recommendations without even looking at the screen.

A better alternative is to use the red and green squiggles that Word uses to mark such errors as a warning system. You might reread these words, sentences, and paragraphs more carefully to be sure you've said what you meant to say and correctly. Remember, though, that there may well be other words, sentences, and paragraphs needing your attention that haven't been identified as problematic by the software.

4. Try answering the following questions; doing so will help you think critically about your draft:

- Does your thesis clearly relay the purpose of your essay?
- Do all of your supporting points support your thesis?
- Have you given some thought to the way you've ordered these ideas?
- Have you supported the claims you've made with specific, concrete evidence?
- Have you checked to make sure you haven't made the same grammatical mistakes you typically make?
- Did you read the essay to yourself from start to finish? (Try reading it out loud.)
- Did you solicit feedback from your professor, a peer, and/or a staff member at the writing center?
- Did you try to use impressive-sounding language? If so, it is generally better to use simple and concise language.

5. Of course, revising means paying attention to grammatical issues as well. Perhaps the most typical grammatical errors are sentence-level errors, including run-on sentences, comma splices, and sentence fragments. Although a discussion of grammar is beyond the scope of this chapter, use a writing handbook, such as *The Prentice Hall Reference Guide* by Muriel Harris, in which you will find an explanation of these errors along with suggestions for avoiding them. It is equally important that you familiarize yourself with the grammar errors you usually make, identified on graded papers that have been returned to you.

6. The easiest mistakes to find and correct in your writing are spelling mistakes. If you have any question about how a word is spelled—signified by a hesitation in thought when writing or typing the word—all you need to do is look it up in a dictionary or use the spell check within your word processor. For this reason, teachers of all disciplines frown on spelling mistakes. These errors signify a less-than-discriminating (i.e., lazy) writer. Make a list of words that you usually misspell, so you can eventually learn the proper spellings and avoid making the same mistakes.

USING FEEDBACK TO BEST ADVANTAGE

You can receive **feedback** on your written work in several ways: on the graded paper itself, during faculty office hours, through peer review, and via a consultation at the writing center. Each is valuable, and these methods should be used in combination to be most beneficial.

Your Faculty Provide Feedback via Graded Papers

Professors typically spend a great deal of time responding to the writing their students produce. Depending on the length requirements of a particular assignment, it is not at all unusual for a professor to spend a half an hour or more reading and commenting on a single paper.

Their responses usually include four components: intertextual markings, marginal comments, an end comment, and a grade. **Intertextual markings** include an inserted comma, a crossed-out semicolon, a notation of "sp" above a word to identify a misspelling, or a phrase deleted for conciseness. These markings are placed within the text itself, that is, on top of, underneath, or covering your actual words. In fact, these markings are the reason you are often asked to double-space your assignments, leaving a space between each line of text. **Marginal comments** occur in the (typically) one-inch margins surrounding your text. Here, you might find a question your professor has asked in response to what you've written. You might also find arrows to suggest a better organizational approach. And you may find some of the same types of comments as you would within intertextual markings, although these comments are usually a bit more global, looking at least at sentence meaning and often at the significance of entire paragraphs.

End comments are even more global. Professors usually include an end comment at the end of the paper, indicating its major strengths and weaknesses. This comment is based on the intertextual markings and marginal comments and is, in fact, an attempt to summarize them. The purpose of this end comment is to help students understand what they should continue to do in future papers as well as what they should work on improving.

Typically, the end comment is situated next to the numerical or letter *grade* that the paper has earned. This is unfortunate because this proximity often results in the end comment going unread. Students are tempted to focus solely on the grade, regardless of whether it is an A, B, C, D, or F. Of course, it is important to focus more on the written feedback because it will help you improve your work and/or enjoy continued success.

Of course, faculty may offer feedback relative to your graded work in other forms. Your professor might insert written or verbal commentary within an electronic version of your paper. He or she may also offer verbal commentary via an audiotape or other recording medium. Such alternative feedback methods are used at times to allow professors to go into more detail regarding observations because typing and speaking are faster than writing longhand.

Faculty Can Also Provide Feedback During Office Hours

Faculty hold weekly **office hours**, scheduled times when they are in their offices waiting for students to drop in with questions and/or for student appointments. Additionally, many faculty respond to student e-mails during office hours. It is a good idea to use these opportunities to get feedback on your writing. Clearly, the most useful time to do so is before the paper is due. You can solicit advice from your professor at any point in the process of writing: understanding the assignment, refining a thesis statement, organizing ideas, drafting, and so on. Consider this person your primary resource when working on writing for that particular course.

Your Classmates May Provide Feedback During Peer Review

Of course, professors are not the only resource for writing support. For example, you will likely be asked to perform peer review in one or more of your classes. **Peer review**, also known as peer group workshop, acknowledges the collaborative nature of the composing process, the understanding that writers and readers work together to construct meaning from text. Peer group workshops allow authors the opportunity to see how readers will respond to their texts, and to make changes based on these responses. To benefit from these workshops, be willing to listen to others' advice, remembering that your classmates will offer you suggestions. It is up to you to decide whether or not to implement them.

Understanding that your professor will usually explain the goal(s) desired and methods to be used in a particular peer review session, we offer some general advice here to help you make the most out of these experiences. There is no one right way for you to review another student's paper, but there are some things to keep in mind. The first is to have respect for your fellow classmate's work. Even though honesty is important when responding to what the author has written, intimidating and/or embarrassing remarks won't convince the author that your suggestions have merit. Such remarks result in a defensive posture, a situation that prevents constructive changes from taking place. To ensure your advice is taken the right way, try phrasing your comments in question form. Do not—under any circumstances—give the "Looks good to me" response. Although such a comment seems polite and neighborly, it won't help the author at all when it comes time for the piece to be judged a second time.

Another thing to keep in mind is that your advice will be far more on target if you take the time to read the entire paper before commenting. Focus on larger issues before mentioning issues like missing commas and confusing phrasing.

If your professor hasn't provided you with a list of questions to answer regarding your classmate's writing, you might consider some or all of the following:

a. Is the piece focused on the assignment? How does it (or doesn't it) fulfill the guidelines? Can the author do anything to meet the criteria more successfully?

b. What is the structure of the paper? Work backward to create a logic outline from the draft you are reading. Are the supporting points all relevant? Are there any overlapping points?

c. Gaps are places where more explanation and/or examples are needed to give the reader a clear understanding of what the author is trying to convey. Are there any gaps in this particular writing? Remember that although the author is present and available to answer questions during your reading of her or his paper, this will not be the case when the paper is collected to receive a grade. Make sure these questions are addressed.

The Writing Center Is Another Great Place to Get Feedback

Your campus **writing center** can help you make writing assignments more manageable. When assigned an essay, report, research paper, or other type of writing, you may be tempted to put off getting started, telling yourself that you "work well under pressure."

Remember, this is the credo of the die-hard procrastinator. Just as with studying, procrastinators put less time into writing their papers compared to nonprocrastinators. A successful paper requires a sufficient amount of time and effort. The question here is "Have you planned your time appropriately to put the necessary work into writing a good paper?" Here is evidence that time management is linked to your writing process.

It is strongly suggested you start your papers early—as opposed to, say, the morning the paper is due—meaning you should start to think seriously about an assignment the day you receive formal instructions from your professor. Professors don't haphazardly assign writing in their courses; they have reasons for giving you the lowdown on your team project two months in advance. One reason, of course, is that they think it should take a student that long to produce a paper that adheres to the stipulated guidelines.

Once you receive your instructions, try breaking the paper or project down into a series of deadlines in your daily planner. Force yourself, for example, to have an informal outline in a week and a rough draft in two weeks. If you do so, you'll find you have plenty of time to visit your professor during office hours and meet with members of your writing center's staff *and* have time to make necessary changes once you've received feedback. Too often students find themselves disappointed and frustrated because they realize too late that they haven't answered the question their professor asked, and their paper is due in two hours. Take this advice, and you'll reduce your chances of being in this rather hopeless situation.

Ultimately, you will learn more about yourself as a writer if you leave yourself time to reflect on what you are writing. You'll get more out of each writing assignment if your writing process includes getting feedback from someone on the writing center staff, and doing so requires planning ahead.

The goal of any writing center is to help students become better writers. What these facilities offer writers is an opportunity to have readers of their work before that work is assessed for a grade.

Notice that writing centers don't offer only struggling writers this opportunity; these centers can benefit *all* writers. This is an important distinction because many think of writing centers as remedial resources, as places where poor writers go to get extra help. The truth is that poor writers don't often seek readers of their work; that's part of the reason their writing is less than effective.

If you aren't required to use your writing center through your first-year writing program and/or individual faculty, you can use the center as you see fit. You may visit the center multiple times for a single assignment, or you may stop by when you are getting started to be sure your ideas are focused. You can visit the center to get started on a paper, to get feedback on a draft, to develop confidence about your writing, to clarify MLA or APA citation formats, or to reword a sentence for clarity. You might come to the center to use one of the reference books available. You may come to the center to write. Writing centers are *for* writers.

Although writing centers function differently from institution to institution, those who work there generally help writers become more aware of their writing strengths and challenges through focusing on the ways in which they compose text. For this reason, you would be likely to overhear a discussion about process on visiting a writing center, namely the process students go through to arrive at the notes, outline, brainstorming, plan, and/or draft they brought to the session. Staff members also like to talk with students about what they plan to do with their work once they leave. Another common component of a writing center session is the discovery of new strategies, new ways of approaching writing, better ways to react when writing is assigned. If a student claims, for example, that he has never needed to brainstorm, that ideas are always plentiful, but the writing center staff member sees the student's paragraphs lack development, the staff member might suggest he give brainstorming another try. These suggestions are typically offered in the context of specific assignment guidelines.

Your preparation for, and active participation during, a session at the writing center will help you get the most out of the experience. Remember that you are in control of what will happen. Here are some tips to help you get the most out of the time you spend:

1. *Be open to suggestions.* The writing center staff is not the writing police. Their goal is to help you become a better writer. This can only happen when you are both willing to talk about your writing and willing to listen to suggestions about that same writing.

2. *Provide the necessary background.* Your instructor has certain expectations for the paper you are trying to write, and those expectations can often be clarified by reviewing the assignment sheet during a consultation. By bringing notes, planning, and drafts, the center staff can see the journey your writing has taken and suggest where you might step next.

3. *Be prepared to explain the assignment.* You can visit your writing center at any stage in the writing process—whether that be deciding on a topic, organizing ideas, writing an introduction, or revising a draft. Wherever you happen to be, however, you need to make a serious attempt at understanding the assignment. Be prepared to answer questions about the assignment and about your writing.

4. *Let the staff member know what kinds of feedback you've received from your professor.* Although the session will focus on the paper you're currently working on, it will be helpful to both the writing center staff member and yourself to review the comments your instructor has made on your past work. What has your instructor identified on these papers as needing improvement? You'll want to be sure the paper you're working on doesn't repeat problems you've had in the past and that it *does* repeat the things you've done successfully.

5. *Be realistic about what can occur in a single session.* What would you like to understand once the session is over? What bridge are you having difficulty crossing? What problem would you like to solve in a half an hour to an hour? Don't hesitate to relate your goals for the session to the staff members with whom you are working; they will appreciate that you are using the time wisely.

PARTICIPATING IN CLASS DISCUSSION

O f course, you will learn and demonstrate understanding (and misunderstanding) verbally and in writing. This will occur in various contexts, including a discussion with a classmate after class, a group meeting at the library, and an argument over a reading of the story "Young Goodman Brown" in your residence hall room. In addition, many college classes require or encourage student participation in class discussion. Examine the syllabus from each of your classes to determine how class participation is defined and what emphasis the professor has placed on this activity. Many students resist participation, choosing not to ask questions or contribute to an in-class conversation. Here, we explore the rationale behind class discussion so you can make a more informed decision about whether you will be a regular participant.

In 1970, the educator and theorist Paulo Freire criticized what he termed the **banking model of education**. Ira Shor (1992), a Freirian scholar, explains this model: "Banking educators treat students' minds as empty accounts into which they make deposits of information, through didactic lectures and from commercial texts" (p. 31). One of the problems with this banking model is that it fails to consider the idea that students are not "empty accounts," that they, in fact, bring with them ideas, perspectives, doubts, and aspirations. Thinking of students as being acted *on*, and not actors in the sense that they can affect change, is a dangerous notion. Adrienne Rich, in *Claiming an Education,* felt so strongly about the difference between students acting versus being acted on that she characterized it as the difference between life and death. Instead of adhering to a banking model, Freire poses what he calls the "problem-posing approach":

> Problem-posing education affirms men as beings in the process of *becoming*—as unfinished, uncompleted beings in and with a likewise unfinished reality. . . . The banking method emphasizes permanence and becomes reactionary; problem-posing education—which accepts neither a "well-behaved" present nor a predetermined future—roots itself in the dynamic present and becomes revolutionary. . . . Whereas the banking method directly or indirectly reinforces men's fatalistic perception of their situation, the problem-posing method presents this very situation to them as a problem. (qtd. in Shor, 1992, p. 35)

So what does all of this have to do with class participation? Well, Freire would support student participation in the construction of knowledge, an idea that fits in nicely with the theme of claiming an education. Freire would argue that the opportunity to ask questions, to challenge statements made by the professor and/or other students, is crucial to a democratic education. Opting not to participate should be a conscious choice, one made with the understanding that in-class contributions will add to your own learning as well as that of classmates and faculty.

Of course, not all classes include a class participation component. In others, professors assign a grade based on participation. Some professors don't assign a class participation grade but welcome questions during class. As an active participant in your education, you must be clear on the way class participation functions in each of your classes. Do you understand what your participation grade will be based on, for example? What constitutes a successful contribution? How frequently are you expected to participate? Have you discussed classroom rules for respecting the views and opinions of others? If you don't have answers to these questions—or if you have other such questions—you should seek answers.

Some students are anxious about speaking in class. Take Justin, for example. Justin decided during his first day of class in political science that he would forgo the 10 percent of his grade for class participation. He doesn't feel comfortable talking about things he doesn't really understand, and he doesn't want to look like an idiot—or teacher's pet—in front of his friends. This isn't a big deal, he thinks, because he can still get a 90 in the class, and an A—isn't bad at all.

But what is wrong with Justin's logic? To begin with, to earn that A— without contributing to class discussion, he'll have to get a perfect score on each exam and paper in the course, an unlikely possibility. Another problem is that he is basing his decision on avoiding discomfort. Anxiety can lead to avoidance; Justin should seek to confront his anxiety, not avoid it. As a marketing major, Justin is working toward a career in which he must ask and respond to questions. Indeed, it is difficult to think of a career in which communication isn't an integral component. What we've been emphasizing is that college students need to be open to change, an attitude typically accompanied by discomfort. In other words, Justin should be seeking to move out of his comfort zone.

For Justin and others like him, confidence will come with practice. This means, of course, that, at least for these students, initial contributions to class discussion will be anxiety inducing. If you are among this population, try taking some of the stress out of these situations by coming up with a question or two outside of class. Anticipate the focus for your next class; what will your professor likely discuss? What central ideas, concepts, and/or examples do you expect to be the center of discussion? Preparing in advance, even practicing the phrasing of your questions or observations, should help when it comes time to raise your hand in class. After all, if you do so, you'll likely be in a better position than many of your classmates, giving you additional confidence. You may even want to observe the students who participate in class discussions regularly and model after those who do so with confidence.

Once you've developed your confidence, you'll be more willing and able to share comments and ask questions that came to you during class, things you hadn't prepared in advance. If you don't participate in class, you are missing a terrific opportunity to process material by discussing it and talking through difficult concepts. This mode of learning and studying material is the favored one for auditory processors. In a sense, they are doing some studying while in class. At the same time, however, all students can benefit. As pointed out, the most sophisticated learners figure out ways to cross over all three learning modalities in their studies. Participating in class provides you with the opportunity to cross into the auditory processing mode.

WRITING THE RESEARCH PAPER

W hat is the point of a research paper? A research paper consists of your contribution to an ongoing conversation (remember the Burkean Parlor?) about a particular topic or problem, in effect a demonstration of your intellectual curiosity. The best research papers involve true discovery. Although it is typical to have a hypothesis at the start of the research process, don't ignore your findings. You may very well end up trying to prove something different from what you originally imagined.

The research papers you write will be discipline specific. What follows here, then, is not a how-to-write a history, literature, psychology, or economics paper, but some advice that is applicable, for the most part, to research papers in general. What follows are guidelines on (1) formulating a research question, (2) finding sources, (3) evaluating sources, (4) outlining and note taking, (5) using evidence effectively, (6) the ethics of research, and (7) using MLA and APA format.

Formulate a Research Question

Oftentimes professors offer students a list of research topics from which to choose or in some way assign guidelines regarding topic selection. When this happens, resist the urge to just grab a topic and run with it. Instead, make your selection in a more calculated way. Choose several that particularly appeal to you, that you are genuinely interested in learning more about. You can then perform an initial library and/or Web search to see what is available about each of the topics you've selected. Acquire a few of these sources and skim them. Learning more about each of the topics will help you make a more informed decision. You are also discovering how easy or difficult it is to find information relating to that topic.

Once you've decided on one of the topics offered, you'll usually have to *narrow your focus*. If, say, you've decided on television violence as your topic, you might consider a focus such as "Television violence causes children to behave violently." You would find after doing some research, however, that there are many different types of shows exhibiting violence and these shows are viewed by individuals of widely differing ages. Depending on the length of your paper, you would need to decide whether to narrow your focus down to a subset of violent shows and their effect on one particular age group. It would be easy to find plenty of information relating to the broader focus for, say, a three- to four-page paper, but the paper would be doomed to fail because it is impossible to cover the material sufficiently in such a limited space. That focus is beyond the scope of the assignment.

Should you not have been given a list of possible research topics from your professor, you will need to formulate one on your own. To do so, you might want to consider the topics of conversation in class. Perhaps you could complicate or extend a point discussed in this forum. You might also want to familiarize yourself with the topics most often explored in the particular field you are studying. Once you generate a few possible topics, it would be wise to do some of the preliminary research mentioned previously as well as to visit your professor during office hours to discuss the possibilities. It's always a good idea to make sure you're headed in the right direction before becoming too invested in a particular topic and/or focus.

Find Appropriate and Useful Sources

Once you have a focus/main idea in mind for your research paper, you'll need to conduct a more thorough *search for relevant information*. There are a couple of ways to find books and articles that relate to your focus. One is to visit the library. Ideally, the library is somewhat familiar to you, but, if not, reference librarians are always glad to help you find what you need. These people know the library they work in better than you know your own home, so use their expertise to your advantage. If you want to begin on your own, you can search using the library's computerized databases, such as Ebsco Academic or Lexis-Nexis. These databases include information about magazine and journal articles that could be useful for your paper. By typing in keywords, you can search through thousands of articles in seconds. Many campus libraries offer workshops for students about how to access and search computerized databases.

Once you've found books and articles, use them to find others. If there is a references page at the end of the work, and there usually is, scan it for other relevant sources. These authors have done their own thorough searches for information, so use their work to cut down on yours.

The Internet is another place to find sources. Through keyword searches similar to those you would perform to access information via the library's databases, you have access to incredible amounts of data through the Web. This searching is done with search engines such as Infoseek, WebCrawler, and Yahoo!, but hyperlinks within Web pages can lead you to additional sources, similar to looking through the bibliography at the back of a book. Just as you would assess a printed book or article to verify that it is a credible and reliable source, you must do the same for Internet materials. Look for the name of the author, the date of posting, the last time the material was updated, and the citation of supporting evidence within the document. Your research must support the points you'll make in your paper, and the secondary sources you find should have evidence that supports the authors' statements. Be critical of what you read.

Evaluate Your Sources

All sources are not created equal. Your evidence could be critiqued as dated, irrelevant, biased, inconsistent with other findings, or otherwise unreliable. To be sure that you don't leave yourself open to such critique, use these strategies:

a. Check the copyright date if current sources are important.

b. Be aware of bias within sources: Do the authors have a stake in the issue? Do they benefit from their findings? For example, was the study showing that secondhand cigarette smoke isn't all that harmful performed by the Laramie Cigarette Company?

c. Search for professional publications (e.g., *Journal of Economic Literature, Political Science Quarterly, Black American Literature Forum*) because they are usually perceived as more credible than those in nonprofessional publications such as widely circulating magazines (e.g., *Newsweek*).

d. Scan a book to determine its relevance. Be deliberate. Check title, subtitle, major headings, indexed terms, and the bibliography.

e. Scan an article to determine relevance. Again, check title, subtitle, major headings, and the bibliography. You might read the introduction and/or conclusion as well.

f. Read and take notes actively. Be sure you don't use information out of context.

You aren't reading for pleasure when you are looking for evidence; you need to read efficiently and carefully. This means scanning a source to identify especially useful sections. Once you are aware of these sections, you can make a point to read them more than once so you have as clear an understanding of them as possible.

As you are reading, take notes, similar to what you would do when annotating text. These *notes* can take many forms: underlining phrases, bracketing lists, writing in the margin of a photocopied article or book chapter, writing on self-sticking notes, or color coding based on an outline. These notes should be made as you read; think of it as having a conversation with the text—make comments, ask questions, agree or disagree, interrupt. These notes will help tremendously, especially if time passes between when you read these sources and when you write the paper.

Read with a clear sense of what you are looking for: answers to questions you've formulated based on the preliminary outline you've generated. You are looking for information that deals with the focus you've chosen. Remember this when you are ready to take notes. Ask yourself, "Does this have to do with my focus?" or "Where could I use this information in my paper?"

This is by no means an exhaustive list of techniques, but ideally these suggestions provide you with the means to begin gathering evidence in support of the focus you've tentatively chosen. Remember to ask questions—of your professor, of librarians, of tutoring center and/or writing center staff. They are all valuable resources who can help you smooth out the path to a successful paper.

Select Potential Material from Your Sources

After gathering a few articles, assess their usefulness by analyzing the title, abstract, and/or the first couple of paragraphs. Decide whether the article will offer you insight regarding the topic you've selected. Once you've gathered what seem to be appropriate sources, it's time to start taking notes. As mentioned earlier, this initially entails bracketing, underlining, or using sticky notes to identify useful information within these sources. Jotting down notes in the margin will be extremely helpful when it comes time to organize this information. Notes such as "?," "possibly good for intro," "the opposition makes a good point here," "possible supporting point," or "important" will tell you more than highlighting alone when you revisit these articles.

Before you begin compiling your notes in a more organized and useful fashion, make a list of the sources you plan on using so you will have the bibliographic information necessary to do the references section of the paper. Consider this list a work in progress because it will most likely change as you reread the notes you've made; you will decide some are more relevant than others and that you will need to acquire additional sources to fill in some gaps.

Once you've read through your articles and have identified the useful information within each one, you need to decide on a method of organization. How will you arrange the information you've found? You may decide to use index cards. You may choose scissors and tape. Other choices include markers or crayons, word processing software, a three-ring binder, or color-coded sticky notes. Some of these possibilities are discussed here, and there are many others. Find a system of organization you're comfortable with; remember, this system is supposed to make the process easier, not more difficult!

Here one of the systems, specifically the *index-card system*, is explained in some detail. This system basically involves putting each piece of useful information on its own 3 × 5, or 4 × 6 index card. By doing so, you will be able to shuffle them based on the main ideas found on the individual cards. On each card, in addition to the information, indicate which source you've cited from as well as the page(s) on which you found the information. Doing so will save you time later. When writing the information onto the cards, you can *quote, paraphrase,* or *summarize.* Each use of ideas will need to be documented in your research paper. When you copy down exact words from a source, put quotation marks around them on your note cards. This will remind you to do so in your paper. If you paraphrase, you are putting someone else's language into your own words, but you still need to give credit to the original author for her or his idea. Summarizing means reducing a long passage into a sentence or two—of course, doing so still requires documentation.

After you've generated all of your note cards, read through them one by one to determine what is on each of them. Identify somewhere on the card (on the back, say) how/where you think you'll use the information it contains. Does it include general information that might appear in your introduction? A specific example that illustrates one of your supporting points? Statistics that would strengthen part of your argument? Concluding thoughts? For example, if you've identified a quote that you think you might use in the opening section of your essay, write "opening." If you are researching the effects of Barney the dinosaur on his young viewing audience, you might identify a certain quote dealing with how the show instructs through repetition, so you might write next to it, "repetition."

This brief summary will help you organize your stack of index cards into smaller stacks, and, incidentally, create a pseudo outline of your argument if you haven't made one already. After you've finished labeling this information (and you will, most likely, want to alter these labels at one time or another, which is *fine*), it is usually helpful to make an informal or even a formal outline before sitting down to start writing a first draft. Such an outline might look something like this:

Thesis: The children's television show *Barney* should change its instructional approach.

Supporting Point Number 1: Teaching involves more than just getting children to repeat what they hear.

Supporting Point Number 2: The show doesn't adopt a multicultural perspective, alienating many ethnic groups.

Supporting Point Number 3: Gender biases are being perpetuated through the show's themes and lessons.

When you write a section of the paper, you can have the stack of cards related to that section next to you, allowing you to manage your evidence effectively. If you get stuck, as writers often do, you can read through the relevant stack of cards for inspiration.

Whatever method you choose, the process of organizing this information should cause you to think about the reasoning you'll be using in the research paper itself. In other words, the points that other authors have made should help you think about the points *you* want to make.

Utilize the Evidence You Have Collected to Your Best Advantage

Research papers set out to prove a point or sometimes a number of points. These papers are thus, to some extent, persuasive. It is up to the writer to be as convincing as possible, which can be accomplished in part through the effective use of evidence.

Why Include Documented Information?

Besides the fact that doing so is often a requirement of the assignment, using evidence, which supports your ideas, is helpful for at least two reasons. First of all, this evidence can lead you to think about your subject differently. Material you read during the research process strongly influences which points you will make as well as the conclusion you will come to. Also, if selected for its relevance and included in the essay in strategic locations for logical reasons, this material can strengthen the argument you are making.

What Makes Evidence Relevant?

Another way to phrase this question might be, "How do I know what information to use?" Including evidence within a paper means being selective. Quoting or paraphrasing goes beyond showing you've read the texts in question: use them to verify what it is you are trying to say. Provide specific examples, whether they be a word, sentence, or passage, to illustrate the more general point you are making. Decide if the information in question adds significantly to what you are attempting to communicate; in other words, would including it simply be redundant? Or does the passage in question introduce a new angle you can elaborate on further?

How Should I Incorporate Borrowed Material into an Essay?

Be concise. Quote only as much of the text as is necessary to impress a point on the reader. Resist the urge to fill up your paper with borrowed material because this paper-lengthening tactic is obvious to instructors and highly discouraged.

> **Student Portrait**
>
> **Joe:** "Quotes are great, are you kidding? If I have to get, like, four pages or something, double spaced, a few long quotes really help. Know what I mean? I usually try to use about four quotes, about one in each paragraph."

Discuss or elaborate on every quote included. Remember that in citing material, you have taken it out of its original context. This means you have the benefit of reading the words, sentences, or passage in relation to the rest of the essay, story, novel, or other type of work while the reader of your paper probably has not. For this reason, it is helpful to introduce quotes to the reader, sometimes identifying the person speaking in the quote, sometimes hinting at its content or relevance. After including the quote, discuss how it adds to what you have been (or will be) saying. Never let the quote speak *for* you because it might say something you don't want it to say.

Here is a brief example of how to introduce, cite, and elaborate on a quote:

> *Women are portrayed as housewives and sex objects in television advertisements. One television critic argues, "Women are portrayed exclusively as floor scrubbers, Band-Aid appliers, dish washers, and stain removers when they aren't strewn on a beach half-naked or drying off after a shower" (Smith 25). These portrayals of women limit how they are viewed by society as a whole, mainly as dutiful housewives, nurturing mothers, and enticing sex partners. These ads ignore the large number of women who are in charge of multimillion dollar companies or are professors at prestigious universities.*

Conduct Your Research Ethically

You must give credit for others' ideas when writing. Whether quoting, paraphrasing, or summarizing a source, remember to use both in-text and bibliographic citations. Doing so will help you avoid plagiarizing, using someone else's words as if they were your own.

Academic writing often requires incorporating others' ideas. If these ideas are attributed to the appropriate sources, not only will you avoid plagiarism, but you will also demonstrate an ability to join a conversation in progress, as in the Burkean parlor, and make a contribution—in the way of summary, analysis, or synthesis, for example. To incorporate the ideas of others, you'll need to quote, paraphrase, or summarize. **Quoting** is appropriate when you'd like to use the exact phrasing found in the original source:

> ### Student Portrait
>
> **Margaret:** "I never know what I'm supposed to put in quotes. My English teacher used to tell us you don't have to use quotes if it's common knowledge. I mean, most of this stuff makes sense to me when I read it, so why

Quoting Example

> *Richard Light's (2001) survey of more than 1,600 Harvard University students indicated that participation in extracurricular activities is quite common: "Seventy percent of all students are involved in two or more activities, and 14 percent are involved in four or five. Of those participating in any extracurricular activities, 68 percent invest more than six hours per week on average, and 34 percent spend more than twelve hours per week" (p. 28).*

Paraphrasing is used when you'd rather change the original phrasing, either for conciseness or to integrate the idea more clearly with what you said previously. When paraphrasing, be sure to indicate the source in an introductory phrase:

Paraphrasing Example

According to the results of Richard Light's (2001) survey of more than 1,600 Harvard University students, the vast majority of undergraduates participate in extracurricular activities, with some devoting more than twelve hours per week to these activities.

Notice in the example that information was left out of the original quote, and choices were made regarding what it was most important to reveal. This is similar to what happens when using summary, the difference being a matter of scope. Although you might paraphrase a sentence or two, **summarizing** takes on larger portions of a text:

Summary Example

Richard Light's (2001) survey of more than 1,600 Harvard University students produced results indicating that there were definite factors influencing whether students had a positive undergraduate student experience. These factors include connections on campus, mentoring and advising, effective classes, engaging faculty, and campus diversity, among others.

Plagiarism, intentional or not, can have serious consequences. Lawsuits, failing grades, expulsion, and humiliation are all possible consequences of plagiarism. To avoid such disastrous consequences, see your professor or a member of your writing center staff if you have any questions regarding whether to cite material.

The Function of Citation Formats

Investment bankers, psychologists, linguists, and other professional communities share systems of communication. These systems typically include, among other things, jargon that allows members to reference complex concepts quickly. They also include accepted rules for formatting particular types of documents; **MLA** and **APA citation formats** are two such sets of rules. These accepted standards allow members of particular professional communities to communicate more efficiently. These standards help define the community: to identify easily who *is* a member of the community as well as who clearly *is not* a member. In other words, if you'd like your work to be taken seriously by your peers, you need to familiarize yourself with, as well as demonstrate a mastery of, the conventions of that particular scholarly community.

For your reader to be able to access the sources you've referenced, you'll need to provide some information. Both MLA and APA formats utilize a cross-referencing system, and the elements of that system are in-text citations and post-text citations. In-text citations occur when you reference the ideas of others within your own narrative. Whenever this occurs, it is important to let your reader know the source of the reference idea(s). An in-text citation gives the reader limited information. In MLA style, the author's(s') last name(s) and page number of the reference are listed, whereas in APA style, the author's(s') name(s) and the date of the source are listed. For a direct quotation in APA format, an in-text citation must also include a page number (citing electronic sources complicates this a bit).

The other important element of this cross-referencing system is the post-text citation, a more detailed compilation of information regarding each particular source. If you reference a source in the body of your paper, there will be a post-text citation offering the details regarding that particular source in your references page(s) for APA format and in your works cited page(s) for MLA format.

A grammar handbook or MLA/APA style guide offers a more thorough explanation of how to format in-text and post-text citations. These manuals are much broader in scope and include information on formatting, grammar, and other important topics. Equally important, these manuals include guidelines regarding citation format and offer examples for reference. The *Publications Manual of the American Psychological Association* is currently in its sixth edition, and the *MLA Handbook for Writers of Research Papers* is in its seventh edition. You can find these texts at your library or college bookstore.

MAKING IN-CLASS PRESENTATIONS

Much like an essay or research paper communicates your understanding about a particular topic or set of topics, an *in-class presentation* communicates what you have learned about a subject. You may be asked to do a presentation by yourself or with a group of students. These presentations may range in length from five minutes or less to an hour or more. You may be asked to summarize an essay, state a problem and pose solutions, present a business plan, or conduct other presentations that require you to do ample preparation beforehand and keep other things in mind during the presentation itself.

Professors typically offer guidance regarding these presentations, but there are some things you should know that would help you in most such situations. When students prepare for an in-class presentation, they usually focus on the points they'd like to make and the evidence they will use to support those points, much as they would in an essay. Having a clear focus and support is not bad, by any means. Students also plan to have some type of overarching message, again, like a thesis statement in an essay. Remember, however, that there are significant differences between communicating in writing and communicating in person.

In addition to thinking about the logic of the presentation, also consider the way in which the audience will perceive the speaker. When communicating in person, your audience will make judgments about your credibility, sincerity, and interest in the subject. If the goal of your presentation is to have the audience support your conclusions, then you will want to consider how you present yourself to them. If you don't seem to have considered the evidence fairly and objectively, if you don't seem to truly care about the subject about which you are speaking, do you think your audience will receive your message in the way you intended?

There are ways to focus your audience's attention during the presentation and maintain a confident persona. As you may be aware, making eye contact with members of your audience will help you gauge the extent to which they are understanding what you have to say. You can also vary your vocal delivery. Try speaking more softly to emphasize a point or more slowly. You might also try getting out from behind the podium or desk, to assume a more personal relationship with your audience.

Here's a checklist for making in-class presentations:

- make eye contact with your audience,
- vary vocal delivery,
- vary physical proximity,
- utilize visual aids,
- prepare talking points instead of reading,
- provide transitions between speakers in a group presentation, and
- practice your presentation beforehand, in front of an audience if possible.

In addition to using nonverbal communication, consider doing some audience analysis. Think about your audience as you prepare for your presentation. Why would your audience be interested in the topic(s) you'll discuss? How can you make your presentation particularly relevant for them? If you can engage your audience, your professor is likely to take notice.

If at all possible, elect to use talking points as opposed to a script. Reading out loud—whether from an $8\frac{1}{2} \times 11$ paper or from PowerPoint slides—will make it more difficult for you to engage your audience, make eye contact, and demonstrate your mastery of the subject matter. Your delivery would be greatly improved if, instead, you prepare talking points, that is, notes to remind you about the points you want to mention. Of course, you'll need to be familiar enough with the material that you'd be able to speak effectively about the topic from memory. Having such familiarity will require ample practice.

You'll likely be asked to do some *group presentations* in college. Because there will be multiple speakers during these presentations, there are additional preparatory activities. First, at least one of the group members should look through the notes for each speaker. The goal in doing so is to identify any contradictions and unplanned redundancy. Another thing to consider here is how to make the entire presentation flow. For instance, plan for transitions between speakers: The second speaker can summarize the first speaker's comments and mention how the upcoming information relates to earlier comments. For example, "As Sarah explained, it is important to identify possible training issues early on. I'll now discuss other potential problems with introducing a new software package, including compatibility issues and stability." Transitional phrases help your audience make the connections you want them to make, increasing the likelihood they'll see how your supporting points and evidence support your overall message.

Finally, don't perform the presentation for the first time in front of the class and your professor. Recently, a group of four students gave a presentation on tutoring. The group was overly confident and didn't perform a run-through of the presentation prior to the actual event. This proved disastrous. They began with their first point, but they hadn't remembered to introduce the members of the group or the title of the presentation to the audience. Ten minutes into the presentation, they recognized their error and took time out to do belated introductions, making their presentation seem fragmented and disjointed. The lesson here is to practice your presentation as many times as necessary beforehand to work out any problems and to ensure things will go smoothly when it is time for your work to be assessed. It would probably be helpful if you could have an individual not affiliated with the group and/or class to give constructive feedback. Chances are, if that individual has trouble understanding how a piece of evidence is relevant or needs clarification regarding a particular statement, your classmates—and professor—could very well respond the same way.

This chapter challenged you to reflect on your communication skills and how you will need to work on honing them to meet the heightened expectations of your professors. With that in mind, you have been provided with a variety of sound suggestions to respond to the various forums in which you will need to demonstrate your communication skills. One important question remains: "Will you heed the advice offered in this chapter?" That is, will you change the way in which you use feedback, how you approach writing papers, and will you make a concerted effort to participate in class discussions? You have control over your answer; you can change or stay stuck in the familiar.

FIRST-YEAR DIARIES:
ADJUSTMENT REFLECTIONS

Adjusting to Using the Writing Center ~ Abby

Having to write my first college-level paper was difficult, but I used the Writing Center to master it. The extra time, effort, and resources aided me in bring my papers to As. After writing my first college paper, I realized my courses with writing were the hardest ones, not what I would have originally predicted.

Adjusting to Receiving Feedback ~ Barry

I have been told on multiple occasions about my choppy writing. This was the result of multi-tasking while trying to write a paper. Now, whenever writing is required, I find a quiet place with no distractions to write my assignments. With my choppy writing, I knew I needed to hone my writing style and ensure I was staying on track in my writings. I went to writing workshops and used the information from there to improve.

Adjusting to College Level Writing ~ Kassara

In high school, I was accustomed to receiving A's on each essay that I wrote. Exerting the same effort, on essays in college, I was surprised to see that I was only receiving Cs. I quickly realized that college requires more time and effort. Hearing from other students in class discussions made me realize this problem is common. It takes most students an entire semester to become acquainted with and adjust to the new classroom environment.

DISCUSSION QUESTIONS

1. In one of the student portraits in this chapter, Melodie talks about feeling intimidated by her professor's response to her writing. How do you imagine professors will respond to your writing? How have you handled feedback in the past?

2. What types of patterns have you observed in the way that teachers respond to your writing? What types of comments typically emerge?

3. What do you do with the graded papers professors return to you? Do you ever react emotionally? Why or why not? How does using feedback relate to active learning? If you wanted to discuss a writing assignment with your professor, what would you bring to her or his office hour?

4. Do you always use the same process regardless of what you are writing? How does your process differ depending on the writing task? How do the stages in writing processes presented in this chapter compare with those you use?

5. How do you go about finding useful information for research papers and projects? How do you take notes for a research paper? How do you organize the information you find? What is plagiarism? How do you know what is common knowledge and what needs to be cited?

6. What is the purpose of research? What do research papers have in common with other types of writing you have been asked to compose? What makes research papers different from other types of writing?

7. Describe what happens during peer review. Is this a useful exercise? Why or why not?

8. When should you visit the campus writing center? What should you expect to happen during this session?

9. How could you work backward from the due date of a paper in your daily planner? How could you slice up the work into manageable chunks?

10. In this chapter, Justin decides to avoid class participation because he isn't comfortable talking in class. What aspects of college make you uncomfortable? What would it take for you to move out of your comfort zone? What differentiates you from students like Justin? What do you have in common with him?

ACTIVITIES

6.1 Practice criticizing your own writing. This activity involves creating a meta-text for a piece of writing you've composed recently. Using a paper you have already submitted for another course, create an accompanying document that explains how you went about composing the original piece. Describe your writing process for this particular paper by answering the following questions as specifically as possible:

- How did you arrive at your focus/thesis?
- Did you have an organizational plan? (If so, how did you decide on this plan?)
- Did you draft the paper in a single sitting or in multiple sittings?
- Where did you work on this paper? (This can include more than one setting.)
- Did you solicit any feedback while working on this paper? (If so, from whom? How did you use the feedback?)
- How happy were you with the outcome?

6.2 This activity requires you to seek feedback regarding a piece of writing on which you are currently working. You may visit your professor during office hours or meet with someone at the writing center. After you've done so, record your thoughts regarding the experience. Was the meeting productive? Did a second set of eyes help you see things you couldn't on your own? How could the meeting have been improved? What did you learn about yourself as a writer?

6.3 Logic outlines are a great way to ensure that your writing stays focused and organized. Create a logic outline for a paper you have not yet drafted *or* create a logic outline from the draft of a paper on which you are currently working.

6.4 Compose a journal entry in the form of a letter to an incoming student at your college or university. Offer this individual insight into what she or he should expect when writing a college paper. What have you learned so far about professors' expectations? What tips could you give this student?

6.5 Take a trip to the library. Conduct an initial library search to see what is available about one of the topics you will be researching for another course. If you haven't yet been assigned a research paper or project, simply choose a topic you are interested in learning more about. Search a database such as ProQuest to find sources related to your topic. Don't hesitate to ask the reference librarian for help if you need it. Print out a list of four or five relevant sources, including one journal article.

6.6 When searching the Web for information, we certainly hope that what we find will be reliable and useful. Write about the ways you verify the reliability and usefulness of a website. Here are some questions intended to deepen your response:

- Can the reliability of information found via the Web be determined?
- What about the nature of Web pages might make them less reliable than, say, an article in a scholarly journal?
- Should we be more critical of websites than of more traditional publications?
- What distinguishes a reliable website from an unreliable site? The author? The scope? The date published? The absence of grammatical errors?
- Are commercial sites a better source of information than private sites?
- Are so-called official websites somehow more valid than nonofficial sites? Why or why not?

6.7 When you have a draft of a paper you are working on, try reading your work out loud to yourself, as if you were giving a speech. What did you notice about your writing as a result of this exercise? Does this seem like a useful technique that you might repeat in the future? Why or why not? How might you modify this technique to reveal more about your writing?

REFERENCES

Light, R. (2001). *Making the most out of college: Students speak their minds.* Cambridge, MA: Harvard University Press.

Olson, G. (1999). Toward a post-process composition: Abandoning the rhetoric of assertion. In T. Kent (Ed.), *Post-process theory: Beyond the writing-process paradigm* (pp. 7–15). Carbondale: Southern Illinois University Press.

Shor, I. (1992). *Empowering education: Critical teaching for social change.* Chicago: University of Chicago Press.

Additional Readings for Students

Class Participation

Burchfield, C. M., & Sappington, J. (1999). Participation in classroom discussion. *Teaching of Psychology, 26*(4), 290–294.

Hyde, C. A., & Ruth, B. J. (2002). Multicultural content and class participation: Do students self-censor? *Journal of Social Work Education, 38*(2), 241–257.

Reinsch, R., & Wambsganss, J. R. (1994). Class participation: How it affects results on examinations. *Journal of Education for Business, 70*(1), 33–38.

Trosset, C. (1998). Obstacles to open discussion and critical thinking. *Change, 30*(5), 44–50.

Collaborative Learning and Group Work

North, S. M. (1984). The idea of a writing center. In R. W. Barnett & J. S. Blumner (Eds.), *The Allyn and Bacon guide to writing center theory and practice* (pp. 63–78). Boston, MA: Allyn & Bacon.

Critical Thinking/Problem Solving

Trosset, C. (1998). Obstacles to open discussion and critical thinking. *Change, 30*(5), 44–50.

Writing to Learn/Journal Writing

Connor-Greene, P. A. (2000). Making connections: Evaluating the effectiveness of journal writing in enhancing student learning. *Teaching of Psychology, 27*(1), 44–46.

Mio, J. S., & Barker-Hackett, L. (2003). Reaction papers and journal writing as techniques for assessing resistance in multicultural courses. *Journal of Multicultural Counseling and Development, 31*, 12–19.

Skinner, J., & Policoff, S. P. (1994). Writer's block—and what to do about it. *Writer, 107*(11), 21–25.

Zacharias, M. E. (2001). The relationship between journal writing in education and thinking processes: What educators say about it. *Education, 110*(2), 265–270.

Additional Readings for Faculty

Collaborative Learning and Group Work

Bourner, J., Hughes, M., & Bourner, T. (2001). First-year undergraduate experiences of group project work. *Assessment & Evaluation in Higher Education, 26*(1), 19–40.

Hampton, D. R., & Grudnitski, G. (1996). Does cooperative learning mean equal learning? *Journal of Education for Business, 72*(1), 5–8.

Tinto, V., & Goodsell-Love, A. (1993). Building community. *Liberal Education, 79*(4), 16–22.

Walker, A. J. (1996). Cooperative learning in the college classroom. *Family Relations, 45*, 327–335.

Writing a Research Paper

Foley, J. E. (2001). The freshman research paper. *College Teaching, 49*(3), 83–87.

Leckie, G. J. (1996). Desperately seeking citations: Uncovering faculty assumptions about the undergraduate research process. *Journal of Academic Leadership, 22*(3), 201–208.

Writing to Learn/Journal Writing

Fulwiler, T. (1987). *The journal book*. Portsmouth, NH: Boynton/Cook.

Jurdak, M., & Zein, A. (1998). The effect of journal writing on achievement in and attitudes toward mathematics. *School Science and Mathematics, 98*(8), 412–419.

Maloney, C., Campbell-Evans, G., & Cowan, E. (2002). Using interactive journal writing as a strategy for professional growth. *Asia-Pacific Journal of Teacher Education, 30*(1), 39–51.

Mannion, G. (2001). Journal writing and learning: Reading between the structural, holistic, and post-structural lines. *Studies in Continuing Education, 23*(1), 95–115.

Spiller, D., & Fraser, D. (1999). Writing to learn: A collaborative endeavor. *Innovations in Education & Training International, 36*(2), 137–144.

Stonewater, J. K. (2002). The mathematics writer's checklist: The development of a preliminary assessment tool for writing in mathematics. *School Science and Mathematics, 102*(7), 324–334.

CHAPTER SEVEN

Reading and Taking Notes for Optimal Performance in Lectures and on Exams

In This Chapter

Adjust Your Mindset

- How can you be sure you are prepared for an exam?
- Why are study groups a popular study strategy?
- How do you know when you've figured out what's *really* important during a class lecture?

Adjust Your Strategies

- What are the best ways to take notes in college?
- How can you best reconcile class notes with out-of-class notes on the reading?
- What can you do to improve your performance on true-false, multiple-choice, short answer, and/or essay questions?

Y ou will face many points in the semester when your professors will ask you to demonstrate mastery of course material. That is, they will expect you to show them what you have learned. Some of the places where you will showcase your knowledge are on quizzes, tests, and exams. Facing the testing situation in college is inevitable; thus this chapter covers the major facets of testing: test preparation, test taking, and self-evaluation.

Unlike in high school, you can no longer afford to think of test preparation as what you do the night before a test. In college, test preparation includes all of the activities you accomplished before sitting for the test, basically all of the study strategies you applied starting from the very first day of the semester. To do well on your tests in college, you have to think about how you prepare for tests as well as how you take tests. Essentially, you must employ your metacognitive and critical thinking skills: thinking about how you tend to learn material for your tests and questioning how your methods impact your test performance.

You'll need to ask yourself a variety of questions: "Did I do all of my assigned readings?" "Did I fully understand everything I read?" "If I had questions regarding the reading, did I seek out answers on my own?" "Did I visit my professors during their office hours?" "Did I take adequate notes in lectures?" "Did I design and take practice tests to be sure I understood the material?" "Did I seek out learning assistance, such as requesting a peer tutor to help me when a term or idea was unclear?" The list of questions here goes on and on. The point to all of these questions is for you to **self-evaluate** to be completely sure you did everything within your power to prepare adequately for the test. Evaluating your test preparation strategies gives you valuable feedback. If you can honestly say you did everything within your power to prepare adequately for a test, and you still are not successful, you would know that your area of weakness in testing is not with test *preparation* but may be with test *taking*.

After you evaluate your test-preparation strategies, general approaches for taking multiple-choice and essay tests are discussed. Having a general approach to tackle a multiple-choice or essay exam will help reduce your anxiety when you are in a test-taking situation. Having a plan of action always helps; however, what is often more powerful is learning from past mistakes.

The best way to determine whether your testing challenges come from the test preparation situation or the test-taking situation is to diagnose your errors on a test or exam on which you have received feedback. Look at the items marked incorrect. Can you determine the location of each of these items in your text or notes? Answering this question is crucial. If you cannot find the correct answers, your notes are probably incomplete. You would then know that note-taking is a skill you need to develop. When it comes to questions on a test derived from readings, you will have to determine why you may have missed the important

Student Portrait

Phil: "I studied for the material. I thought I had the material down enough before the test. I got the test, read through it and realized I didn't understand the stuff enough to take the test. I got nervous and brought the test up to the professor and said I couldn't take it."

What habits and personality traits do you possess that may be preventing you from applying the strategies you have learned?

information, and analyze your reading skills in relationship to the strategies outlined in this text.

Perhaps the most powerful information that self-evaluation and diagnosing errors on your tests will give you is a reality check as to whether you are actually using the study strategies you have been taught. At this point in the semester, you have likely learned at least a few new study strategies and know what you should be doing; the real question is whether you are actually doing these things. If not, you may need to reflect on your motivation and attitudes again: what habits and personality traits do you possess that may be preventing you from applying the strategies you have learned?

THE COMPONENTS OF TEST PREPARATION

A s mentioned, test preparation begins on the very first day of class. What you do daily ultimately affects how you will perform on an exam. Study skills specialists and psychologists have observed and researched what the best college students do regularly that allows them to perform to the best of their abilities. Consistent patterns have emerged among the top students in various schools and among students of widely divergent backgrounds and abilities. Although many succeed in academic settings, certain study techniques stand out that any student, no matter how well prepared in high school, can apply. The following study techniques address how savvy students read, take notes, study, and participate in classes, all activities that contribute to adequate test preparation (White, Milecky, & Emery, 1986).

> ### Student Portrait
>
> **Rupa:** "I can't believe I didn't start studying until the night before. I stayed up until five in the morning and didn't even hear my alarm clock. Why do I always have to pull all-nighters before every test?"

Be Aware of Course Objectives

First, successful students focus their attention on the *course objectives*. This may seem obvious, but it appears that the average student has the attitude that "If it's in the course, I have to memorize it." Most professors introduce too much information to allow for memorization. Also, most professors are not impressed with simple memorization of details. They want to know whether you can apply, compare, and employ the concepts and thinking strategies presented in the course. How can you find out what the course objectives are? Professors usually relay this information in the course syllabus, at the beginning and end of classes or lectures, and in directions for assignments. What you will want to do is consider how the course objectives might be used as questions on a test or exam. For example, if one of the goals of your Earth Science course, "Human Impact on Land and Life," is to develop a thorough understanding of the issues involved in the misuse of land and wildlife management, you can expect to see an essay exam question that might read, "Describe four key issues involved in the misuse of land in the Brazilian rain forest."

Take Comprehensive Notes

This brings us to the second characteristic of highly prepared students: they take **comprehensive notes** in classes and lectures. Comprehensive means complete notes with all levels of information, including generalizations, examples, explanations, transitions, questions, introductions, summaries, and repetitions. Students will say, "But my teacher told me just to write down the important things." The professors can say that because they already know what the important things are, and they are so familiar with their fields that they are able to remember details. Students can't always tell what is important, and they will likely forget a significant portion of the lecture if they don't write down enough information. So, as one study skills specialist advises, "Write as much as you can down, and figure it out later. You can't write down everything!" Many students find that by going into a lecture with the objective of writing down everything and by writing continuously during the lecture, they can record almost everything they need. Two additional advantages of writing everything down are that it forces you to use your kinesthetic learning modality and it keeps you listening actively throughout the whole lecture. Note taking is addressed more extensively a bit later in this chapter.

Connect Important Ideas

Another skill successful students possess is the ability to *make connections* between the whole and the parts. That is, they can usually identify what the most important ideas, concepts, or relationships in a reading, laboratory, lecture, class, or work of art, *and* they figure out how each part is related to the main points. For example, if the notion of self-concept is presented in a lecture, these students watch and listen for examples of self-concept in readings and class discussions. Good students figure out what's important and/or anticipate what will be expected. An effective strategy for figuring out what's important is synthesizing notes and readings, that is, taking your class notes and checking their consistency with information in your text. Doing this will allow you to find out whether you've missed any important points.

Gather Internal Feedback

How do you know when you've figured out what's *really* important? That's another strategy of good students: they establish **feedback procedures** to find out whether they understand the subject. The most common sources of feedback are study groups, professors, upperclass students

EXHIBIT 7.1 *Feedback Cycle*

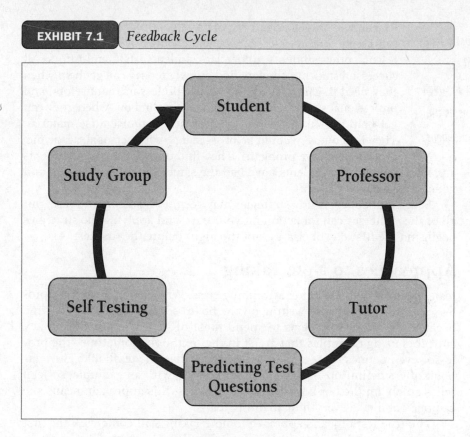

who took the course, and tutoring center or other learning assistance staff. Students can gather internal feedback by using some of the following strategies: predicting the questions that might appear on examinations, making summary sheets, tutoring other students, and self-testing, in other words, closing the notes or textbook and *saying* everything aloud (for auditory learners) or writing down everything you remember (for kinesthetic learners).

Ask Questions

Perhaps the single most significant characteristic of the best students, and the way in which they prepare for exams, is that they *ask a lot of questions*. These questions fall into two categories. First, in reading and listening, these students silently ask questions of the author or lecturer. Put another way, they form hypotheses and then read or listen to see if they have predicted correctly what will be said next. This is where your text annotation comes in again. For kinesthetic learners, writing down the questions in the margins of their books will help them remember the information more readily.

Of course, questions can also be asked of other people: in classes, tutorials, conferences with professors, and in meetings with learning specialists.

Perhaps the single most significant characteristic of the best students, and the way in which they prepare for exams, is that they ask a lot of questions.

Remember, this is a learning style strength favored by auditory processors. Auditory learners benefit greatly from questioning professors, other students, upperclass students, staff, and tutors. All successful students, though, find out where they can get help when they need it. They get to know their professors, counselors, and professional staff by talking to them. They find out where they can get help for study skills, reading, math, and/or course material. They find out who could be of assistance with personal, academic, or administrative problems. They find out who the best students are, which upperclass students have had the same course or professor, and which tutors can help them.

Successful college study strategies may seem to be common sense, but all of the strategies call for action on your part, and applying the strategies begins on the first day of classes, not the night before the first test.

Approaches to Note Taking

Jean doesn't take notes in her astronomy class. Writing down what the professor is both saying and writing on the board seems like a waste of time because the professor seems to spend most of her time illustrating key concepts using examples that aren't in the textbook. Sometimes the professor even defines these concepts differently than the textbook. The textbook offers definitions for each key term along with an example, so Jean relies solely on the book for her notes. Besides, this approach means she can relax and take everything in during class.

The true test of Jean's approach to note taking will come with the first astronomy exam. Jean is making some rather flawed assumptions:

1. that the textbook's definitions supercede those of the professor,
2. that the examples offered in the textbook are sufficient toward illustrating each concept,
3. that the examples offered in class are similar to those offered in the textbook (i.e., redundant), and
4. that the exam will be based on the textbook and not class notes.

Other potential problems with this approach to (not) taking notes is that Jean will likely be less engaged in the class and more likely to daydream, do other work, or not attend class. Participating in class discussion will be more difficult for such disengaged students. Finally, Jean's professor is likely to notice this behavior, depending on the size of the class, and attribute it to laziness, disinterest, or perhaps even disrespect.

It Is Important to Have an Organized System of Taking Notes

Students should have a system of note taking and a notebook that keeps their notes organized. Many students find that using a three-ring binder with several pockets for notes and other materials is the most efficient way to be organized (Lister, 1993). Using a three-ring binder is efficient because it allows you to keep notes and handouts in order. If you get a handout that goes with a particular lecture, you can three-hole punch it and keep it in your notebook alongside the lecture notes. This method also enables you to record your reading notes and/or study group notes on loose-leaf paper, so you can place that information with your lecture notes as well. Keeping all relevant material together will make life easier when it comes time to study for tests.

Good note taking requires being attentive and employing active listening skills during lectures. Students should develop a personal system of note taking that works for them. Judicious use of a highlighter to make certain information stand out in notes is useful. Just as the author of a textbook highlights important information in bold print, you can use a highlighter to mark information that you deem important in your own notes, making it easier to locate important information. There are several other techniques you can use to take better notes:

- Some time during the semester, you will begin to get used to your professors' various lecture styles. At this point, try listening for signal words in a lecture, rather than trying to write everything down. Signal words provide directional clues to alert you to important information. Listen for clues such as, "The two areas are. . .," "One key feature. . .," or "In conclusion . .," If ever a professor raises a question in a lecture, write it down and listen for the answer. You can almost guarantee this question will appear on an exam (Longman & Atkinson, 1991).
- Don't necessarily copy notes over to make them neat. Instead, write neatly to begin with. This is another strategy to keep you on task with your listening comprehension during lecture. If you begin to write sloppily, you are likely losing concentration (Lister, 1993).
- Don't erase mistakes, but rather draw a single line through the error. That will prevent you from losing your thoughts during the lecture (Lister, 1993).

Also develop your own abbreviations for taking notes, your own shorthand.

Use Shorthand When Taking Notes

Taking notes in class requires you to record information quickly and accurately. Because it is impossible for most of us to transcribe a lecture verbatim with no errors, you need a system to make note taking more manageable.

One such system is to formulate a key that allows you to abbreviate major concepts and commonly used words and phrases. These concepts and commonly used words and phrases will change, to some extent, from class to class, and it may take some time to develop the key.

Sharon Alex (1999), a study skills specialist at Becker College in Massachusetts, offers a sample key for an introduction to chemistry course:

Major Concepts Key

Enz	= Enzyme	P	= Products	Mol.	= Molecule
Sub	= Substrate	R	= Reactants	Engy	= Energy

Common Words Key

b/c	= because	w/	= with	2′	= two
+	= and	t	= the	⟶	= follow
*	= important	c	= with	rt	= right
\	= therefore	b/f	= before	dn't	= didn't
w/o	= without	2	= to	cont.	= continue
intro	= introduction	a/f	= after	lf	= left

Used with permission of the author.

Exhibit 7.2 shows notes written using this sample key.

You'll want to keep your key handy because this method won't be very effective if you forget how to translate your own shorthand. Try translating the following statement using the keys offered above:

*b/c he dn't ⟶ t * directions b/f going to class t student was :.unable to cont t class.*

In addition to developing a more efficient system of taking notes in class, consider using a note-taking system that allows you to synthesize your class notes with notes you've generated from course readings. One system designed for this purpose is the Cornell system of note taking.

EXHIBIT 7.2   *Example of Taking Notes Using Personal Shorthand*

Enz Function

Sub are R in chemical reaction
Enz 1. Lower temp
    2. Engy ↓
    3. pH
Sub + Enz → P + Enz
(React)

Specificity—Active site

Coordinate Your Class/Lecture Notes with Your Reading Notes

The **Cornell system of note taking** allows students to coordinate their lecture notes with their reading notes. This approach to note taking involves following certain procedures. To begin, you can try one of two techniques: you can either write down your notes only on the right side of your notebook and leave the left side for a worksheet (or vice versa if you are left handed) or divide the paper on which you are taking notes into two columns (see the student sample in Exhibit 7.3). In each case, implement the Cornell system, the components of which consist of the five Rs: record, reduce, recite, reflect, and review.

Record

Take your notes during a lecture on the side of the page you have designated for that purpose.

Reduce

Either in the left margin or on the left side of your notebook, summarize your notes as soon as possible after the lecture.

Recite

Cover the column where you took your notes in class. Using the summary in your reduce column, see if you can recall the information.

Reflect

Think about the material discussed during the lecture. Try to formulate a question that may be asked on a quiz, test, or exam. Record the question in the reduce column, a question that your notes in the record column answer.

Review

Review your notes regularly. You may actively review your notes by comparing your notes with what the text says about the same topic or concept. You may want to write down the text material in your notes but in a different color, so you can easily distinguish the source of information. Jot down the page number for a quick reference; that will save time when you study.

Exhibit 7.3 illustrates a page of student notes using the Cornell system of note taking. Notice the way the page of chemistry notes is broken up into sections, the possible exam questions listed in the left margin, and the notation of page references.

EXHIBIT 7.3   *Cornell System of Note Taking: Student Sample*

REDUCE	RECORD
State the differences between Protons, Electrons, and Neutrons (pg. 24)	I. Atoms: The Stuff of Life (pg. 24)
	A. Protons—positive charged sub-atomic
	• weight 1 amu (atomic mass unit)
	• found in nucleus
	Electrons—negative charge
	• no weight
	• found in energy levels (orbits)
	Neutrons—no charge
	• weight 1 amu
	• found nucleus
	• it stabilizes nucleus
	number of protons determines atomic number of an atom
What is atomic mass? How is it found? (pg. 25)	Atomic mass=sum of protons and neutrons (pg. 25)
What is electricity?	Electricity—Flow of electrons (pg. 24—25)
	Opposites—attract
	Likes—repel
What is an Isotope?	B. Isotopes (pg. 25)
	• atoms with a different number of neutrons
	Some elements exist as mixtures of different isotopes
	Deuterium—hydrogen atom with 1 neutron
	[Hydrogen atoms do not have neutrons]
	Tritium—hydrogen atom with 3 neutrons
	Energy levels (pg. 29); 1st—2 3rd—18
	2nd—8 4th—32
What is the rule of Octet?	Rule of Octet—most atoms like 8 electrons in outer energy level
	This makes the atom Happy:O)
	Chapter 2
What is PH?	PH (pg. 37)
	• hydrogen ion concentration
	Hydrogen w/out electron is an ion
	The more you have the more acidic it gets
What is a hydroxyl?	OH—hydroxyl—oxygen & hydrogen
	W/extra electron base or alkaline
	PH scale (pg. 37)
	Anything below 7 acid [lower the # stronger it gets]
	anything 7—neutral; above 7—base
	Acid released hydrogen ion or proton
What is a base?	Base—something that takes on protons
	Ex. Bio cd (7.35 ph)
Explain a buffer.	Buffers (pg. 38)
	• help to maintain PH
	• take H ions out to make acid
	Co in H20 make carbonic acid Most of the time naturally produced
What are the waves from? Weakest to strongest?	Alpha—weakest; Beta—stronger
	Gamma—starting to get dangerous; X-ray—can be very dangerous

Information added from text

Information added from text

le-
H⊙◄————HYDROGEN (H)

1P ◦le-

1P   le-

Information added from text

To Read Actively, Take Notes *Before* You Read

Besides active reading and text annotation, there are additional reading methods to help you prepare for tests. One way is through engaging in pre-reading strategies. These activities will help you better understand what you are reading—the first time through—as well as help you generate organized and efficient notes from the reading.

By this point in the semester, you've probably realized you are expected to do *lots* of reading in college. You're probably expected to read several chapters (or more) every night. Despite the volume of reading, your goal shouldn't be to see how quickly you can tear through a chapter. Reading passively often results in simply staring at words that have ceased to have meaning—reading "in the zone," so to speak, where your eyes are seeing but your brain isn't processing.

You'll be a more effective and more efficient reader if you engage in some preliminary activities before your "word-by-word" reading begins. The list of prereading activities that follows is designed to help you become a better reader of college textbooks. Performing these tasks will, admittedly, take some time, but you will find doing so means you will have a fuller understanding of what you read.

The first of these preliminary, or prereading, strategies is to look at the title of the chapter. Besides recording this information in your notebook as the beginning of an outline, also use the title to predict what you will be reading. Are you familiar with any of the words or phrases used in the title? What do you already know about these concepts? This reflection will give you a foundation on which to build an understanding of new information.

In addition to considering what you already know about the topics suggested by the chapter title, also situate this chapter among other chapters in the text as well as other material presented in class or referenced on the course syllabus. Here you are concerned with understanding how the chapter you are about to read relates to the totality of material you will be reading for the course.

Another useful prereading strategy is to skim the introduction to the chapter, listing key points, sequencing ideas, and perhaps even writing your own brief summary paragraph. Doing so will help prepare you for what is to come, and it is a particularly effective exercise for kinesthetic learners.

Before you read the chapter in earnest, consider creating an outline. By this point, you've already recorded the chapter title. Now add the first main heading, subheadings, and, under each subheading, the content vocabulary words (i.e., those words emphasized in bold or italics). Be sure to record page numbers next to each item so you can easily access the information in the textbook as necessary. Exhibit 7.4 provides an example of a chapter outline that employs this method.

Finally, after creating a chapter outline, it can be used for additional studying. You might try, for example, putting the outline into paragraph form. You could also study the outline and then self-check your understanding of the material by seeing how many questions you can answer at the end of the chapter.

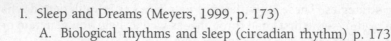

EXHIBIT 7.4   *Sample Chapter Outline with Note*

I. Sleep and Dreams (Meyers, 1999, p. 173)
    A. Biological rhythms and sleep (circadian rhythm) p. 173
    B. The stages of sleep p. 174
        1. REM sleep
        2. Alpha waves
        3. Hallucinations
        4. Delta waves
    C. Do we need sleep? pp. 176–7
        1. The effects of sleep loss
        2. Sleep theories
        3. Sleep disorders pp. 178–9
            a. Insomnia
            b. Narcolepsy   } A potential
            c. Sleep apnea   multiple-choice
            d. Night terrors   question

Study with a Group

Although we have focused in this chapter, for the most part, on what you can do to study on your own, there is no need to study in isolation. In fact, many students create study groups for this purpose, and these study groups can be quite beneficial. Simply discussing course material with others is a great way to learn—as opposed to memorizing—new concepts and practice applying new analytical methods. Study groups also have the benefit of multiple students' perspectives on classroom lectures, discussion, and text readings. Each member can have a more comprehensive set of notes through the efforts of the group. In other words, if you were unable to transcribe the professor's example in class, chances are one of your group members has the example recorded.

Of course, groups don't just originate instantly and begin to work at the height of productivity. It is inevitable when groups of people live, work, and study together that they will progress through certain developmental stages. According to Bruce Tuckman (1965), a theorist interested in how groups evolve, these stages are forming, storming, norming, performing, and adjourning. **Forming** involves a group getting together to work toward a collective goal and determining members' strengths and weaknesses. Here the group discusses how to approach the task at hand. **Storming** occurs when conflict arises, an inevitable occurrence. The group must resolve these conflicts before proceeding to norming, the next stage. **Norming** is when the group agrees on guiding principles or rules that each group member must abide by for the group to function most productively. In the **performing** stage, the group performs effectively and productively, that is, if they reach this stage. **Adjourning** involves establishing closure for the particular project involved.

When you are assigned a group paper or project, or even when you are assigned to work in a group in a classroom setting, your group will naturally progress through some or all of these stages. The roles of each individual member will affect the group's ability to progress through these stages.

To consider how you might function as a group member in college, it might be helpful to think about the first group of which you were likely a member, your family. Oftentimes the role you play in your family will emerge when you participate in other groups. If, for example, you were the mediator of disputes in your family, settling arguments among siblings or between siblings and parents, you might be inclined to want to resolve disputes in your marketing group. If you were the oldest member of your family and took responsibility for taking care of your younger siblings, you might be compelled to take care of your group members. You might, for example, feel the urge to follow up to make sure your group members complete their tasks. To use a popular culture analogy, the characters on the television show *Friends* fulfill specific roles in their group. Chandler is the group clown, always telling jokes to relieve tension. Ross is the responsible, level-headed one. Monica is the obsessive caretaker. Do you know what role you occupy within your family and/or your primary group of friends? How might this role affect your participation in a group project or study group?

The stages of group development can tend to be a long, laborious process. The college semester is roughly 15 weeks long, so if you decide to join a study group or you are assigned a group project, you don't have the luxury of allowing your group to proceed naturally through these stages.

For the group to be as productive as possible, consider setting some rules and procedures. These rules and procedures could include information about meeting length, frequency, and location. The group might also decide that food, drink, and music aren't conducive to a serious businesslike study situation (White, Milecky, & Emery, 1986).

The group should also agree on a structure for meetings (White, Milecky, & Emery, 1986). The group might decide, for example, that each meeting will be a review of the readings and lectures for the week. Everyone in the group must complete the readings and review notes before the meeting, so the meetings can focus on identifying and mastering key concepts. The study group might also decide collectively to draw up a summary sheet for the course, listing main topics and important subtopics. Each topic on the sheet would be discussed and thoroughly understood by all members of the group.

BENEFITS OF EMPLOYING THESE APPROACHES TO STUDYING

N ow that you've been exposed to a variety of study strategies to prepare you for exams, the question is "Will you use them?" Better yet, will you use them starting from the first day of classes? It is time, once again, to reflect on your attitudes toward learning and studying. There are many advantages to taking a systematic approach and implementing all of the strategies you've learned:

- *Encourages the use of all three learning modalities:* outlining your chapter will create a visual representation of the concepts and allow you to see the part-to-whole relationships in the text, a visual processing activity. Active listening and questioning in lectures will tap into your auditory processing mode. Taking comprehensive notes is your kinesthetic activity.

- *Creates a schema to guide reading comprehension:* outlining your chapter and recording key terms will help you create a mind map of the information. This will enable you to check your vocabulary and begin to familiarize yourself with difficult terms and concepts. Once you see the big picture with your outline, you'll be better able to learn the supporting examples and details that relate to the new concepts.

- *Increases listening comprehension for lectures:* the exercise of outlining your chapter prepares you to listen well in lectures. When the professor mentions a new concept in lecture, your familiarity with the concept and its relationship to other concepts will facilitate greater understanding.

- *Generates a list of all key terms and concepts:* many times students say, "I have no idea what's going to be on the test." Using the outlining strategy produces a list of all the concepts in the chapter you'll need to know.

- *Discourages memorization (unlike flash cards) and taps into higher-order thinking skills:* memorization is a lower-order thinking skill. Higher-order thinking skills are application, analysis, synthesis, and evaluation.

- *Helps predict test questions:* taking the headings and subheadings in your text and turning those statements into questions may give you some insight into what will be asked on the test. While you are at it, design some multiple-choice questions using those words in bold print.

- *Assists in time management practices:* for example, if you outline on Monday, go to class and take notes using the Cornell method on Tuesday, synthesize your notes and your readings on Wednesday, and review material with your study group on Thursday, you are breaking your study time up over a few days (spaced practice) instead of cramming (mass practice).

What follows now is a step-by-step study process that can be implemented from the first day of classes:

| EXHIBIT 7.5 | *Study Strategy Steps* |

Mastering Your Course Materials Step-by-Step

Step One: Outline Your Chapter(s)

When to Implement: Over the weekend or before you attend class
Primary Learning Modality: Visual Kinesthetic
Bloom's Taxonomy of Critical Thinking: Memorization and Application
Advantages:

- Gives a visual representation of chapter concepts
- Creates the ability to see the part to whole relationships among concepts
- Creates a mind map of the information
- Increases your listening comprehension in lecture
- Familiarizes yourself with new vocabulary
- Lists key terms and concepts that *may* appear on a future test
- Focuses on examples to represent concepts
- Increases listening comprehension in lecture
- Helps predict test questions

Step Two: Attend Your Class

When to implement: Follow your class schedule
Primary Learning Modality: Auditory and Kinesthetic
Bloom's Taxonomy of Critical Thinking: Application and Evaluation
Advantages:

- Draws connections between your outline and the lecture
- Creates a list of questions on material you did not understand
- Examines what was both discussed in lecture and appeared on your outline; this is likely to be test material

Step Three: Coordinate Class Notes with Your Readings

When to Implement: As soon as possible after you attend class
Primary Learning Modality: Visual and Kinesthetic
Bloom's Taxonomy of Critical Thinking: Synthesis (brings material/concepts together) and Analysis (examines the parts and the whole)
Advantages:

- Provides opportunity to compare and contrast the two sources
- Compares the different vocabulary used to represent concepts in lecture to how your readings addressed those same concepts
- Discourages memorization
- Reveals possible gaps in lecture notes

(Continued)

EXHIBIT 7.5	*Continued*

Step Four: Study Group

When to Implement: As soon as possible after you attend class
Primary Learning Modality: Auditory and Kinesthetic
Bloom's Taxonomy of Critical Thinking: Memorization, Application, Synthesis, and Analysis
Advantages:

- Allows comparison of your understanding of material to others in class
- Provides for comprehension check; what you may not have understood, a study group member can clarify and vice versa
- Gives you time for auditory rehearsal of information
- Compares your notes and outlines to others in your group

Step Five: Self-Test

When to Implement: Before the next week of new material/As soon as possible after you attend class
Primary Learning Modality: Visual and Kinesthetic
Bloom's Taxonomy of Critical Thinking: Analysis and Evaluation
Advantages:

- Reveals to what extent you understand the material
- Gives insight into concepts to focus on more and study further
- Allows you to evaluate if you are prepared for a quiz, test, or exam

APPROACHES TO TEST TAKING

E very test is unique, and so there are limits to the advice offered in the remainder of this chapter. The following two sections are designed to give you insight into two of the more common types of test questions: the multiple-choice question and the essay question/prompt.

Here Is Some Advice for Taking Multiple-Choice Exams

Savvy students find out what the test format is before the test or exam because they recognize that the format will influence how they study for the test. If a test is multiple choice, some students gear up for tough study sessions because they know from past experience that this test format is an area of weakness for them. Many students, however, breathe a sigh of relief when they hear the test will be multiple choice. They think, "Phew, I won't have to study as much now. All of the answers are right there, and all I have to do is choose the right one. I'll have a one-in-four chance of picking the right one." In this manner, some students lull themselves into complacency when it comes time for multiple-choice tests.

Most multiple-choice tests tend to be derived from readings (textbooks in particular) as opposed to class notes, which means good reading comprehension is the key to success on these tests. For those who have procrastinated, avoided their readings, or haven't bothered to try some of the college-level study skills presented in this text, multiple-choice tests in college will likely present a problem. To do well on a multiple-choice test, knowing the structure of your textbook and corresponding notes is a must. Look back at the outlining strategy illustrated in Exhibit 7.4.

Now focus on a particular section of the outline. Doesn't C.3. look like a multiple-choice item? Using this outline strategy helps you identify the possible source of your test questions. "Sleep disorders" is part of the potential stem of the item, and a., b., c., and d. are among the potential answers. Insomnia, narcolepsy, sleep apnea, and night terrors were the concepts that appeared in bold print in your chapter.

Imagine that all you did was memorize these definitions, however. Say, for example, you made a flash card, putting the word "insomnia" on one side of the card and the definition, "a sleep disorder involving recurring problems in falling or staying asleep," on the other. This strategy may have worked in high school, where you might have seen a multiple-choice question that tested you on recall of memorized information, perhaps looking something like this:

1. The following is a sleep disorder involving recurring problems in falling or staying asleep:

   a. Insomnia

   b. Narcolepsy

   c. Sleep apnea

   d. Night terrors

In college, you are likely to see a more complex question, one that tests your higher-order thinking skills like application, synthesis, and analysis. The question that follows, for instance, requires you to think about the concepts more deeply:

1. All of the following sleep disorders have the potential of threatening a person's physical safety except:

   a. Insomnia

   b. Narcolepsy

   c. Sleep apnea

   d. Night terrors

For this question, you'll need to think critically about each possible answer. In class, it was mentioned there was speculation that the captain of the ship involved in the *Exxon-Valdez* oil spill was an insomniac, which caused extreme sleep deprivation. He may have fallen asleep while piloting the ship. This example (application) was discussed in class and did not appear in the text. Knowing the danger insomnia poses, in this case, requires that you compared your notes and your readings as you studied (synthesis).

According to the text, narcolepsy occurs when a person has uncontrollable sleep attacks and lapses into REM sleep at inopportune times. The text states,

> Those who suffer from narcolepsy—1 in 1000 people, estimates the National Commission on Sleep Disorders Research—must live with extra caution. As a traffic menace, "snoozing is second only to boozing" says the American Sleep Disorders Association, and those with narcolepsy are especially at risk. (Myers, 1999, p. 170)

Understanding examples is the thinking skill of application.

In your notes, you have recorded that sleep apnea is when people stop breathing during their sleep. Sounds dangerous; that could certainly be a physical threat. You choose "d." as your answer because you didn't read the text and have to rely solely on your notes. If you had read the text, you would have found this explanation regarding sleep apnea: "A sleep disorder characterized by temporary cessations in breathing during sleep and consequent momentary re-awakenings" (Myers, 1999, p. 170). Sleep apnea causes irritability the following day, and spouses of sufferers complain about the snoring common to this disorder. You need to analyze this. Nowhere in the text did it mention physical threats to the individual with sleep apnea.

Finally, you look at night terrors. Night terrors happen mostly to children. Unlike nightmares, they are characterized by high arousal and an appearance of being terrified. Sufferers may get out of bed and walk around even though they are still asleep. This poses a danger to small children inflicted with this disorder who could fall down the stairs or trip and fall on something. You now go back to the stem and reason that the only sleep disorder that is likely *not* a physical threat to the sufferer is sleep apnea. The process of reasoning through this college-level test item is quite a bit more complex than the first sample item.

What if the multiple-choice question looked like this sample? This question relies on recall but is complicated by the vocabulary found in the text:

2. A sleep disorder characterized by temporary cessations in breathing during sleep and consequent momentary reawakenings is:

   a. Insomnia

   b. Narcolepsy

   c. Sleep apnea

   d. Night terrors

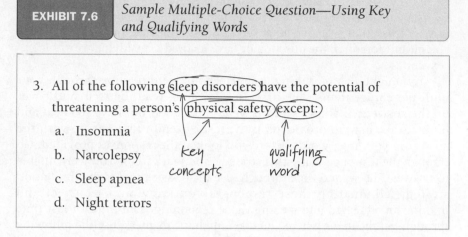

| EXHIBIT 7.6 | Sample Multiple-Choice Question—Using Key and Qualifying Words |

3. All of the following sleep disorders have the potential of threatening a person's physical safety except:

   a. Insomnia

   b. Narcolepsy

   c. Sleep apnea

   d. Night terrors

key concepts

qualifying word

You are back to relying on your notes. Your notes say that sleep apnea occurs when people stop breathing during sleep. Although question 2 is a recall question, you didn't read the text and aren't sure what "cessation" means. It sounds like it might mean "stopping." You're a little nervous taking the test because you know you avoided the reading. Seeing the unfamiliar vocabulary word makes you feel even more panicked and contributes to your test anxiety. If only you had synthesized your text and notes, you would have seen the word *cessation* before and given yourself the chance to clarify its meaning. The bottom line: what separates the most successful students from the rest is that they are intimately familiar with their readings and notes. They are close to 100 percent mastery of the material that has been presented to them whether it's from the lectures or readings. They also have a strategy for taking multiple-choice tests; what follows is one such strategy, referring to the multiple-choice question in Exhibit 7.6.

Read the stem of the question, namely, "All of the following sleep disorders have the potential of threatening a person's physical safety except:" and note any qualifying words, in this case, "except." Next, determine the key concepts in the question, in this case, "sleep disorders" and "physical safety." Determine the exact context in the course. For this item, you recognize that this item has been derived from a chapter titled "States of Consciousness" and appeared under the main heading "Sleep and Dreams." You have now established the part-to-whole relationships. If you know the answer, answer in your own words before you get confused by the distracters, different phrasing, or vocabulary presented in the potential responses.

Check *every* answer. See if you can determine whether each answer is true or false. Insomnia has the potential of threatening a person's physical safety. True or false? If you get confused, go back to the stem and try to answer the question in your own words and then find the closest meaning. Be careful about distracting answers that may be from the same context but irrelevant, are from similar concepts, or have qualifying words or prefixes.

After the first test in a course, you can often see what kind of distracting answers are being used. If there is more than one answer, choose the one that is more true. After selecting an answer, always check the stem quickly to see you haven't forgotten the question or have ignored a qualifying word such as "except."

You might also try taking the thrice approach to going through your multiple-choice items. The first time through, read the stem and cover up the answers. If you've studied well, you should not have to cheat and look at the answers provided on the test. Attempt to come up with the answer in your own words before you look at the responses provided. Go through the test once using this strategy, and mark items you were unable to answer. The second time through, use the classic process-of-elimination strategy, eliminating those responses you know aren't correct and making an educated guess using those remaining. The third or last time through, on the items where you can only hope to guess, use the following method: resist choosing absolutes like "all of the above" and "none of the above." Eliminate similar choices, and choose the longest, most detailed answer. Remember, use this last method *only* when you are forced to guess.

Here Is Some Advice for Responding to True-False Questions

Many students get very nervous about true-false items on objective tests. Providing your preparation was adequate, in other words, you have used the suggested reading and study strategies outlined thus far, there is a way to approach true-false items. Read the item as if it is a rule that has no exceptions:

1. (T/F) All of the tissue in the central nervous system is neural tissue

First, answering this item correctly requires the test taker to understand two concepts: (1) the brain and spinal cord make up the central nervous system and (2) neural tissue is a tissue consisting of neurons or nerve cells. Knowing this information depends on the level of your test preparation (what you did before the test) as opposed to test taking (what to do when taking the test, what you are learning about right now: tips for reading true-false items). Assuming you are prepared, your job is to see if you can come up with an exception to the rule:

All of the tissue in the central nervous system is neural tissue

If you are unable to identify that exception, then the item is true. If you can come up with an exception, the item is false. In this case, the item is false. You know this because some, albeit very little, of the tissue in the central nervous system is connective tissue. You identified an exception. Consider the same rule with just one word altered:

Most of the tissue in the central nervous system is neural tissue

With true-false items, changing one word can change the correct answer. In this case, constructing the item with the word *most*, instead of *all*, accounts for the exception(s). Awareness of this requires you to read each item carefully, noting any limiting words or phrases just as you would with a multiple-choice item. A successful true-false question strategy, then, involves these steps:

- reading the true-false item as if it is a rule with no exceptions;
- checking your level of preparedness, making sure you understand the concepts (key words or phrases at the heart of the item) clearly;
- noting any limiting words or phrases like *some, many, all*, or *few*;
- identifying any exceptions to the rule, accounting for the limiting words and/or phrases; and
- answering based on the presence or absence of exceptions. If you are unable to identify that exception, then the item would be true. If you can come up with an exception the item would then be false.

In-Class Essay Exams Don't Have to Be So Daunting

Professors often require students to compose an essay in response to one or more prompts on an exam. These essay responses constitute all or part of the exam, which might also include other types of questions, such as multiple choice, identification, true or false, matching, or short answer questions.

Essays written in this particular situation tend to invoke anxiety from a substantial number of students. It isn't difficult to imagine why this might be the case, in large part because this writing situation is different from that of a take-home writing assignment. Comfort level, space, immediacy, and available time are all limited during in an in-class essay exam, more so than with a take-home writing assignment. You may very well feel less comfortable in these situations. This is partly because you aren't likely to know precisely which topic(s)/question(s) you'll be asked to respond to on the exam. You also aren't able to write in a space of your choosing. Writers often have one or more spots where they do their work, but composing an essay exam response usually means writing at a less-than-comfortable desk with pen and paper. There won't be the poster you look at to help you focus your thoughts at the library or the computer with which you write more quickly. In fact, you may find yourself distracted by the classmates writing around you ("He's done already?!") or the sounds of maintenance workers outside your classroom window. This situation also means you can't decide when you'd like to get started writing. You have a limited amount of time, and you need to begin the process as soon as possible. This process is often modified due to time constraints.

Because much of students' anxiety surrounding in-class essay exams is a result of such situational differences, it makes sense that these anxious feelings might be diminished if the situations weren't so different. What, then, can you do to make in-class essay writing more like take-home essay writing? For one thing, you can try to make yourself as comfortable as possible within the confines of a classroom environment where respect for the professor and fellow classmates is expected. A cup of coffee, favorite pen, or lucky sweatshirt might help these exams seem a bit less daunting. A seat toward the front of the room may limit the extent to which you are distracted by everyone else working on their own exams.

One other way you can make in-class essay writing more like take-home essay writing is to engage in some of the same writing activities. Although time, admittedly, is limited, much can be done with a little time management. Consider a 50-minute exam period, for example. If you normally do some brainstorming before creating an outline and draft, you might give yourself 5 to 10 minutes to brainstorm, 5 minutes to create a draft, and 25 to 30 minutes to compose a draft. If you write on every other line, you'll leave yourself room to go back and revise/edit—and you'll have 10 minutes remaining in which to do so.

Here are some additional suggestions for taking essay exams:

1. Make sure you understand the question or prompt; if you don't, get clarification.

2. Don't assume that structure, transition, and grammar don't count. These are all important because they allow your reader to understand the ideas you are attempting to convey in the manner in which you want them understood.

3. Don't try to tell your teacher anything and everything that you know. Stay focused on answering the question or responding to the prompt.

4. Be specific when possible. Offer examples and illustrations that demonstrate a more thorough understanding on your part.

5. Be aware of how much time your professor has allocated to the essay(s). If you are finished too early, your professor might be looking for a more developed response than the one you've provided. Use the extra time to provide an additional supporting point and/or to illustrate existing points with detailed examples.

6. Write legibly. This is something you can check for when you review your work. Your professor can't commend what she or he can't read.

Self-Evaluation of Preparedness for Tests and Exams

Think you are ready for your next test? The following questions, developed by Heidi Brown (1996), formerly a social science learning specialist at Boston University, are designed to allow you to self-assess how prepared you are for an upcoming quiz, test, or exam. If you can answer "yes" to most of these questions, you are probably well prepared. If you find yourself responding "no" to some of these questions, you may want to engage in some additional preparation and/or plan on doing things differently for the next such examination.

1. Did you spend a portion of your study in a group of at least 3 people?   YES NO

2. Did you study by units? Did you coordinate readings with lectures?   YES NO

3. Did you write questions in the margins of your class and laboratory notes, questions that the notes were answers to?   YES NO

4. If yes, did you use these questions to test yourself after having studied the notes?   YES NO

5. Did you use the class and lab lecture outlines to test whether you could summarize the entire lecture in a few minutes (i.e., look at the outline and recite the major points of the lecture)?   YES NO

6. Based on the class lectures and the readings of each unit, did you make a list of all the terms, concepts, and theories you should know?   YES NO

7. Did you restate all definitions, concepts, etc., *in your own words* (orally or in writing)?   YES NO

8. Did you work at linking authors and their ideas/theorists and their concepts?   YES NO

9. Did you use all of the study guides you may have received?   YES NO

10. Did you review past tests, quizzes, etc., and determine your areas of weakness?   YES NO

11. Did you discuss past "problem" quizzes, etc., with your professor in an individual meeting with him/her?   YES NO

12. Did you *actively* read *all* of the assigned readings, restating main points in the margin in your own words, summarizing sections, making outlines, and relating them to lectures?   YES NO

13. Did you use your texts and/or a dictionary when a term or idea was not clear?   YES NO

Used with permission of Heidi Brown.

In many ways, this chapter asks you to think about all that you've learned from the *Foundations for Learning* text. For instance, "Is the night before your first test in college the time to begin thinking about whether your high school level study strategies will serve you in college?" In effect, you begin preparing for your tests and exams the minute you step into the classroom at the start of the semester. The testing situation will raise a variety of issues for students. The decisions you make regarding how you take notes, how you read your texts, and whether you join a study group will have a greater impact than drinking a pot of coffee to cram the night before the exam.

FIRST-YEAR DIARIES:
ADJUSTMENT REFLECTIONS

Adjusting to Synthesizing Notes and Readings ~ Frank

I found that bringing my textbooks to class gave me a greater understanding of the course material and allowed me to start practicing better outlining and note-taking strategies so that I could do well while still in class. This method consisted of taking lecture notes on the right side of my binder and using the left side to add key points from the textbook and other important dates, chart information including the page numbers. This made it a lot easier to focus on which information was important and what was not, which was in essence my main issue.

Adjusting Note-Taking Strategies ~ Bryce

After my first accounting exam, I realized that I needed to start using a different form of note-taking. What I did was take the Cornell system and made some alterations to it to better suit my class. I set up sections of my notes based on different segments of the chapter we would be covering in class based on concepts such as formulas or processes and then would expand on the topic with more in-depth notes. I kept copies of these notes in both hardcopy in my notebook as well as an electronic copy in a notebook on my laptop for a quick reference and an easy way to search for more obscure material. After using this new note-taking strategy, I saw a noticeable decrease in the amount of time it took me to complete my quizzes as well as an increase of about 70 points on my following two exams.

Adjusting to Outlining ~ Morgan

I tried outlining the reading. I always thought outlining was for writing papers, not extracting important facts and material from the readings to make it easier to grasp and retain. Outlining was the best strategy I adopted this semester. It led to more strategies that I now utilize such as writing my outlines by hand and making mental connections of material. Outlining my readings made it easier to, not only retain the material, but also to organize my notes and pick out what was important in each chapter.

DISCUSSION QUESTIONS

1. What makes memorization a problematic study technique?
2. How do you approach multiple-choice test questions? How efficient and effective is this approach?
3. What should you do if you earn a lower grade than you expected on a quiz, test, or exam?
4. Do you take notes in the same manner in each of your courses? What are your reasons for doing so or not doing so? How might your professor's instructional methods affect the notes you produce?
5. This chapter reviewed a system for synthesizing textbook and class notes called the Cornell system of note taking. What other system(s) could provide the same function? How do you currently combine class and textbook notes?
6. When you reach the point where you feel you are prepared to sit for a test or exam, how do you know you are ready? What kinds of feedback techniques do you use?
7. What test format(s) do you prefer? Why do you think this is so?
8. Compare your preparation techniques for a test on which you performed well with your preparation techniques for a test on which you performed poorly. What were the key differences?

ACTIVITIES

7.1 Practice for an upcoming essay exam. Generate questions that you think may appear on the exam, and, after studying, attempt to answer the questions in the time allotted for the actual exam. This exercise will help you see where you should focus your remaining studying.

7.2 After a test has been returned to you, see if you can diagnose your efforts. Look carefully at the items you got wrong. Were the items derived from the text, lecture, or supplementary materials? Bring your test to a learning specialist and have him or her help you determine your areas of weakness.

7.3 Do some preliminary studying for your next test. Generate a list of questions you would like to have clarified. Bring the list to a tutor or professor to seek answers.

7.4 Form a study group and create a mock test for one of your classes. Have each member pitch in a designated number of questions. Self-administer and grade the test you created.

REFERENCES

Alex, S. (1999). *Note-taking shorthand* [Pamphlet published by Becker College, Worcester, MA]. Used with permission.

Brown, H. (1996). *Self-evaluation of preparedness for tests and exams* [Pamphlet]. Used with permission.

Lister, R. (1993, February 21). Good study skills can and should be learned by everyone. *The Boston Globe,* p. 37.

Longman, D. G., & Atkinson, R. H. (1991). *College learning and study skills.* Minnesota: West.

Myers, D. G. (1999). *Exploring psychology.* New York, NY: Worth.

Tuckman, B. (1965). Group development: Developmental sequence in small groups. *Psychological Bulletin, 63*(6), 384–399.

White, W., Milecky, B., & Emery, R. (1986). *Study groups* [Pamphlet]. Used with permission.

Additional Readings for Students

Collaborative/Cooperative Learning and Group Work

Beaudin, J. A., & Free, L. (1999). Building teamwork. *American School & University, 71*(12), 101–104.

Beckman, M. (1990). Collaborative learning. *College Teaching, 38*(4), 128–134.

Bruffee, K. A. (1984). Collaborative learning and the "Conversation of mankind." In R. W. Barnett & J. S. Blumner (Eds.), *The Allyn and Bacon guide to writing center theory and practice* (pp. 206–218). Boston, MA: Allyn & Bacon.

Cooper, J. L. (1995). Cooperative learning and critical thinking. *Teaching of Psychology, 22*(1), 2–9.

Walkner, P., & Finney, N. (1999). Skill development and critical thinking in higher education. *Teaching in Higher Education, 4*(4), 531–548.

Additional Readings for Faculty

Study Strategies

Bol, L., Warkentin, R. W., Nummery, J. A., & O'Connell, A. A. (1999). College students' study activities and their relationship to study context, reference course, and achievement. *College Student Journal, 33*(4), 608–623.

Hadwin, A. F., & Winne, P. H. (1996). Study strategies have meager support. *Journal of Higher Education, 67*(6), 692–715.

Longman, D. G., & Atkinson, R. H. (1991). *College learning and study skills.* Minnesota: West.

Matt, G. E., Pechersky, B., & Cervantes, C. (1991). High school study habits and early college achievement. *Psychological Reports, 69,* 91–96.

Purdue Research Foundation. (1993). *Academic success skills workshop: Lecture notetaking* [Motion picture]. West Lafayette, IN: Purdue University Continuing Education.

Purdue Research Foundation. (1994a). *Academic success skills: Guidelines for taking multiple choice exams* [Motion picture]. West Lafayette, IN: Purdue University Continuing Education.

Purdue Research Foundation. (1994b). *Academic success skills workshop: How do I show what I know?* [Motion picture]. West Lafayette, IN: Purdue University Continuing Education.

Purdue Research Foundation. (1994c). *How can I organize my textbook reading? Or unraveling the textbook maze* [Motion picture]. West Lafayette, IN: Purdue University Continuing Education.

Purdue Research Foundation. (1994d). *How do I know what to study?* [Motion picture]. West Lafayette, IN: Purdue University Continuing Education.

Purdue Research Foundation. (1994e). *Increasing reading efficiency: Rate and comprehension* [Motion picture]. West Lafayette, IN: Purdue University Continuing Education.

Ryan, M. P. (2001). Conceptual models of lecture learning: Guiding metaphors and model-appropriate notetaking practices. *Reading Psychology, 22,* 289–312.

Schwartz, M. D. (1992). Study sessions and higher grades: Questioning the causal link. *College Student Journal, 26,* 292–299.

Thomas, J. W., Bol, L., & Warkentin, R. W. (1991). Antecedents of college students' study deficiencies: The relationship between course features and students' study activities. *Higher Education, 22*(3), 275–296.

Turner, G. Y. (1992). College students' self-awareness of study behaviors. *College Student Journal, 26*(1), 129–134.

CHAPTER EIGHT

Taking Responsibility in College and Life

The theme of *Foundations for Learning* focused on taking responsibility for your education as you transitioned to college. To begin with, you were asked to develop an understanding of the new environment in which you would be living and learning and how the choices you made in this new environment would affect your ability to be successful. You were encouraged to reflect on decisions you made about relationships, how you managed your time, and how your personality and attitudes would influence these choices. As you made decisions and choices, you were urged to modify strategies and perspectives to help with the transition to your new situation.

With new situations come new experiences, challenges, and perhaps even a little bit of anxiety regarding how to make sound decisions when facing the unknown. Indeed, college is a new situation, and with any new situation, it is up to you to handle the successes, challenges, setbacks, and accomplishments. To be sure, you will encounter all of these in college and beyond. Any time you experience something new, whether it be sophomore year, changing your major, studying abroad, or starting a new job, you will have to make certain choices and take responsibility for your experiences and actively claim them. If you were a little nervous about a class, for instance, we suggested asking for tutoring if you were concerned or beginning to struggle. For some of you, having to reach out for help may have been something new but perhaps necessary to achieve success in a particular class. Possessing humility and the ability to ask for help can be applied beyond your college years. Let's say you begin a new job, and your supervisor gives you a project deadline that you think is unrealistic based on time and resources. A situation like this may call on you to ask your boss or coworker for some advice and help. Someone who is not used to asking for help initially may find doing so difficult. In some cases, asking for help is a positive, sound choice and can save you time and alleviate stress. Rather than viewing asking for help negatively, you were encouraged to change your perspective, your mindset.

Another key to success in college is the willingness to change. One thing the text asked you to do was to change past study habits and try some new reading and studying strategies designed for college-level courses. Essentially, you were asked to take some risks by trying something new and moving out of your comfort zone.

How can this experience be applied after college? Imagine you are offered a job in another country where you are required to speak another language and adapt to a different culture. Will you be willing to take the risk and move? Will you be willing to change your behaviors to adapt to another culture's customs? Will you be willing to ask for help if you are struggling to learn the language? A key to success during your first year and beyond is the willingness to change.

Another suggestion made was that you develop a heightened consciousness of how you are using your time. In high school, you were in structured classes for nearly six or seven hours per day as opposed to the three hours per day you'll be in classes in college. Being aware of what you do with the rest of your time each day is a necessary part of regulating your own learning. You'll need the discipline to get your work done—without anyone reminding you to hand in assignments, get up for class, or attend activities. Using your time in such a disciplined way will pay dividends beyond college, of course, whether you are developing a business plan, drafting a building sketch, touring a city while on vacation, or balancing work, family life, and your relationships in these two arenas.

Another significant challenge for many students is forming healthy relationships with people who are going to support their academic endeavors as opposed to people who sabotage their ability to do well. Recall that procrastinators, for example, recruit others to procrastinate with them so they feel less guilty about not being productive. An academic environment as well as a professional environment requires motivation and productivity. You know the old expression "Misery loves company?" In college you may encounter individuals whose hearts are not entirely committed to succeeding. You are likely to experience the same dynamic in the workplace after you graduate. For instance, you may encounter a frustrating coworker who is less productive than you or an office mate who doesn't care for your boss and gossips all the time. You may be challenged in this case to maintain a positive attitude. Indeed, you will face challenges similar to those you experienced in college in your professional life. Just as you make a commitment to be successful in college, you will be challenged to motivate yourself to work hard in your professional life. Working hard includes persevering when challenged. And challenge is something you should expect because college should challenge you to grow as a person and as a student.

How you will grow as a person is entirely up to you. Just as you have been encouraged to take responsibility and claim your education, after you graduate you will be challenged to take responsibility for the important decisions you make throughout your life. Life beyond college will be filled with many new challenges. You were encouraged to adopt a growth mindset instead of a fixed mindset with the understanding that a growth mindset will serve you as you traverse through changes, transitions, and new experiences, such as in your career and in personal relationships. Possessing the ability to be self-reflective about your decisions and approaching them with a growth mindset will enable you to develop the habits of mind to be successful in life after college.

FOUNDATIONS FOR LEARNING THEMES: DEVELOPING THE HABITS OF MIND FOR SUCCESS IN COLLEGE AND LIFE

1. Possess humility.
2. Ask for help.
3. Have the willingness to change and take risks.
4. Cultivate critical thinking skills.
5. Form healthy relationships and practice healthy habits.
6. Develop a heightened consciousness and self-consciousness.
7. Manage your time and behavior.
8. Respect diversity.
9. Take responsibility.
10. Develop a growth mindset.

FIRST-YEAR DIARIES: ADJUSTMENT REFLECTIONS

Adjusting to New Habits of Mind ~ Will

Entering a University as a non-traditional student from a community college at twenty-nine years of age, I was faced with the reality that I was going to be required to perform academically on a higher level than I was accustomed to. I needed to develop "habits of mind" and face reality—get my education done once and for all or I would be sweeping floors for the rest of my life. Before coming to the university, I was scared academically. I knew I was attending a challenging university and my prior community college experience was nothing compared to what I was about to face. At twenty-nine, I had feelings that I was not going to fit in socially as well as not being as technologically advanced as other students. Being implored to "develop habits of mind" this semester helped me to overcome my feelings of anxiety.

Possessing humility came when I decided to go back to school and finish my degree in the first place. For the last eleven years, I was in and out of school, going part-time, and easily persuaded to skip semesters and go to work. As the economy started to fail and jobs were scarce, I realized I must complete my education or I would be up a creek...another moment of humility. Once unemployed, I said to myself, "If I had completed school when I should have, I may not be in the position I am now." This is when I decided to go full speed ahead and come to the university. By doing so, it proved to me, my family, and my friends that I had the willingness to take risks and change.

Academic autobiography: Your academic history, which includes your development as a student and the characterization of the type of student you were in elementary, middle, and high school.

Academic self-concept: The component of your self-concept that includes all of the thoughts and feelings that might affect and define you as a student.

Achievement motivation: Murray (1938) defines this as the "need to succeed" or the desire for significant accomplishment, for mastering skills or ideas, for control, and for rapidly attaining a high standard.

Active learners: Individuals who believe they are primarily responsible for their own learning, that they are agents in their own educational process.

Active reading: General approach to textbook reading aimed at assisting students of all learning styles. The process involves utilizing multiple learning modalities: visually processing what you are reading, summarizing passages in your own words, and questioning yourself about your level of understanding.

Adjourning: Last stage in group development, which involves establishing formal closure for a particular project, study group, or meeting.

American Psychological Association (APA) citation format: System of accepted rules for formatting particular types of documents. The association publishes a handbook outlining the particulars of this system. These accepted standards allow members of particular professional communities to communicate more efficiently.

Annotating text: Process of writing analytical, critical, and/or summative notes in response to written work. This activity involves writing comments, notes, and questions in the margins, essentially establishing a written conversation between reader and text.

Anxiety: Feeling of being tense, apprehensive, unsettled, and unsure why.

Attitude toward intelligence: Dweck and Leggett (1988) identify two implicit theories of intelligence, an entity view and an incremental view. People with an entity view believe intelligence is a fixed, single ability. Thus ability, not effort, is the key factor that determines performance. People who hold an incremental view believe intelligence involves a set of skills that can be improved through effort.

Auditory learners: Individuals who tend to favor their ears as the primary mode for learning. They are most likely to remember what they hear and what they say.

Automatic thinking: Term used by Friedman and Lipshitz (1992) to describe remaining entrenched in old habits and in old ways of thinking and learning. They explain that students sometimes are immobilized to learn new information because of past experiences.

Balance theory of wisdom: Robert Sternberg argues that a wise person, when faced with a real-life situation, balances interests and responses to environmental contexts in relation to wisdom.

Banking model of education: Paulo Freire describes this educational model as one in which educators attempt to dump information into the minds of students via lecture and textbook reading.

Bias-incident: An action that is motivated by a person's real or perceived race, religion, national origin, ethnicity, sexual orientation, disability, or gender.

Brainstorming. Process of letting ideas flow from your mind through your hand onto paper without making judgments as to how to say things perfectly, how to arrange the ideas, or whether or not you *really* want to include a particular idea. Brainstorming is about recording as much of what you are thinking as possible so you can make these judgments later.

Campus resources: Departments, people, and programs on college or university campuses that support students outside of the classroom.

Clustering: Also referred to as *branching*, a process that involves a more visual approach to prewriting. Here ideas are presented graphically as they relate to one another.

Comprehensive notes: Complete notes with all levels of information, including generalizations, examples, explanations, transitions, questions, introductions, summaries, and repetitions.

Cornell system of note taking: System of note taking that allows you to coordinate lecture notes with reading notes; an approach that involves, among other things, listing possible exam questions based on the notes gathered.

Daily schedule: Prioritized list of activities and/or tasks you need to accomplish derived from your semester and weekly schedules; if used correctly, it enables you to meet the deadlines you've set for yourself.

Defense mechanisms: According to Sigmund Freud, ways in which individuals distort reality to reduce anxiety.

Delay gratification: The ability self-disciplined individuals possess to restrain impulses in order to put work first and then have fun.

Die-hard procrastinator: Individuals who tend to get stuck in a rut to the point where they are completely immobilized.

Drafting: Process of turning less-than-cohesive thoughts into coherent phrases and paragraphs.

8-8-8 formula: For optimal balance with time management practices, the 24 hours in a day can be broken down into three components for college students: eight hours for sleep, eight hours for studying, and eight hours of leisure time.

Emotional intelligence: Daniel Goleman's (1995) challenge to the way our culture quantifies intelligence. Emotional intelligence includes self-awareness, impulse control, persistence, and self-motivation.

End comments: Forms of instructor feedback typically found at the end of a paper and are global in nature; comments that usually provide a summary of intertextual markings and marginal comments.

Entity view: Belief that intelligence is inborn and a fixed, single ability.

External locus of control: Generalized expectancy or feeling that outcomes are largely beyond our control and are a result of luck, fate, chance, or powerful others.

Feedback: Response you receive from instructors, learning assistance staff, or peer tutors regarding your academic work, studying, or behavior; a mechanism used to revise existing academic practices.

Feedback procedures: Methods of discovering your level of understanding of a particular subject. The more common methods include study groups, professors, upper-class students who took the course, and writing center or other learning assistance staff.

Fixed mindset: The belief that basic qualities are carved in stone.

Forming: Initial stage in group development involving a group getting together to work toward a collective goal and determining members' strengths and weaknesses. The point at which the group discusses how to approach the task at hand.

Freewriting: Form of prewriting that include the formulation of sentences and paragraphs instead of the list of ideas that would result from brainstorming.

Growth mindset: The belief that basic qualities can be cultivated through individual effort, that you can change and grow through application and experience.

Hate crime: A criminal act including physical assault or vandalism when the victims are targets because of their real or perceived race, religion, national origin, ethnicity, sexual orientation, disability, or gender.

Incremental view: Belief that intelligence involves a set of skills that can be improved through effort.

Intellectual curiosity: Defined by Peggy Maki (2002) as "the characteristic ability to question, challenge, look at an issue from multiple perspectives, seek more information before rushing to judgment, raise questions, deliberate, and craft well-reasoned arguments" (¶ 6).

Intellectual discourse: Ability to have a rational discussion about a particular subject with interested others.

Intellectual property: This property is unique in some way: it contains some new concept or data set, or perhaps argues against a previously established correlation. Intellectual property can be utilized by individuals other than the originator with permission.

Internal locus of control: Generalized expectancy or feeling of being reasonably in control over outcomes; attributing outcomes to your own hard work and effort.

Intertextual markings: These markings are placed within the text itself, that is, on top of, underneath, or covering your actual words.

Learning style: Pattern of personality and environmental factors related to how one learns.

Learning styles theory: Addresses the ways in which a person learns best and tailors approaches to learning and studying based on individual.

... s of control: Involves a generalized ...ancy that people hold regarding the ...o which they control their fate.

Logic outline: Outline that includes a thesis statement, a sentence that reveals the purpose of the paper, as well as the points the writer will offer in support of that thesis, the supporting points.

Marginal comments: Markings that occur in the (typically) one-inch margins surrounding your text. These comments are usually a bit more global in scope than intertextual markings, looking at least at sentence meaning and often at the significance of entire paragraphs.

Metacognition: Strategies that allow students to plan, monitor, evaluate, and revise learning strategies whenever needed in studying and learning new materials; literally, thinking about how you think.

Mixed modality learners: Individuals who are able to function in more than one learning modality.

Modern Language Association (MLA) citation format: System of accepted rules for formatting particular types of documents. The association publishes a handbook outlining the particulars of this system. These accepted standards allow members of particular professional communities to communicate more efficiently.

Moral courage: The behavioral expression of authenticity in the face of the discomfort of dissension, disapproval, or rejection.

Motivation: Expression of your attitude toward achievement.

Norming: Third stage in group development when the group agrees on guiding principles or rules that each group member must abide by for the group to function most productively.

Office hours: Scheduled times, typically posted on a course syllabus, when professors are in their offices waiting for students to drop in with questions and/or for student appointments.

Paraphrasing: Refers to the practice of putting someone else's language into your own words but still giving credit to the original author for her or his idea.

Passive learners: Individuals consciously or unconsciously subscribing to the philosophy that others are responsible for teaching them what they need to know.

Peer review: Process of reviewing work with peers in a classroom setting.

Performing: Fourth stage in group development that occurs when/if the group performs effectively and productively.

Plagiarism: Practice of presenting someone else's ideas as if they were your own.

Portfolios: Collections of student work, with an emphasis on metacognition, requiring those who keep a portfolio to consider what it will include and how it will be organized.

Prewriting: Action of recording ideas with an emphasis on getting ideas in a form that you can see or hear them. Prewriting is more about *what* you might say than *how* you might say it.

Procrastinate: Act of putting off working on an activity because it seems too complex, difficult, time consuming, and overwhelming.

Procrastination: Putting off doing something until a future time or needlessly postponing or delaying doing something.

Quoting: Refers to the practice of using quotation marks around exact words that you copy down from a source.

Rationalization: Justifying undesirable behaviors with excuses.

Reciprocal determinism: Notion that there is an influential relationship between people and their environments.

Reflective journal: Collection of thoughts written down whose purpose is to help the author think through ideas by writing about them. The act of keeping a reflective journal involves making regular entries and collecting them together to illustrate thinking over a period of time.

Replacement activities: Activities in which individuals typically engage other than those that should be priorities; activities that are typically engaged in during the process of procrastination.

Research: Investigating what others have said and/or written about topics of interest. Research can be done in many ways, including a search at a library or via the Internet, and by talking with experts in a relevant field.

Responsibility: Literally, your response-ability, that is, your ability to choose a response.

Revision: Writing process activity that involves carefully reviewing your work and making changes because a word, sentence, or paragraph in the writing interferes with the meaning(s) you were trying to convey to your audience. It is a good idea to look for grammar and spelling errors when reviewing a piece of writing, but there are other things to look for as well. Of at least equal importance are unclear and/or underdeveloped ideas that could be interpreted by an audience in ways you didn't intend.

Schema: Term used in the context of active reading. Schema refers to what you already know about the subjects that you find in your reading. Any new information presented will be interpreted/understood based on this prior knowledge.

Scholarly community: Group of people working toward intellectual pursuits.

Self-concept: Our understanding of who we are, a conceptualization that encompasses all of our thoughts and feelings.

Self-efficacy: Belief that you are capable of producing desired results, such as mastering new skills and achieving personal goals.

Self-evaluation: Process of developing an understanding of your studying practices and procedures; that you did everything within your power to prepare adequately for a given test.

Self-regulation: Ability to monitor your own learning and study procedures; a process under your control that is *your* primary responsibilit

Semester schedule: Use a daily planner or electronic planner to record due dates for papers, projects, and presentations, and enter midterm and final exam information into the appropriate dates for an entire semester.

Spaced practice: Also referred to as chunking, spaced practice is learning material in small parts, ahead of time.

Storming: Second stage in group development that occurs when conflict arises. The group must resolve these conflicts before proceeding to the next stage, norming.

Student-directed environment: Learning environment in which students are expected to adapt to the different demands of each class on their own.

Summarizing: Activity involving reducing a lengthy passage into a sentence or two while remembering to document the original source.

Supporting points: Ideas offered in support of a thesis.

Switching cognitive gears: Transitioning from one mode of thought to another.

Syllabus: Document describing a course, outlining desired course outcomes, and detailing other relevant information, such as topics and readings.

Tactile/kinesthetic learners: Individuals who prefer learning when they are physically involved in what they are studying. These learners want to act out a situation, create a product, or work on a project. They understand and remember best when they physically do something.

Teacher-directed environment: Learning environment in which teachers help students adapt to the different demands of each class.

Test preparation: Includes all of the activities involved in preparing for an exam, including reading techniques, note-taking techniques, study techniques, class participation, and other contributory activities.

Theory of multiple intelligences (MI theory): Howard Gardner's (1983) idea that intelligence is not a single capacity that equips a person to deal with various situations. He argues that people use at least seven intelligences: linguistic, musical, logical-mathematical, spatial, bodily-kinesthetic, interpersonal, and intrapersonal, to approach problems and create products.

Thesis statement: Sentence or two that reveal(s) the purpose of a piece of writing.

Three-tier time management system: Consists of completing a semester schedule, weekly schedule, and daily schedule/to-do list.

Time management: System for using your time in an efficient and effective manner.

To-do list: Prioritized list of activities you need to accomplish based on your semester and weekly schedules. It is up to you to meet the deadlines you've set for yourself.

Visual learners: Individuals who use their eyes as the primary mode of learning. They want to see a picture; they want to actually see the words written down. These learners tune in to the physical environment.

Weekly schedule: Tool used to identify how much of your time is available for study. It is designed for writing in fixed commitments such as classes, labs, and job hours, listing times for eating, sleeping, grooming, transportation, leisure, and outside employment; then tentatively blocking out large spaces of time for studying.

Writing center: Resource on many college and university campuses designed to help students become better writers. In such a facility, a student can expect to work one on one with a tutor to work on a piece of writing in progress.

INDEX